HOW TO

Profit In Commercial Real Estate Investing

JOHN B. Allen

Real Estate
Education Company
a division of Dearborn Financial Publishing, Inc.

While a great deal of care has been taken to provide accurate and current information, the ideas, suggestions, general principles and conclusions presented in this text are subject to local, state and federal laws and regulations, court cases and any revisions of same. The reader is thus urged to consult legal counsel regarding any points of law—this publication should not be used as a substitute for competent legal advice.

Publisher: Kathleen A. Welton
Acquisitions Editor: Patrick J. Hogan
Associate Editor: Karen A. Christensen
Senior Project Editor: Jack L. Kiburz
Interior Design: Lucy Jenkins
Cover Design: Michael S. Finkelman, Shot in the Dark Design

Published by Real Estate Education Company,
a division of Dearborn Financial Publishing, Inc.

Printed in the United States of America.

93 94 95 10 9 8 7 6 5 4 3 2 1

Library of Congress Cataloging-in-Publication Data

Allen, John B.
    How to profit in commercial real estate investing / by John B.
Allen.
        p. cm.
    Includes index.
    ISBN 0-79310-190-5
    1. Real estate investment—United States. I. Title.
HD1382.5.A374 1993   93-10462
332.63′24—dc20   CIP

Preface

This is a book about how to invest in commercial real estate and do it right. After you have read it, you will know more about commercial property investing than 95 percent of those who invest in it regularly.

One of the attractions to real estate investors, both individual and institutional, is the seductive simplicity of the investment process. The product types—apartments, office buildings, retail stores and industrial buildings—seem to be simple to understand. There also are thousands of individuals and organizations ready to make it easy for you to put your capital into real estate. Even so, long-term success as a real estate investor is often elusive. Success won't be elusive after you read this book and apply the principles set forth here.

Many differences exist between those who almost always make money investing in real estate and those who seldom are able to do so. Perhaps the biggest difference is that the "winners" know that the "hard" way is ultimately the easiest way to make money consistently. This is a paradox that few people seem to understand.

The hard way, as it turns out, is not all that difficult, but it does involve more work than simply calling your broker or adviser and telling him or her to find you a good real estate investment.

The problem, of course, is not that some investors are unwilling to make an effort to ensure their investment success, but rather that there has been no clearly defined path for those investors who are willing to do what it takes to succeed. This book is that path.

Acknowledgments

The author wishes to thank the Grubb & Ellis Company, San Francisco, California, for permission to reprint material from *Investor Outlook,* a quarterly newsletter on real estate investment activity. Chapters 1 through 13 originally appeared as editions of *Investor Outlook.* They have all been revised and updated for this book.

Contents

Introduction

How To Profit in Commercial Real Estate Investing is divided into three main sections. Part I has four chapters covering apartment buildings, office buildings, retail and industrial investments. Part II contains complete information on many of the minor investment types, with chapters on factory outlet stores; the self-storage investment; elderly care facilities; hotels, motels and resorts; and the golf course investment. Part III is devoted to financing structures and nonfinancial influences on investment values. This section contains a valuable chapter on what the environmental movement means to the commercial real estate investor as well as chapters on financial analysis, financing and sources of information.

Those who want to profit most from the ownership of commercial real estate will read the entire book, probably more than once. It is not necessary, however, to read it in the sequence in which the subjects are presented. You can easily go to those subjects of the greatest current concern to you and find the answers you need.

There are numerous tables, graphs, charts and examples throughout the book. It is not possible for any book to stay current when so many facts are presented within it. And though no data can be provided beyond the date of publication, this will not render the book obsolete. Historical accuracy and the methods set forth are what matter.

Every reasonable effort has been made to present the reader with a solid factual background for the broad factors that influence investment value. To the extent that such information is historical, the data will not change; conclusions that stem from it may or may not change depending upon recent trends. Having reliable historical information available will save you the time it would take to gather broad background data; all you have to do is update the data by a telephone call or two. The factual material also serves as a valuable example of what you need to know on a regional and local level before you commit capital to an investment.

Regardless of its merit, the data is not the decision. Two of us looking at the same data easily could come to differing conclusions. Few succeed, many struggle; it is interpretation that makes the difference.

This book provides you with a factual framework and examples of the kinds of judgments that are made from the data by those who make money investing in real estate. For instance, in early 1985 it was abundantly clear to any careful investigator that investment in a hotel was a very chancy business. All the signs of the impending space surplus that would lead to declining income were solidly in place. Many astute investors avoided hotels, but many did not; in fact, the years from 1985 to 1990 saw one of the greatest hotel-building booms in U.S. history. Billions were lost by uninformed investors. Billions will be made by those who knew the market truth and waited.

This book is written from the perspective of someone with extensive and unique experience in real estate investing. That experience, combined with exceptional research, assures you of a guide to real estate investing that is complete and easy to understand.

—John B. Allen
   Villa Park, California

PART
I

Common Commercial Real Estate Investments

CHAPTER
1

The Apartment Investment

If you invest in apartments, you're in good company; they are the most popular commercial real estate investment in the United States. And they are likely to retain their number-one ranking for decades to come.

Here are some quick facts: Multifamily housing makes up one-third of all improved real estate in America; the total market value of this investment exceeds $6 trillion. Over 80 percent of the multifamily product is owned by individual investors, and 20 percent is held by institutions. This heavy concentration of ownership in individual hands ensures an active resale market; it makes apartments more liquid than other types of investment real estate. The ratio between individual and institutional ownership could change, of course. Some analysts think that the ownership of apartments is in the process of being "institutionalized"; they predict a 40 percent ownership by institutions by the year 2000. That forecast seems very aggressive. However, it is just one of many indicators that investor demand for apartments will tend to be strong for the rest of the 1990s.

This chapter has two main parts:

1. The nonfinancial analysis of the apartment investment
2. The financial analysis of this investment type

The chapter ends, as do all chapters, with a list of trends.

The Nonfinancial Analysis

Nonfinancial or non–balance sheet factors are the broad base upon which the financial condition of an apartment property rests. This is true for all types of real estate, but in spite of the fundamental importance of the nonfinancial considerations, most investors are unskilled in uncovering and evaluating such data. One of the differences between this book and others is the emphasis placed upon the importance of the nonfinancial side of real property investing. If anything characterizes those people who just never seem to do well investing in real estate, it is their lack of attention to these factors.

It could be argued, of course, that anything that affects the performance of an investment property is part of its financial character, and therefore there is no such thing as a distinct group of factors labeled "nonfinancial." People who think that way are usually better at arguing than they are at investing in real estate.

Throughout the book, anything that influences supply/demand balance is recognized as a nonfinancial factor; we also include decisions about such diverse matters as location, building design and investment timing as non–balance sheet items.

It is not possible to maximize profit from an apartment investment unless you can reason from the nonfinancial facts that will determine occupancy, rent level and cash flow during your holding period.

Supply and Demand

The major nonfinancial elements of the apartment house investment are supply and demand data and the influences upon it. A careful analysis of these items is vastly more important than "crunching the numbers" for a particular property.

In the area of supply and demand, national and regional data are used to illustrate critical points; no local information is used anywhere in this book. You must be familiar with the facts for your own marketplace, because it is the relationship between supply and demand locally that really matters. You can't afford to ignore the wider-ranging figures, however, because they are the ones you need to rely on for your baseline data.

Some investors may feel that an emphasis on supply and demand shortchanges other important considerations. For example, what about economic activity and diversity in the area? That, too, is important; however, many successful investors have found that if they have a strong supply and demand situation and the indications are that it will stay that way for a few years, they can study the other economic indicators at their leisure.

Supply and demand is an unchanging basic of real estate investment; this law rules the marketplace. At times it may seem as if the law of supply and demand has been suspended, because its effect is occasionally distorted by "easy money" conditions or periods of highly favorable tax treatment for apartments or for real estate in general. But the law of supply and demand is immutable. It never goes away. In the long run, no investor can afford to ignore its workings.

One reason the law of supply and demand is of such overwhelming importance is that apartments, like all real estate, are long-term investments. Most purchasers have an investment horizon of seven to ten years; over a decade, almost all temporary influences on supply and demand are absorbed or washed away by the relentless movement of this law. Let's look at the recent history of supply and demand to see what we can learn from the facts.

From 1983 to 1986, apartments experienced a construction boom. During those four years new supply far exceeded effective demand, and a surplus built up. That surplus was absorbed in most major markets, and apartments entered the 1990s with a good relationship between supply and demand and strong prospects for providing investors with a favorable and steady return on investment through 2000 and, perhaps, slightly beyond.

The facts seem to favor investing in apartments. As you investigate any real estate investment, it is not unusual to find that what the majority of people seem to believe—almost accept as an article of faith—is simply

Table 1.1 Multifamily Housing Starts in the United States by Type and Region: 1964–1991 (in thousands of units)

Year	U.S.A.		Northeast		Midwest		South		West	
Type	2-4	5+	2-4	5+	2-4	5+	2-4	5+	2-4	5+
1964–69*	83	445	16	78	18	112	22	161	26	94
1970–79*	103	522	12	68	23	109	31	214	39	129
1980	109	331	8	30	20	56	50	165	30	80
1981	91	288	8	25	15	40	46	153	23	69
1982	79	320	7	31	12	99	45	357	17	61
1983	113	522	10	35	17	48	61	317	27	121
1984	122	544	11	35	16	60	64	274	31	175
1985	94	576	15	55	15	77	38	240	25	204
1986	84	542	16	50	17	91	28	201	22	200
1987	65	409	15	50	14	81	20	129	17	148
1988	59	348	12	42	14	66	17	115	15	125
1989	55	318	9	37	14	62	18	109	16	108
1980–89*	87	442	11	39	15	68	39	206	22	129
1990	38	261	6	21	10	50	9	99	12	91
1991**	24	219	2	22	4	27	11	101	7	70

* = Average for the period
** = Grubb & Ellis Company estimate
Source: Department of Commerce, Current Construction Reports, Series C-20 (Washington, April 1991).

wrong. The truth about population growth, discussed under "Demand," exemplifies this difference. Such discoveries add an air of excitement to a tedious job. The fact that discovering the truth might also make you rich doesn't hurt, either.

One of the easiest ways to see supply and demand principles at work is to look at the complete history of new supply for apartments. It is not a long history. Federal records of new apartment starts have been kept only since 1963 and were first published in 1964. Table 1.1 shows a condensed version of the data since 1964, rather than the year-to-year figures for all four decades. You can get the yearly figures at your local library or from the source cited. The average data used allow about the same conclusions as would be reached from the yearly figures.

Despite all the publicity concerning the easy-money, frantic-building eighties, this table illustrates that the popular impression of this decade as an undisciplined and out-of-control era may not be entirely accurate. Those who invested based on the often unfavorable reports they read in the daily newspapers could easily have missed out on some good investment opportunities. Far more apartment units were built in the seventies (6,251,00) than in the eighties (5,069,000 units). The decade of the eighties was only 81 percent as productive as the previous ten years. Looking even farther back, into the sixties, you can see that the pace of new supply construction has been declining for more than 20 years. This persistent decline has not been good news to developers, but it was very good news indeed to the holders of existing multifamily projects. However, only those who studied the data really understood what was going on.

Before leaving Table 1.1, please note the often considerable differences in the supply picture among areas of the country; the same phenomenon can occur in a local area, where the data between neighborhoods can vary greatly. The important lesson here is not to be a casual user of market data. Not everything you read in the daily paper is helpful in pointing you toward a smart investment. Look into the facts thoroughly. You will nearly always be happy with the decisions you make, as many of them will lead to a profit. It is also worth noting the differences in the patterns for 2–4 units and for 5+ units. It is possible that small-unit holders will do relatively well in the next several years.

It would be quite simple if all there was to studying supply was to look at its history, but there is more to it than that. Before any building can be built, it must go through a process that involves getting local governmental approvals, such as proper zoning and density requirements, and the developer must get a permit to build it. These preliminaries are applicable to all types of real estate, not just apartments.

Three vital areas can give you a more complete "read" on supply. They are the planned, permitted and under-construction phases of development. These figures represent potential and fairly near-term additions to supply and are easily obtained at the local and regional level. You can often find planned units by talking with the city or county planning departments that hold the necessary hearings before any permits can be issued. It is not unusual for developers to get development rights that do not have to be exercised immediately. Such rights are like supply time bombs; they will explode into the market when the financing situation is right. The number of permits issued is a matter of public record, as is the number of projects under construction. If you gather these statistics, you will quickly discover the difference between the number of "planned" buildings and those that actually get built. In some product types this difference can equal 50 percent. The permitted and under-construction numbers are important, because they can represent a quick increase in supply.

You will also want to know what is occurring in the rehabilitation and conversion market, because one makes the competition more effective and the other adds to supply. In some markets the conversion of property from other uses to apartments is quite significant. Some analysts have ventured the opinion that, nationwide, the conversion market is almost as large as the new construction market. An offset to these numbers is the number of units that are being razed.

Certain influences on supply have a powerful impact and seem to operate in spite of the law of supply and demand, which theorizes that the market is always searching for balance. Governmental actions and the environmental movement, particularly the "Not In My Backyard" (NIMBY) faction, act to distort the supply/demand relationship. Let's take a brief look at one or two of those governmental actions.

Government influence on supply. In 1986 the federal government passed sweeping tax law changes, commonly called the Tax Reform Act of 1986 (TRA 86). One of the results of this tax law was the death of the real estate syndication industry, which eliminated a huge element of demand. Another result was removal of most of the special tax provisions that had made real estate a particularly good deal for the rich. It was no longer possible, after TRA 86, to offset in the current year all losses from real estate against non–real estate income. Such a radical change drove many speculative investors from the market, and investment demand declined somewhat. Consequently, new supply began to decline. It is unlikely that TRA 86 is solely responsible for the decline in supply that followed 1986, but it was one of the factors.

Government action to encourage the development of low-income housing also can be a significant factor in increasing supply. Subsidized housing has been in decline for the past ten years, and the signs are that it will not stage a sudden comeback. A program you should know about is the federal tax credit program designed to stimulate construction of low-income to moderate-income housing. It is available in all 50 states. The tax credit program does not provide federal dollars to build housing. Instead, it is a credit that reduces tax liability. The effect on the federal budget is to reduce tax revenues and, at the same time, distribute economic benefits without actually mailing out checks. No subsidy dollars show up in the federal budget, and because of this, the program is expected to enjoy wide and continuing congressional support. Here is a brief outline of how the program works:

1. Congress authorizes a maximum amount of tax credits that can be issued in the program; the credits have a ten-year life and "roll over" from one year to the next if not completely allocated in any one year. This means that the amount allocated for any given year can be much more than 10 percent of the total tax credit pool. The original total authorization was $3.125 billion, but that was increased to $5.25 billion early in 1991 for use over the next 10 to 13 years.

2. Tax credits are awarded to qualifying developers by their individual states. To get a tax credit, a developer must deal with the state and local housing authorities and follow the bureaucratic trail they map out. The tax credits have an immediate present value and can be sold to raise equity dollars for the apartment project.

3. Potential investors in tax-credited low-income to moderate-income housing should be aware that the project must be substantially rented to tenants who are earning no more than 60 percent of the area's median income. If the median income in the project area is $30,000 annually, tenants will not be able to earn more than $18,000 per year. If you assume that 30 percent of gross income is spent on rent, this means a monthly rent of $450. This amount may be somewhat lower than what non–tax credit facilities are charging. Rents can rise as incomes rise, and the program must stay in place for 13 years. The framers of this program felt that the 60 percent rule encouraged building activity in the areas with the greatest need for decent housing. However, it may also focus lender attention elsewhere. It appears likely that there will always be unused tax credits available for those who can find a way to make the program work.

4. The amount of apartment housing that could be built under the program is estimated as follows:

Assume that the present value of the tax credit is approximately 45 percent of its face and that a loan-to-value ratio of 70 percent could be achieved; such a ratio may be wildly optimistic today.

Present value of $5.25 billion @ 45% = $2,362,500,000
Total value of new construction @ 30% equity ($2,362,500,000 + .30) = $7,875,000,000

Total units @ $50,000 average ($7,875,000,000 + $50,000) = 157,500

If 150,000 units get built each year as a result of this program, it will be the single greatest supply driver in the market. Given the rent-level limitations, it seems unlikely we will see that kind of production. The program may be one of those that looks good, sounds good, but does little good for those it is designed to help. From an investor's viewpoint, it does not seem to threaten any massive increase in the supply of "bread and butter"–type units.

Demand

Without effective demand, it is difficult to make a satisfactory return on your investment. Your investigation into the strength of demand ought to proceed from the national and regional to the local, just as it did for supply. Many of the sources are the same.

At times the demand picture offers investors reason to feel confident about the short-term, mid-term and long-term prospects for multifamily housing. Now is one of those times. Demand is reasonably steady, and it appears this will be the case in at least three of the four major regions of the country for the next eight to ten years. The 1990s should be a period of stability (at the very least) and growth (at the very best) for apartment investments. Don't panic if there are brief periods of weakening demand; the long-run picture is good for most areas.

The key to demand is people with money to spend. It is easy to find reasons to expect a bleak future. The fact that population growth is at a historic low is certainly one of these reasons. It is also an example of why you need to look beyond the "easy" national figures into their structure to see the real story. Table 1.2 is one such look. It shows the pattern of

Table 1.2 Regional Share of U.S. Population: 1990 to 2010 (in percent)

Area	1990	2000	2010
Northeast	27.6	20.4	18.4
Midwest	34.6	24.0	20.9
South	32.2	34.4	37.2
West	5.7	21.2	23.4

Source: U.S. Department of Commerce, 1990 Census Profile, No. 1, *Population Trends and Congressional Apportionment* (Washington, March 1991): 1–4.

population distribution from 1990 to 2010, and it becomes fairly obvious that not all regions will be treated equally in the years to come; they never have been where population growth is concerned.

A 90-year trend has continuously favored the South and the West; Table 1.2 indicates that trend will continue. While some forecasters look at national slow-growth forecasts and predict a sluggish apartment market, others, looking behind those numbers, can find plenty of opportunity.

The average U.S. population growth rate until the year 2000 will be approximately .73 percent annually, or about 1.8 million persons per year. Immigration is expected to account for 700,000 of that total. With slow growth like this, it is especially important to look behind the numbers to see if certain population segments will be affected. The age groups that comprise the largest number of renters are the 18–24 and the 25–44 segments. Table 1.3 shows what is likely to happen within those groups both nationally and regionally. Once again, there are significant differences between regions, just as there will be within your own marketplace. About 85 percent of the 18–24 age group are renters, while 55 percent of 25- to 44-year-olds rent. These are national tendencies; local numbers will vary. Table 1.3 illustrates that minor population changes will occur in the high-propensity-to-rent groups in the Northeast and Midwest, while the South and West will continue to experience a fairly strong demand.

Occupancy rates are of continuing concern to careful investors. A thorough investigation into this area is always worthwhile. No other real estate statistic contains so much misinformation published by so many people. Fortunately, the truth is not that hard to find if you know where to look. And look you must, or you will either fail to make an investment

Table 1.3   Population* Projections By Region and Selected Age Groups: 1990 and 2010 (in millions)

				18–24 Years		25–44 Years	
Area	1990	2010	Change	1990	2010	1990	2010
U.S.A.	250*	282	+32	66	72	66	77
Northeast	51	52	+ 1	10	9	10	9
Midwest	60	59	– 1	14	12	14	12
South	87	105	+18	31	36	31	38
West	52	66	+14	11	15	11	18
Totals	250	282	+32	66	72	66	72

*All population projections are from the middle series of estimates.
Source: U.S. Department of Commerce, Bureau of the Census, *Current Population Reports, Series P-25*, O.S. 519, 917, 1022 (Washington, July 1990).

at the right time or jump into one without proper information and suffer the losses common to the uninformed.

Even though most investors plan on a holding period of from seven to ten years, they are often seriously influenced by current vacancy rates. A fixation on a short-term phenomenon in what is essentially a long-term investment is a serious error that will lead to poor investment decisions. To put it bluntly, if all you know about vacancy rates is what you read in some journal, that paper is going to be a lot more interesting reading than your financial statement ever will be. Fortunately, you don't have to rely on such fleeting information.

There is a long history of reliable national and regional data on vacancy rates available to you. Similar information can be obtained for any locality or neighborhood. Table 1.4 shows the rental unit vacancy history in the United States by region since 1960. This data came from the U.S. Department of Commerce as a result of one telephone call; they even faxed it to me. Once again the data includes both national and regional information and creates a solid basis for comparison with your metropolitan and neighborhood information.

Table 1.4 indicates that the highest vacancy rate recorded since 1960 is about one-half the persistent average rate for office buildings in most of our major metropolitan areas. Multifamily housing offers much better occupancy numbers than do many other types of real estate. If hotels ever

Table 1.4 Rental Unit Vacancy History in the United States by Region: 1960–1991

Year	Region and Vacancy Percent				
	U.S.A.	Northeast	Midwest	South	West
1960-65*	8.2	5.3	7.8	9.3	11.5
1970	5.3	2.7	5.8	7.2	5.6
1975	6.0	4.1	5.7	7.7	6.2
1976	5.6	4.7	5.6	6.4	5.4
1977	5.2	5.1	5.1	5.7	5.0
1978	5.0	4.8	4.8	5.5	4.8
1979	5.4	4.5	5.7	6.1	5.3
1970-79*	5.4	4.3	5.6	6.4	5.4
1980	5.4	4.2	6.0	6.0	5.2
1981	5.0	3.7	5.9	5.4	5.1
1982	5.3	3.7	6.3	5.8	5.4
1983	5.7	4.0	6.1	6.9	5.2
1984	5.9	3.7	5.9	7.9	5.2
1985	6.5	3.5	5.9	9.1	6.2
1986	7.3	3.9	6.9	10.1	7.1
1987	7.7	4.1	6.8	10.9	7.3
1988	7.7	4.8	6.9	10.1	7.7
1989	7.4	4.7	6.8	9.7	7.1
1980-89*	6.4	4.0	6.4	8.2	6.2
1990	7.2	6.1	6.4	8.8	6.6
1991**	7.5	7.0	6.9	8.8	6.6

* = Average
** = Annualized from Quarter One 1991 data.
Source: U.S. Department of Commerce, Household and Household Economics Section, *Rental and Homeowners Vacancy Rates by Area:* 1960–1991 (Washington, 1991).

achieve the occupancy levels that apartments have demonstrated, there will be a lot of new billionaires. The data in this table is for all types of apartments, and that may not be as close to the investment you are considering as you would like.

Table 1.5   Income, Expense, Net Operating Income for Unfurnished Garden
Apartments in Dollars per Square Foot: 1973–1990

Year	GSI	Coll Rent	V & C Loss %	Oper Exp	NOI Pre-Debt	NOI % of GSI	NOI % Coll Rent
1973–79*	2.91	2.71	6.9	1.38	1.34	46.1	49.4
1980	3.86	3.60	6.7	1.73	1.81	46.9	50.3
1981	4.24	4.00	5.7	1.93	2.00	47.2	50.0
1982	4.67	4.37	6.4	2.07	2.24	48.0	51.3
1983	4.94	4.58	7.3	2.18	2.33	47.2	50.9
1984	5.21	4.80	7.9	2.31	2.44	47.0	48.1
1985	5.43	4.91	9.6	2.45	2.44	45.0	49.7
1986	5.61	5.03	10.3	2.51	2.48	44.2	49.3
1987	5.77	5.08	12.0	2.62	2.47	42.8	48.6
1988	5.96	5.31	10.9	2.66	2.62	44.0	49.3
1989	6.05	5.45	9.9	2.71	2.73	45.1	50.1
1980–89*	5.17	4.71	8.7	2.32	2.36	45.7	49.8
1990	6.36	6.02	5.4	2.86	2.73	43.9	45.3
1973–90*	4.36	4.01	7.8	1.98	1.98	46.1	49.4

* = Average; Year (Col. 1) is the year in which data were first reported; GSI (Col. 2) = Gross
Scheduled Income; COLL RENT (Col. 3) = Total Collected Rent, which includes miscellaneous
income not included in GSI; V & C Loss (Col. 4) = Vacancy and Collection Loss as a percent of
GSI; Oper Exp (Col. 5) = All Operating Expenses; NOI Pre-Debt (Col. 6) = Net Operating Income
before debt service; NOI as % GSI (Col. 7) = NOI Pre-Debt/GSI × 100; NOI as % Col Rent
(Col. 8) = NOI Pre-Debt/Coll Rent × 100.
Source: National Association of REALTORS®, *Income and Expense Analysis Conventional
Apartments,* 1973 through 1990 Editions (Chicago).

The National Association of REALTORS® (NAR) has maintained records
on all types of multifamily units in all major cities for many years. You
can access this information by working with a REALTOR® or by purchasing
NAR's reports from The Institute of Real Estate Management in Chicago.
Table 1.5 is an example of what NAR has to offer.

What you see in this table are the figures for garden-type (the most
common) multifamily projects. The vacancy range is a little wider than
that shown in Table 1.4, but it is still an acceptable picture taken alone or
when compared to other investments.

Table 1.6 New Household Formations in the United States: 1960–1999

Time Period	New Households per Year
1960 to 1969	1.05 Million
1970 to 1979	1.48 Million
1980 to 1989	1.37 Million
1990 to 1999	1.17 Million

Source: U.S. Department of Commerce, Bureau of the Census, Household and Household Economics Section (Washington, April 1991).

Other Demand Indicators

It is not possible to cover all the areas of supply and demand that investors may want to consider. Before we leave this area, however, let's discuss the two major, and several minor, demand areas.

The pace of new household formations is an important demand indicator. Table 1.6 shows some of its recent history. It is necessary to look at this statistic over a long time period, because it is highly elastic and quite sensitive to economic downturns and booms. The data show what has happened since 1960 and what is likely to happen until the end of this decade. The number of new households formed averaged 1.3 million from 1960 to 1989. The formation rate for the 1990s has been forecast at 1.17 million per year. If you are in the business of building new multifamily housing, this decline translates into less opportunity in the 1990s than in the 1980s. Owners of existing apartments, however, may see this number as one that translates into an average yearly new demand of about 400,000 units. (At 2.4 persons per household, it is actually about 487,000 units.) This number becomes significant, and encouraging, only if the rate of new supply is less than the rate at which new households are being formed. Some think that new supply (Table 1.1) will average 200,000 units per year in the 1990s. These figures may also point to an opportunity in the rehabilitation market. Any conclusions should, of course, be tempered by judgments on the state of financing availability throughout the period. If "easy money" prevails, new supply could quickly double regardless of the facts about demand.

Housing affordability is often cited as one of the drivers of multifamily demand. For many years, an approximate 2:1 ratio has existed between owners and renters in the United States. It varies significantly in the West, where it is only 1:1 in some areas. Virtually every survey taken about what people really want shows that 80–85 percent want to own a home. This means that at least 20–25 percent of the apartment market is made up of reluctant renters who would fly off into home ownership if they could ever afford it. Hence the importance placed by some investors on affordability data, such as that published monthly (in *Realtor News*) by NAR. The real importance of affordability to an investor is not in what some short-term survey shows, but rather in any long-term change from what has been established as normal. If, for example, it can be shown that home ownership will increase to 70 percent, then we would have a serious decline in demand for apartments. No such trend is being forecast for this century.

Occasionally you will read about the importance of immigration, migration and mobility as factors in apartment demand. Immigration is part of the total population figure and will be fully considered if you get complete population data. What may be missing from official statistics is reliable data on *illegal* immigration, which can be a major demand element in some areas.

The movement of groups of people from one region to another or within regions can also affect demand but, once again, it is a relative effect. Migration and mobility have always been a fact of American life; their importance arises only when they depart from the norms. There is no sign that any significant changes in these numbers are expected.

Other Elements

You cannot maximize profit from a multifamily investment unless you are able to reason from the non–balance sheet and non–income statement items that will influence occupancy, rent levels, and cash flows during your expected holding period. The facts relative to supply, demand, location, building quality and investment timing are far more important than the often more carefully scrutinized financial statements, yet many investors are unskilled in gathering and evaluating such data. We have already discussed supply and demand. In this section we will address the neighborhood, the building and the timing of the investment decision. Each chapter includes pertinent data on supply, demand and other non–

balance sheet factors. You will, by reading a chapter, have a reasonably good appreciation of the importance of these factors as they relate to the particular product type; however, you should read all chapters to get a strong, overall view that will allow you to form your own opinion on the importance of the nonfinancial elements of an investment.

Many nonfinancial analysis factors seem too simple or obvious to even mention. By ignoring these simple considerations, however, you create bargains for the more careful investor. If value increase is your goal, the first rule of apartment investment is that bad locations don't get any better. It is better to buy the worst building in a great area than it is to do the reverse.

Most of us have little trouble spotting top-quality locations and, similarly, it is not too difficult to know where the worst spots are. But what of the marginal areas? How can you know if an area is in decline? Popular wisdom—i.e., local reputation—can tell you a lot, but prudent investors prefer to depend on what they see for themselves. If an area is in decline, one or all of the following signs will be present:

- A general sense of overcrowding
- Graffiti
- Inadequate landscaping and poor landscape maintenance
- Heavy on-street parking with a significant number of old and/or abandoned vehicles
- Lack of occupancy balance; very few homeowners
- Poor exterior maintenance

In addition to these obvious signs, you would be justified in rating an area as poor if it is subject to noise pollution, smog (bad air quality), on or near a former toxic waste dump site, near a jail or close to heavy traffic–generating public facilities.

A building should not be judged by cosmetics alone, as cosmetics are really not that important at the time of purchase. Interior and exterior maintenance conditions are fairly easy to fix and are often not too expensive. If the price is right, they can be minimized in your decision-making process. A structurally unsound building, however, will eat up all your profits and ask for more. Get a professional inspection of the roof; the foundation; the exterior walls; electrical, plumbing, and heating and cooling systems; elevators; and any other mechanical system.

It is a profit-destroying error to buy properties with major systems or building component problems unless you get a price discount more than sufficient to bring the building up to standard. Money you spend on a new roof or other structural items will not increase occupancy or rent levels.

While cosmetics are relatively unimportant at the time of purchase, they can be important to a prospective tenant. "Curb appeal" is one of the strongest drawing cards a property can have, but it is easy and economical to achieve if the property is basically sound.

The caution against buying buildings that are not structurally sound could work against the consideration of older properties and, indeed, it does for many investors. Older buildings can be a reasonably good investment if they are bought and sold at prices that reflect their true operating costs and their limitations on attracting top rents. Such properties often occupy good locations, and the individual apartments are sometimes much larger than those found in newer buildings, which appeals to some tenants.

The space, the location and the amenities are what the tenant is willing to pay for. The average size of new apartments has been close to the figures listed below for quite a few years. If you want to know the average size for your area or for the nation, you may get this information from the U.S. Department of Commerce. Here are some guidelines:

Studio	475 square feet
1 Bedroom	650 square feet
2 Bedroom	850 square feet
3 Bedroom	1,000 square feet

The amenities most often found in new buildings are dishwashers (90 percent), parking (97 percent), gas utility service (54 percent) and swimming pools (72 percent). These figures are also available yearly from the Commerce Department.

Timing the decision to buy or sell can be as important as buying the right building. Our brief look at supply and demand shows that the multifamily market cycles between oversupply, market balance and slight undersupply. By studying the facts, you can determine where the cycle happens to be and time your decision to buy or sell to maximize your advantage.

The Financial Analysis

If the supply and demand situation is favorable, the net income produced by multifamily investments should also be good. We are assuming, of course, that management is at least adequate. The net income from unfurnished garden apartments has been steady at an average of 46.1 percent since the early seventies. A decline was registered in 1990, but this was quickly erased by the effects of a lower supply of new units. The main reference for this section is the NAR publication *Income and Expense Analysis: Conventional Apartments,* which is published annually. This is a valuable national data series but of limited value on a local level. You need to have good communication with an experienced, local apartment specialist who will, in big markets, have highly detailed income and expense data on a minimum of 200 to 400 buildings.

There is no nationally accepted terminology for the items in an apartment house chart of accounts. Most real estate brokers use the following:

Name	*Meaning*
Gross Scheduled Income	Total possible income from rental units
Vacancy and Collection Losses	Vacancy allowance, nonpayment of rent
Adjusted Gross Income	Money left after vacancy and collection losses
Expenses	All operating expenses
Net Operating Income	Net income before loan payments
Loan Payments	All mortgage payments
Spendable Income	Pretax spendable income

NAR uses different terminology in its reports, even though the majority of practitioners use the terms listed above. The NAR system is far more precise and, hence, more useful.

NAR's Typical Chart of Accounts

1. Total Possible Income (same as Gross Scheduled Income)
   This includes all revenue from any source related to the building. Typical items are apartment rent (about 97 percent of the total),

parking rent and rent from nonapartment users such as store or office tenants.
2. Vacancy and Collection Loss (often abbreviated to V & C Loss)
3. Total Rent Collected (same as Adjusted Gross Income)
4. Operating Expenses

A classification system, like this one, that divides expenses into four main categories is useful, because it generally follows the NAR terminology and allows you to compare your building to the experiences of about 4,000 other properties throughout the country.

There are other valid data besides that gathered by NAR. Several private organizations provide, for a fee, highly useful operating information. The particular advantage of the NAR data is that they are reliable and have a long history, which helps you to form opinions and have confidence in them. They also have the advantage of being relatively inexpensive. Further, unlike data from some private sources, which seems to appear and disappear as the economy waxes and wanes, the NAR data seem likely to continue to be available.

The four categories used for expenses by NAR are operating, administrative, maintenance, and taxes and insurance. Operating costs include all utility costs such as heating, cooling, electricity and gas, water, sewer and trash removal. Also included are janitorial supplies, building services (e.g., window washing and pest control), the operating cost of all recreational facilities and all miscellaneous operating costs, such as damage not covered by insurance, site signs, etc.

Administrative costs include all management expense both on-site and off-site, wages for administrative employees, advertising, legal and accounting expense, and other payroll.

The expenses included in the maintenance category cover all interior and exterior maintenance, interior painting and decorating, and all grounds maintenance including snow removal, sweeping, and the like.

Taxes and insurance includes real estate taxes, other taxes (except income taxes) and all insurance costs. Table 1.6 provides you with income and expense experience from 1973 to 1992.

In day-to-day practice, the chart of accounts you will generally be most exposed to looks like this:

Real Estate Taxes
All Other Taxes
Insurance (includes all property and liability coverage, workers' compensation, rental loss, etc.)
Utility Expense (all costs not paid by the tenants)
Management Expense (includes both on-site and off-site)
Maintenance Expense (includes landscaping maintenance)
Miscellaneous Expenses

As a general rule, expenses will range from 40 percent to 50 percent of Gross Scheduled Income. After loan payments it is common to have from zero to 10–12 percent spendable. Figures close to zero during the early stage of the investment are not unusual, nor are figures in excess of 20 percent after debt is retired.

For those who want some broad general guidelines on income and expense, here are some "rule-of-thumb" figures:

Gross Scheduled Income	100%
From rents	97%
From parking	1%
From storage rental	5%
From miscellaneous	1.5%
Vacancy and Collection Losses	5–7%
Adjusted Gross Income	93–95%
Operating Expenses	29–44%
Real Estate and Other Taxes	16–22%
Insurance	1–2%
Landlord-Paid Utilities	2–3%
All Management	5–7%
Maintenance	3–5%
Reserves	1–3%
Miscellaneous	1–2%

The range is designed to accommodate buildings of varying age, condition and management style.

Financing

Multifamily projects are generally among the easiest types of real estate to finance. No other property type has such a widely diversified ownership base, nor does any other type of real estate have an information history as old or reliable. Nevertheless, multifamily does get overbuilt periodically, and this leads to temporary difficulty in obtaining financing. The early 1990s were such a time. Many analysts characterized that time as a period of severe credit crunch. Syndication had been destroyed in the mid-1980s, and savings and loans failed by the hundreds in the late 1980s and early 1990s, which left many apartment deals with fewer places to get loans. Commercial banks initially filled the gap, but they were soon overwhelmed by problems of their own. Meanwhile the insurance companies, having gorged themselves on high-risk junk bonds, also were practically out of the market. At no time, with the exception of the Great Depression, had financing been more scarce. Yet apartment deals often got financed. One result of the tight credit markets was that seller-carried financing more than tripled in frequency; this is often the "bridge" that carries the apartment market in such times. More information on financing can be found in Chapter 10.

Investment Values

Investment values will very likely be strong during the 1990s and possibly into the 21st century. The demand from investment buyers of all types is strong, and the demand from tenants should range from steady to intense depending upon the market you are in. The occupancy history of apartments is not without its ups and downs, but it seems to rebound from its "down" periods within reasonable time frames. Multifamily housing is one of the investment types most likely to succeed in the next eight to ten years.

Trends and Conclusions

This section is subdivided into topics for your convenience. The trends and conclusions highlighted come from the chapter and from the research.

Supply

- The affluent renter will be the focus of many new development proposals. This emphasis will inevitably lead to oversupply in this segment.
- New-start level reached its lowest point in history in 1991. It is likely to remain at a slow pace for two to three years.
- This expected low level of new starts will mean a shortage of apartments in many areas.
- The federal government may do a little more to increase the supply of affordable rentals as new supply remains weak and rents start to rise.
- The two-to-four-unit segment will increase its share of the new start total even though it has been declining recently.
- Cost of construction will continue to rise.
- Renovation activity will continue to increase.

Demand

- Vacancy rates will decline nationally.
- Both renter and investment demand will be strong.
- Higher-amenity apartments could show an increase in demand as the renter group ages and their incomes rise.
- Overall renter demand in the nineties will range from stable to slightly rising.
- The yearly demand from new household formations should average 400,000 units.

Finance

- A strong supply/demand profile assures adequate financing in the nineties.
- Difficulty in financing new construction should last into 1993.
- Refinancing will be more difficult to arrange than it was during the 1980s.
- Higher equity (20–30 percent or more) will be needed for years to come.
- Environmental requirements will continue to increase the cost of financing.

Returns

- Rents will increase faster than the CPI; return on investment will rise.
- No-growth and slow-growth movements will assure good returns for existing properties in most communities.
- Less than vigorous growth in wages and salary levels will influence the size of rental increases.

Taxation

- Few substantial federal changes expected. Passive loss limitation rules, capital gain and depreciation will be the targets.

C H A P T E R
2
Office Buildings:
Low-Rise to High-Rise

The office building is one of real estate's most prestigious and prominent investment types. Much is written about it, but much of what is written tells us little about its investment potential. After reading this chapter, you will know more than many experienced investors about this important investment type.

In this chapter you will find information on central business district (CBD) and suburban office properties. Slightly more attention has been given to the suburban properties because they are both more numerous and, for most investors, easier to buy. You will also find a section on the smart building.

In addition, there is a history of the office building followed by sections on investment characteristics, financial analysis, feasibility studies, financing, current conditions and trends. More detail on financial analysis appears in Chapter 10.

Office Building History

America is a young country; our office building history does not really begin until the mid-1700s. What we lack in age, however, we more than compensate for in the quantity of activity and the pace of change.

Much can be learned from the history of office buildings, even though get-rich-quick schemers minimize the importance of the history (even a short one) of any investment product type. These short-term thinkers see real estate investing as an opportunistic, go-for-the-throat activity in which the less you know, the better off you will be. The office building industry was well-populated with such people during the last decade; bankruptcy court is their current venue.

Much has been made of the current oversupply of space, which represented a three- to four-year supply nationally in the late 1980s and rose to about twice that in the recession of the early 1990s. Some areas, however, had a much more serious oversupply; it reached more than 40 years in Tulsa, Oklahoma, at one point.

The national years-of-supply figures in the 1990s pale to insignificance when compared to the 25 years of supply that was under construction in 1926. Overbuilding, it appears, is not a unique problem of modern times but a persistent characteristic of the office building market. These supply gluts create great opportunities for the astute investor. Nevertheless, we should not minimize the present oversupply, which, when combined with falling demand, is quite serious for those who "got in" at the wrong time.

Another lesson gleaned from recent history is what happened after the high-rise fire in the First Interstate Bank building in Los Angeles in May of 1988. This fire spawned numerous proposals for state laws mandating the retrofitting of sprinklers in all office buildings that are currently without them. These retrofits will prove much more costly than was first thought, especially if there is asbestos in the building that might be disturbed during a sprinkler installation. If asbestos has to be removed, you are looking at costs that can be ten to 15 times higher than for a simple sprinkler retrofit.

Figure 2.1 shows a short history of the U.S. office building from the mid-1700s to 1991.

Figure 2.1   U.S. Office Building History

Mid-1700s	Several owner-occupied office buildings built in New York, Boston, Philadelphia.
1853	Elisha G. Otis developed reliable passenger elevator system, making it possible to get good rents for the upper floors of buildings.
1870–1920	Population growth fueled first modern office building construction boom. Demand for office space grew by 100 percent. The emergence of large corporations led to an increase in office space demand.
1871	Chicago fire destroyed much of the city's Central Business District (CBD). Spurred development of new and larger buildings.
1878	First elevator-served building built in New York City.
1883–1885	William Jenney pioneered steel-frame construction method. Ten-story Home Insurance Building built in Chicago.
1904	Fast-operating gearless elevators first used in the Beaver Building, New York City.
1906–1911	Five years of tall-building construction: 1906–1908—Singer Building, 47 stories, 612 feet; 1909—Metropolitan Life Building, 50 stories, 700 feet.
1911–1913	Woolworth Building built—55 stories, 792 feet. The world's tallest building for 20 years.
1925	Another construction boom—95 buildings under construction in 31 cities totaling 12 million square feet. This was a 25-year supply at the prevailing absorption rate.
1930–1931	Empire State Building constructed—102 stories containing 1,790,433 square feet. World's tallest structure for 30 years. Did not rent and was not profitable until World War II. It was called the "Empty State" building during the Great Depression.
	Rockefeller Center was started in 1931. This was one of the first developments to use open space for a park-like setting.
	Total office space occupied in 1931 was approximately 145 million square feet. (It is about two billion square feet today.) Occupancy fell by 11 percent to 130 million square feet in 1933.

Figure 2.1   U.S. Office Building History (continued)

1936–1939	Frank Lloyd Wright's pioneering Johnson Wax Building built (Racine, Wisconsin). One of the first designs to fully consider the daily needs of tenants and guests.
Late 1940s	Mile High Center started (Denver, Colorado). Opened in mid-1950s. Important for the length and intensity of the zoning battle. A harbinger of extensive public involvement in the development process.
Late 1950s	International style of architecture appears.
Early to mid-1970s	The start of the current space glut. Market for huge energy loans disappeared; lenders poured money into real estate development.
Mid-1970s	Energy crisis stimulated construction of energy-efficient buildings. Start of "sick building" phenomenon.
	Use of sprayed-on asbestos prohibited.
	Skidmore, Owings & Merrill promoted atrium-type building.
Late 1970s	New office construction boom began. Many notable buildings built: World Trade Center (New York)—110 stories, 1.4 million square feet; Sears Tower (Chicago)—110 stories, 1.5 million square feet (world's tallest building today).
1980s	Half of our total supply of office space was built in the 1980s. A huge oversupply was apparent, even to the most optimistic, by 1983. Nationally, new construction averaged 489 million square feet annually, compared to an average of 196 million square feet during the period 1960–1979.
	CBDs became intensely developed; in-fill projects became the rage.
	High-rise office rent trends (in early 1980s) encouraged suburban office development.
	Tax Act of 1981 stimulated overproduction.
	Savings and loan industry was deregulated and played a major office building financing role.
	Neo-modernism and postmodernism style emerged.
1983	Smart buildings became popular with developers.

Figure 2.1   U.S. Office Building History (continued)

1984	Office building construction boom began to slow.
1987	Stock market crash in October lessened demand for space from the financial services market segment and signaled a massive adjustment to come throughout the country.
1988	First Interstate Bank building (Louisiana) high-rise fire led to a state law on retrofitting all buildings over 75 feet tall with fire sprinklers. Set up the possibility of huge costs to remove asbestos.
1991	Large oversupply led to cut in new construction activity by more than 50 percent in most major markets. Loans for construction or refinance almost impossible to obtain.
	Empire State Building sold by Prudential Insurance for $40 million.

Classification Systems

The intent of this chapter is to help those who want to own office buildings make a good choice whether the property is in the Central Business District or the suburbs. It is somewhat difficult, however, to clearly distinguish the essential differences between CBD buildings and those in the suburbs, because the basic characteristics of office buildings are similar whether they are low-rise suburban office complexes or CBD skyscrapers.

Office properties can be classified in a number of ways:

- By height: low-rise or high-rise
- By occupancy: single-tenant vs multitenant
- By location: CBD or suburban
- By quality: Class A or Class B

At different times all of these distinctions can be useful. For most investors, however, the common classification combines quality and location.

When investors speak of Class A or Class B buildings, they are seldom speaking in strictly construction terms, such as may be found in the *Marshall Valuation Service* definitions. Class A, to most owners and tenants, means the newest, most desirable high-amenity property in the best location. It is typically a larger building with the highest rents and the best tenants. Class B connotes a good building, often somewhat older than Class A buildings, but well maintained and in a good location. It can also be a new low-rise or mid-rise building in a slightly less desirable location than that occupied by the Class A property. Perhaps it has a mid-block location in the Central Business District or is on the fringe of the Central Business District. In most market areas, Class A and B buildings together account for about 70–75 percent of the supply.

The market can also be simply divided, for investment purposes, into "the best" (Class A and B) and "the rest." In this chapter we do just that by focusing on the investment potential of Class A and B buildings and ignoring "the rest." This does not mean that there is no money to be made from Class C and other buildings; but those kinds of buildings often require a hybrid type of investor who combines both passive and active investing. Class C and lower properties frequently require extensive rehabilitation to bring them up to minimum investment quality. These properties are purchased more for redevelopment than for long-term investment profits.

Supply and Demand Considerations

The evidence of office building oversupply confronts us every day, so there is little reason to detail its size and character here. The facts are that Class A and Class B buildings are showing vacancy levels of 15–20 percent or more in markets across the country. The question is not what the vacancy level is but what it will be. Will demand increase sufficiently to absorb the surplus space and return the office building market to a "normal" 8–10 percent vacancy level? The answer is: Not in this decade.

Demand

A number of demographic and economic trends assure us that this over-supply will persist for eight to ten years. Our oversupply was created by "easy" money and overly generous tax treatment of real estate. We may see friendlier tax treatment of real estate in the future, but we are not likely to see money flowing in the streets as it did during most of the 1980s.

Demand will not rise sharply between now and the year 2000, because the population elements that could increase demand are simply not there. As we saw in Chapter 1, our population is growing at close to the slowest pace in its history—and what's more, many of the components of population do not favor the office building. There is simply no possibility of a booming growth cycle stemming from population dynamics.

The group that makes up the new entrants into our work force, those 15 to 29 years old, will not be getting larger; it will be shrinking as a percent of total population, and this decline will persist through the year 2060. This means fewer new workers will enter the work force in the 1990s, and the demand for office space will be less. Combine this fact with some evidence that companies are using slightly less space per worker now than they did ten years ago and you get an even grimmer picture.

At the other end of the workforce spectrum, the 44- to 59-year-old group is undergoing changes that also do not favor office building demand. In the 1990s this will be the largest, fastest-growing group in the workplace. But many of these people are retiring at 55 or younger, as industry trims its employee rolls in an effort to get and stay competitive. The result of these trends is a multiple hit on office building demand. The source of our population information is *The Statistical Abstract of the United States* and the U.S. Census Bureau's publication *Current Population Reports*.

Population is not the only determinant of demand. Both the type of company looking for space and the number of jobs being created will change in the nineties. On the economic front, America has made huge strides in revitalizing its manufacturing industries and regaining its position as the world's number-one exporter. This restructuring and resurgence has led to changes in space demand. Much of the vitality in manufacturing is coming from small, new companies while big, older companies are downsizing. The office space needs of the newer companies are qualitatively different from those of the shrinking, older firms. These smaller firms are not often interested in moving into worked-over, tired old space. Many—perhaps most of them—want new and highly flexible space in buildings and locations that offer maximum amenities for their employees. Finally, office demand will be weaker in the years ahead because there will be fewer new jobs created in the 1990s than in the 1980s.

The definition of a good location will change as the demand comes from newer and smaller firms. "Best location" may come to resemble what was considered good location for a high-quality multitenant business park in the 1970s. It will be on the edge of a major city, on an expressway near an on/off ramp and highly visible. It will also be in a low-density, strictly controlled development with wide streets and lots of landscaping, including jogging and hiking trails, and with quality buildings offering lots of free parking, good food service on-site and unit sizes ranging from 1,000 to 20,000 square feet. All of this at prices that are significantly below class A rents. Such a change could mean more pressure on rents for existing buildings in both the Central Business District and suburban markets.

The suburbs of cities like Los Angeles, New York, Washington, D.C., Detroit, Chicago, Dallas and Atlanta are areas that could prosper from this trend. The bigger and more economically diversified the market, the stronger demand will be.

There may be smaller markets where you can do well, but as a general rule, trying to "boutique" your way to success is an uncertain course to follow. The bottom line is that demand is going to weaken, and investment choices will have to be made much more carefully.

Investment Characteristics

Demand fluctuates much more for office space than for other types of real estate, such as apartments or single-family residences. Consequently, the risk of vacancies is greater, and they last longer than in most other property types. Even the "great" buildings can't escape the problems of vacancies that have their roots in poor economic times. The Empire State Building did not achieve full occupancy during the first ten years of its life. The other side of the long-vacancy coin is long occupancy. When office space is rented to financially responsible tenants, they generally stay a long time. Leases of five to ten years are common today. Regardless of the length of the lease, the credit risk in "well-leased" office properties has been somewhat less than for most other types of real estate.

There is almost always strong competition for tenants, as the market "norm" is one of being overbuilt; what's more, the oversupply tends to persist for years. Few times in the history of office buildings have there been serious space shortages, and when such times appear, they are kept short.

Office buildings carry a risk of obsolescence that is at least as high as that for retail properties but not as easy to cure. Stretched-out absorption times have given rise to the fear that many new buildings are creeping toward obsolescence without ever having been fully utilized. Buildings with new technology appear in the market regularly, and you cannot meet this competition by simply putting a new facade on your property. The section on "Smart Buildings" at the end of this segment is but one example of the forces leading to technological obsolescence.

Office tenants expect far more service than is rendered to tenants in apartments or industrial properties. They pay for it, but the importance of maintaining tenant comfort through a high level of service is much greater than for any other type of real estate.

Many analysts insist that office building rents are not very sensitive to price competition, because quality tenants are more interested in a prestige building and a convenient location than they are in the rent. Although there is a grain of truth in that, the observation does not square with the facts of an overbuilt market. Since the fading years of the last decade, virtually every prospective tenant has shown a sensitivity to price—and that includes the "best" tenants. In fact, at the height of the oversupply, even prestigious existing tenants (especially those with long leases) were calling their landlords and negotiating a reduction in rent; some of them claiming that the rent being charged under their lease was "unconscionable." It is still true, however, that low rent alone will not attract the best tenants to a poor building.

The investment value of an office building is totally dependent on the strength of its leases. The lease controls every item of income and expense (except perhaps unexpected government-mandated costs), and each one must be carefully reviewed before purchase. The section on financial analysis, later in the chapter, deals more fully with the income stream; you will also find more detail on analysis in Chapter 10.

Quality of location and quality of the building is vital to generating and maintaining steady, long-term returns. The best buildings in the best locations always outperform the average buildings. It is not unusual, in an area with a persistent 10–15 percent vacancy factor, to see one or two of the top-quality buildings maintaining 95–97 percent occupancy.

The Smart Building

It would be difficult to find a major developer or investor who is not familiar with the term "smart building." It is equally difficult to find many among them who have an exact idea of what constitutes a completely smart building.

The smart building is not a revolutionary new concept. Office buildings have been getting gradually smarter for the last 50 years; it is an evolution that most lenders and investors envy. It wasn't until 1983, however, that the smart building became a popular marketing term.

There are numerous definitions of "smart building," and we are not going to add to the list by fashioning one. The Intelligent Building Institute has published a definition, which we paraphrase: *A building that integrates various systems such as lighting, heating, ventilating, air conditioning, voice and data communications to effectively manage resources in a coordinated mode to maximize occupant performance and investment return, effect operating cost savings and provide flexibility.*

This definition is broad enough to let many, if not most, modern buildings lay claim to being smart. In fact there are varying degrees of smartness, which inevitably creates confusion for all concerned. Given the conditions that the industry has been wrestling with for the past several years, some observers have stated that "A smart building is one that is completely rented."

A totally smart building is smart from the ground up. It has four components:

1. A design that accommodates high-technology communications and office automation and that is also aesthetically pleasing.
2. The very best operating systems.
3. A telecommunication system.
4. An office automation system.

While the first two are active contributors to a tenant's comfort and productivity, they are, essentially, passive components. The tenant has little or no influence over them and can be actively involved only by knowing what constitutes excellence so he or she can get more value for his or her rental dollar. With these informed choices, tenants influence how future buildings will be built.

If a building has true excellence in design, structure and building systems, that excellence will pay off over the life of the property by delivering higher income and lowering operating costs. Whether this theory and practice always coincide is debatable. Evidence is mounting that office building useful lives are being shortened because many buildings, even though only 10 or 12 years old, are functionally obsolete; they do not have the technological elements that modern tenants need. When it comes to a decision between competing buildings, however, "smartness" is not the only consideration. Quality tenants want four basic things from a building:

1. A superior location
2. Excellent appearance
3. Competitive rents
4. Ample parking

Parking is not always an important issue when the building is well-served by public transportation.

Investors should not be misled into believing that buildings with high-tech communication facilities and shared tenant services such as office automation will necessarily be more successful in attracting or keeping tenants than will their less fully equipped competitors. It is no longer an "either/or" situation. Many buildings have smart features today. One of the most appreciated is a superior heating, ventilating and air conditioning system (HVAC) that can be custom-tailored to a tenant's space and be controlled by him or her for operation during off-hours. Other features that were originally confined to smart buildings, like high-quality life safety systems, are becoming standard equipment, as are systems that allow a tenant to come and go during the hours when the building is closed to public use. What is not yet common is a high level of telecommunication capability and a full range of office automation services. The latter have not "caught on" with tenants.

Suburban Building Characteristics

Many suburban office buildings are built by owner-users who occupy part of the building and rent out the rest. As the suburban market has grown in importance, it has gained a measure of investor acceptance, and opportunities now exist to acquire properties that rival some of the better CBD buildings for quality of construction and amenities.

Suburban buildings are, on average, smaller than those found in the Central Business District. Total size usually ranges from 5,000 to 100,000 square feet. Some buildings in key locations are 200,000 square feet or more.

The tenant mix has been lawyers, accountants, real estate firms, financial services, insurance agents, doctors, dentists and other local businesspeople. Today, because of advances in communications, you are likely to find branches of major credit firms as well as the head offices of small to midsize companies. It is not uncommon to find a good mix of local and national tenants in the better suburban buildings.

Leases are frequently short; some are for only one year, but three-year to five-year terms are more common. You will find some ten-year leases in the bigger and better suburban buildings.

Location is always important, but it is not quite as critical for the suburban building as access and visibility. Tenants want easy access to the building site as well as convenient access to public and private transportation and to shopping and other services.

Proximity to executive housing is another critical location factor, as it helps to maximize the rent and to minimize tenant turnover. Closeness to worker housing is desirable but not nearly so critical as being near decision-maker housing.

The best locations, in terms of distance from the Central Business District, are those within 10 to 15 miles of that area. Many fine suburban projects, however, are farther from downtown and are successful. Such locations are usually strong because they are in a large suburban area with a population base in the millions and with all the components of the nearby urban center, such as fine shopping, hotels, an airport, an industrial base, entertainment and other cultural activities. The new descriptive phrase for these larger suburbs is "edge cities." There are close to 200 of them across the country.

In some cities the suburban office market contains more space than the Central Business District. In Houston it has almost three times the space, while cities like San Diego, Kansas City and Denver have approximately twice the office space in the suburbs as they do downtown.

The suburban office building offers the investor a measure of stability in the income stream, but it does not yet match the performance, over time, of CBD property. Investors are wealthy individuals, small groups, syndications, small to medium-size insurance companies, smaller pension funds and the previously mentioned owner-user.

Additional Investment Considerations: All Office Buildings

It is very possible to make money in today's market, but in a market of surplus, where values in many areas are static or declining, it pays to consider every aspect of the investment carefully before purchase. Here are some of the questions to consider.

Occupancy.   Is it at, above or below the local average? Why is it at its present level?

There have been cases, for example, in which owners have too many irons in the fire. They might be trying to lease up a brand new building, just a few blocks away, so they can get rid of their construction loan and fund a permanent loan. In such a case it is not unusual for owners to pay more attention to their current project than to one that may already have permanent financing. Special "bonus" commission arrangements are frequently offered to leasing agents in the area, on-site marketing staffs are maintained and very competitive pricing/concession packages are common. This attention to a new project can cause the lease-up of the owner's nearby project to falter. A new owner, by concentrating marketing attention on the previously neglected building, might find that occupancy will rise quickly. Recognizing situations like these allows some investors to buy at slightly better prices.

Parking.   Is there enough of it? Is it convenient, safe, economical?

Most tenants would prefer to have parking that is within the building itself, but the majority of them do not enjoy such good conditions. In some markets, having any kind of parking space is the height of luxury. In general, the farther the parking is from the building, the less desirable that building will be to tenants. There are exceptions to every rule; some nice projects have their parking 300 feet or more from their lobby and are doing fine. But new projects with better parking always come along, and when they do, the older, marginal-parking buildings lose tenants.

Closeness to parking is not the only issue. Adequacy of the parking is also critical. The best ratio is four spaces per 1,000 square feet of rentable area. Many buildings use only 2.5 to 3.0 spaces per 1,000 feet of rentable space for daily tenant parking, and it is common for them to make the balance available for public parking and generate revenue from it. Even though actual average daily tenant use may be 25–30 percent less than what is available, it is still critical to have a generous parking ratio. It may be the investment future of your building.

Location amenities.   Does this building have easy access for users of private and public transportation? Is it highly visible?

A strong location is one of the most important keys to investment success. Easy access to the site and high visibility are good regardless of the type of building. Visibility adds to the prestige tenants feel about being in a particular building; it also makes it easier to do business there.

A location near an expressway and/or close to subways, bus lines or other public transportation not only helps to reduce tenant turnover but also helps to attract some types of tenants. Most government tenants (there are some worth having) will not rent unless the property is near mass transit.

Access to this kind of transportation is created by public works, and when it happens, windfall profits are sometimes possible. Building owners along the Wilshire corridor in Los Angeles, for example, will find it easier to rent once the new subway is finished; they may also be able to increase the rent they can charge. Astute investors study such changes and take advantage of them. In a tight market you can profit from having more information than your competitors.

Support amenities.   Does the building or project have competitive tenant support amenities?

What you are looking for here is things like banks, food services, dry cleaners, service stations and car washes, gift stores and other good retail nearby. Property that is close to quality shopping and a variety of dining and entertainment options will rent better than property that is not so well-situated. Such location amenities are time-savers for executives and other employees and act as a valuable personnel retention factor.

Hazardous waste.   Is there a hazardous waste problem?

The major difficulty has been asbestos contamination, although this problem may be lessening as greater understanding of it develops. You can be certain of this: Many jurisdictions will pass laws (some already have) mandating the retrofit of fire sprinklers. Such laws, under the major remodel test, are tantamount to ordering the removal of asbestos from the decking and possibly other areas exposed and disturbed during installation. This will add substantially to the job cost.

There are other concerns. Even in the case of an office building, which most of us do not associate with hazardous substance use, there are considerable risks of actual or potential pollution for which the building owner could be held financially liable. For this reason, you cannot afford to buy any property today without a proper environmental assessment.

Competition.   Is the building competitive? Are the rents high enough to provide a fair return? Is new construction underway or planned? Is the building efficient? Does it have economical, effective and competitively flexible HVAC? What has been the concession policy? Are Tenant Improvement allowances (TIs) adequate or too high?

A good rule of thumb on TIs (they are almost always a factor in a lease negotiation) is that they should never exceed one year's rent. Thus a building with a $20 per square foot rental rate should not have an improvement allowance that exceeds $20 per square foot.

The country is full of investors who have become involved in some of the very best office real estate in their area and have never seen any cash flow from it. It has not been unusual, over the last 10 to 12 years, for rents to be too low to permit a profit. Today, many investors despair of ever making any money on an office building investment. As rents stabilize or decline, and operating expenses continue to move up at 3–5 percent a year, it is difficult to see how office buildings will be able to deliver much, if any, net operating income for the next seven to ten years.

Other Investment Considerations

The net cash flow from a quality office building is not very high; in some cases it has been nonexistent for extended periods. In recent years the higher the quality of the investment, the harder it has been for it to show a net return early on. Cash flows of 5–6 percent are not uncommon (once the property starts to produce any cash) for the very best buildings in the downtown areas. Overall, however, cap rates of 8–9 percent are more common. The price per square foot associated with these cap rates ranges from $150 to $250. The average (in 51 CBD locations as of June 1991) was about $174, according to the *National Real Estate Index Market History Report.*

The best suburban buildings have produced capitalization rates (Net Income ÷ Purchase Price) of 7.8 to 9 percent. It would not surprise informed investors if these rates rose to 10 percent or more.

If the premier CBD buildings produce so little net return, why is there such a strong demand for them? The demand has come from institutional buyers such as pension funds, insurance companies, foreign investors and wealthy individuals, who see the office building as a long-term investment offering stable returns that improve over time; it is regarded as a premiere diversifying asset in portfolios containing other investments that exhibit considerable volatility. Office buildings are seen as offering safety of principal, stability of income and a chance for price appreciation over the long haul. These beliefs are being sorely tested during the persistent oversupply condition.

There is a wide resale market for high-quality office buildings that are well located within an economically diversified market. Price fluctuations are normally minimal in the majority of well-chosen markets. This does not mean that office buildings do not decline in price; no real estate product type is immune from price declines. In some markets we have seen prices fall, for fine properties, by 50 percent or more because of severe economic problems. In Texas, for example, during the mid- to late 1980s, prices fell to a point that brand new, unoccupied midrise buildings were offered for sale at the same price per square foot that the sellers had been trying to get as rent only a few years before. Price declines of this sort are not good news for the conservative investor, but they are grist for the mill of the contrarian. Speculators love such prices, and many of them have positioned themselves to make fortunes in Texas, Colorado, Arizona, Louisiana and in parts of the Northeast. Timing the investment decision is just about everything in such markets.

The cost of finding office tenants is quite high, and it is not made any lower by the fact that tenant turnover has been high. Collection losses in normal times are usually minor, and rents are seldom the target of local or state rent control.

Although not easy to finance today, office buildings are usually readily financed or refinanced; the frequent periods of space surplus is proof of this.

Under the Tax Reform Act of 1986, there is little tax advantage in owning this type of property. The suburban building has a slight advantage, because its land cost is often a smaller percentage of total value, thus leaving more of the investment available to depreciate. This small advantage could be wiped out by a tax law change that would apply a lower capital gain rate to the land.

Feasibility Analysis

Few office buildings—perhaps none—are built without a feasibility study designed to measure the competitive state of the market at the time the building will be available for leasing. Presumably, these studies justify the construction of the buildings that get built. One cannot help but wonder how, with such a procedure, we ever get a serious oversupply. It is either a flawed process or those who order the studies are ignoring or rationalizing the findings. The smart money is on the "flawed process" option. Too many analysts deliver reports that simply reflect what overanxious lenders and developers want to hear.

In any event, once a building is up, the realities of the marketplace cannot be ignored. Periodic competitive market analyses (these are a continuation of the feasibility study into the operating phase) will have to be made in order to ensure high occupancy and a maximum return on investment. Without current and accurate market knowledge, you will very likely make poor competitive decisions.

Many owners isolate themselves from the market by not studying it and thus, among other things, make erroneous assumptions about the unique character of their property. This leads to asking rents and concession policies that are out of step with the times. Whenever you see an apparently good-quality building lagging behind the market in terms of occupancy, you will probably find an owner who is out of touch.

In spite of what appear to be limitations on its correct use, it is difficult to overestimate the worth of a valid feasibility study. Here is what a good analysis of the market should cover.

The market area.   This should be carefully defined. Normally it is not a difficult job. In the case of a CBD property, the market area is often the Central Business District itself, although in some cases a narrower definition (such as "Golden Triangle area") is justified.

The market area for suburban buildings is that area from which you are most likely to get tenants. The greater the distance the area extends from the property, the greater the chance that your definition of market size is too broad. Office building rental is a highly local business; you will seldom draw tenants from a wide area, and almost never from outside the metropolitan area. It is not uncommon for owners to be charmed by marketing agents who promise extensive efforts to locate tenants from distant cities. In spite of some slight evidence that there are moves from high-rent areas toward lower-rent and lower-wage areas, it is unlikely that such foreign tenants will be much of a factor in filling your building.

The competition.   There is a direct link between the feasibility study and the competitive market analysis (CMA), which you must create and maintain once you own the building. The CMA is a one-time project subject only to periodic updates to keep it useful. The first time it is done is the most time-consuming, although you actually do a large portion of it while you are surveying the market looking for the right location in which to invest. Most investors search a fairly narrow area, and the information they develop on various buildings usually finds its way into their market analysis file.

One of the most difficult and time-consuming tasks is the census of competitive buildings. Many services sell lists of office buildings—what they are, where they are, who owns them and other data. Few services have all the information you need to know, and their data are not always accurate. Once again, it boils down to doing it the hard way. You need detailed information, and the best way to get it is on your own. Here is a short list of items to investigate.

- Address and comments on quality of the location
- Building size—gross and net rentable
- Current occupancy level and list of tenants including square feet occupied, rent paid and lease expiration date
- Age and condition of building
- Building site, lobby and other amenities
- Parking and parking pricing policy
- Asking rent and effective rent
- Concession package
- Tenant improvement policy
- Off-site support facilities such as restaurants, shopping
- On-site support facilities such as food, shopping, secretarial services
- Bay depths, column spacing
- Building efficiency
- Any special advantages of this property from the tenant's viewpoint
- Disadvantages such as poor access or visibility, inconvenient parking or too little parking, poor outdoor lighting, poor HVAC, hazardous materials problems, mediocre or poor elevator service, poor maintenance, inattentive management

Supply and demand.   Many of the supply and demand indicators were discussed earlier in the chapter. At this level, you need to know the total current supply of competitive space in your market area including what is vacant, the amount of sublease space available (the "hidden" supply) and what is under construction or planned.

Your study should also include a look at the type and strength of demand. What type of tenant is looking for space today? What type of space does that kind of tenant need? How much of the total demand do particular tenant types represent?

The net absorption rate must be calculated. It is easy to be fooled by widely publicized accounts of total leasing activity, which is *not* net absorption. Net absorption is the change in the amount of occupied (leased) space in a given time period. That is, if on January 1 the market has 12.5 million square feet of leased space and on December 31 it has 15 million square feet, there has been 2.5 million square feet of net absorption. Total leasing activity might have been five or six million square feet, as tenants move around within the market. Net absorption is market growth; total leasing activity is just expensive turnover.

Finally, a frank assessment must be made of current and future competitive conditions in this market.

The task of putting together a proper feasibility study before you invest, or a useful competitive market analysis after you've made your investment, involves more than sitting at a desk looking at a mass of data compiled by some real estate broker or data service. You must get out and see the competition for yourself. Until you do that, you will always be at a greater risk of committing the kinds of errors of fact or interpretation that have been so commonplace in the recent past.

Financial Analysis

The job of financial analysis is deceptively simple. It is a matter of determining the gross scheduled income, the vacancy and collection losses and the expenses, and calculating a net income that is the basis of value. In practice, however, it is a tedious job requiring meticulous attention to the detail in each and every lease and a thorough examination of all accounting records. It takes dogged determination to get the job done right. For a major building (400,000 square feet or more), it is a job that can easily consume 30 days or more, even when one is using the latest computer software. For a smaller suburban building, a 7- to 14-day investigation into the income stream would not be unusual.

Financial analysis is more complicated today because of the severely overbuilt condition of most of our office markets. It is always important to analyze the building both from an investor's viewpoint and through the eyes of a prospective or existing tenant.

Virtually all tenants have sophisticated computer analysis tools available to compare the effective cost, in present-value terms, of renting space in your building with the cost of renting in any other building in the market. The comparative analysis tools being used by tenants can also be useful to landlords. With such tools the landlord can put together better lease proposals than his or her competitors or, if all deals are about equal, can press nonfinancial points with greater vigor knowing that it is not money but location or other amenities that will tip the scale.

When analyzing a building for purchase, one of the first pieces of information you need is accurate data on the gross and net rentable building area. Presumably, the total of all occupied and vacant space will add up to these numbers. But it is not that simple in some larger markets, where a lot of property is held by relatively few owners. In such situations (New York City is the best example) it is not unusual for the net rentable space in a building to expand and contract with the state of the economy. In some cases the amount of space on which rent is being paid is greater than the amount of space in the property. The possibilities for difficulties that this presents for a new owner in a declining market are quite serious.

Once the gross and net areas have been accurately determined, they should add up to the totals from the leases and the vacant space. If these totals do not balance, many days of work can lie ahead.

The list of income and expense items for office buildings is not complicated; it is the detail behind these items that makes analysis time-consuming. A simplified chart of accounts appears below. You will find detailed information on income, expense and occupancy in Chapter 10.

1. Income:
   - Gross scheduled income—Rents from office and retail space, parking, etc.
   - Vacancy and collection loss
   - Adjusted gross income—Gross scheduled income minus vacancy and collection loss
2. Expenses:
   - Taxes—Real estate, fees, permits, etc.
   - Utilities—Energy, water, trash removal
   - Insurance
   - Janitorial—Supplies, payroll including benefits
   - Maintenance and repair—Supplies, payroll, service contracts

- Management fee—On-site and off-site
- Landscaping and exterior services—Window washing, snow removal, common area cleanup
- Lease commissions
3. Net Income:
   - Adjusted gross income minus all expenses; also called net income before debt service. This figure is capitalized to ascertain value when using the income approach to value. Today you should be able to achieve a current return of 9–10 percent; if you can't, put your money somewhere else.

On a percentage basis, annual expenses range from 40 to 43 percent of gross scheduled income. In dollar terms the range is from $5 for a suburban building to $8.50 a square foot for a CBD building. Per-square-foot expenses vary based upon the region of the country, with the Northeast and the far West tending to have the highest costs. Information on income and expense levels can be obtained from the Society of Industrial and Office REALTORS® and from the Building Owners and Managers Association, as well as from the Institute of Real Estate Management and many local sources.

Financing

The trend is toward much less use of mortgage debt to finance the purchase of office buildings than in the recent past. When credit is used, the loan maturity is shorter than at any time in the last 30 years, and the loan-to-value (LTV) ratio and debt-coverage ratio (DCR) are both higher than they were in the 1980s. It is now common to see equity of 30 percent and DCRs of 1.20 to 1.30.

Many purchases are for cash, although the cash used is often credit from other sources, such as loans made in reliance upon the general credit of the borrowing corporation, or loans that use other real estate as collateral.

The source of many foreign purchasers' investment cash is often loans against real estate owned in their home country. Frequently it is a combination of loans, such as a loan on their domestic assets for 50 percent of the purchase price and a loan against the property being acquired in the United States for the balance. This blends the interest rates from at least two countries and often makes the foreign investor more competitive than domestic buyers. Any use of dollar-denominated loans exposes the investor to the vagaries of the U.S. interest rate market and tends to slow foreign interest in U.S. property when rates are high.

Loan Sources

There are six major sources of financing for office buildings. These sources can be loosely divided into two categories: national lenders and local lenders.

Life insurance companies, major syndicators and credit companies serve a national market. Commercial banks, savings and loans, and some smaller insurance firms work the local market. When the banking industry finishes its consolidation period, you will find banks added to the list of national lenders. Pension funds may serve both local and national markets.

In many respects the life companies and the larger pension funds have similar loan criteria, even though some pension funds limit themselves to loans in their own state or local area. These lenders usually want a loan of $5 million or more; and because they are looking for both safety and stability of income, they often will not fund a loan until a substantial portion (75 percent or more) of the space is leased.

Both life companies and pension funds offer a full variety of interim and permanent loans but tend to favor permanent loans over construction lending.

Commercial banks and savings and loans usually provide construction loans and short-term permanent financing. Syndicators, when they are available, may be approached for just about any type of loan format, including construction financing that later converts to a permanent loan. National syndicators tend to be the best source for creative financing approaches, as local and smaller syndicators normally confine themselves to "normal" deals.

The credit companies provide perhaps the widest variety of loan formats. They will also look at highly specialized projects, such as medical office buildings and other nonstandard developments. Credit companies are not a big factor in the total loan market but can occasionally be useful. Their rates are usually higher than those of other lenders. Table 2.1 shows the percentage of loans made, in the Spring of 1992, by the major loan sources.

Table 2.1   Sources of Office Building Financing

Loan Sources	Percent of Total
Sellers	28
Commercial Banks	32
Insurance Companies	19
Pension Funds	<1
Loan Assumptions	2
Private Investors	4
Syndicators	2
Savings and Loans	13

Source: NATIONAL ASSOCIATION OF REALTORS®, *Financing Investment Real Estate,* Volume 5, Number 1 (Washington, D.C.: Spring 1992), 20.

Types of Loans

Even though financing is more difficult to arrange than it was during the last decade, there is a greater variety of loans available today. What might have been labeled as wildly creative only a few years ago is merely a routine structure today. We have listed the major types of loans, with a brief discussion of each. Before we get into that, however, we need to look at the mechanics of financing an office building.

Most new office buildings are financed in two steps: first a construction loan, and then a permanent loan. It is customary to get a permanent loan commitment when you negotiate the construction loan, or even before, because your permanent loan sets the upper limit of the construction loan.

Permanent loans normally have two parts: the guaranteed amount and the contingent amount. The second part (the maximum loan) will be funded upon attaining a specified percentage of lease-up to approved tenants. The construction loan, of course, will generally not exceed the guaranteed, or minimum, commitment. The permanent loan "takes out" the construction lender at the end of his two-year or three-year loan term or when the agreed-upon lease-up has been reached.

The mechanics of construction and permanent lending lead to a number of loan terms (such as *take out*) and deal structures. One of these is the *gap* loan.

Gap loans, which close the gap between the amount of the construction loan and the total cost of construction, are provided by lenders that are willing to take more risk than traditional financial sources. Such funds could be in the form of equity—but when they are not, gap loans are used. These loans are generally quite expensive, as they are one of the riskiest types of real estate financing.

The most common types of financing are bullet loans, miniperms, floating-rate loans, participating and convertible loans, land-sale leasebacks and joint ventures.

The bullet loan.   Life insurance companies have been the biggest provider of this type of loan. Often their source of funds for these loans is Guaranteed Income Contracts (GICs). Issued to pension funds, GICs guarantee a fixed rate of return for a fixed time period. Hence, bullet loans generally are intermediate-term loans (3 to 12 years) at a fixed rate and are usually amortized beyond their maturity date, so there is a balloon payment. The payment schedule may be flat during the term of the loan or it may vary, with an interest-only payment for the first few years and principal and interest over the remaining term. Terms are subject to negotiation and to the requirements of the GIC that supplies the loan funds.

The miniperm.   This is a fixed-rate loan that normally has an interest accrual feature. Payments may be interest-only for five or ten years. Interest can be one rate at the beginning of the payment schedule and can change to a higher rate later in the term. Unpaid interest (the accrual) is added to the principal balance; there is usually a cap on the amount of principal buildup allowed. This kind of loan is sometimes used to increase cash flow during the early years of a project.

Floating-rate loans with accrual.   In this type of financing, the interest rate is adjustable using one of many available indexes. Occasionally, the borrower is allowed to change interest adjustment methods during the life of the loan. The most common indexes used are:

- the U.S. prime rate; for example, prime plus 2 percent.
- the U.S. Treasury bill rate.
- the London Interbank Offering rate (LIBOR).

In each case, the index used is the base rate, and a premium of 1–2 percent is added.

Debt service is commonly at a fixed amount, with any deficiency in interest payments added to the principal. There is a limit on principal buildup. Loan terms are short; five years is common.

Participating and convertible loans. These loans are offered by life companies, pension funds and syndicators. They all have a *kicker*—a feature that gives the lender a chance to earn extra revenue from any increase in net income and resale value. Such loans are generally popular during periods of financing scarcity and high interest rates, because they frequently have a current rate that is less than the prevailing permanent loan rate. They are often available when other types of permanent financing are not.

A participating loan is just that. It gives the lender the basic interest rate and a participation in cash flow improvement, including resale profit, and nothing more. A convertible loan, however, is very much like hiring a developer to produce a building and paying him not only his development fee but a share of the total cash flow and/or a share of the building's total value. This share in value is calculated at the time of conversion and can amount to 10–15 percent of the total value. The conversion percentage is set by contract when the loan is made.

The convertible loan will often have a favorable loan-to-value ratio, because the lender is secure in the fact that it will convert this loan position to equity at a certain time. The lender receives a cumulative preferred return throughout the loan term and has first call on all cash flow. The developer is usually assigned all the tax benefits. Loan terms are for eight to ten years, with a loan amortization based on 25 to 30 years.

The land-sale leaseback. This device reduces the equity needed to fund an office project. In this type of financing, the lender buys the ground under the project, leases it back to the developer and executes a leasehold mortgage to finance the building.

This type of financing maximizes available depreciation but, of course, eliminates any profit attributable to the land. It can also minimize the tax advantage to the building owners if the capital gain treatment is only allowed for the land, or is at a lower rate for land profits than for improved property profits.

Land-sale leasebacks have been popular with syndicators. Many developers like them because they can sometimes "finance out" of a project and have no equity money invested.

The joint venture.   In a classic joint venture, the lender-investor puts up 100 percent of the funds needed to build the project and splits the ownership with the developer 50/50. Ownership can be divided other ways, too, such as dollar-for-dollar matching contributions. These "matching" joint ventures are the type most favored by Asian investors. In a joint venture, the provider of the funds almost always has a first claim on any income up to the agreed return; any difference is accrued until income is available to pay the proceeds of the funds. The balance of the income is divided between the partners according to the agreed formula.

Trends and Conclusions

Office buildings are a troubled property type. A persistent oversupply combined with steadily increasing operating costs and weak demand makes profitable operation unlikely for years to come. Bargains will appear in many areas, and leverage buyers may find the office building a way to build wealth through equity that gradually increases as their loans pay down.

Supply and Demand: Tenant and Investor

- Oversupply will continue to be the normal state of the market.
- The choices for an office building investment are broader than in the recent past because of the emergence of large suburban centers (edge cities).
- Investment demand for quality CBD buildings may fluctuate but, on average, is likely to remain strong for the balance of this decade.
- In the overbuilt markets, the get-rich-quick investors will go broke the fastest, even though there will be some excellent contrarian opportunities in the Northeast, as well as continuing opportunities in Florida, Texas, Colorado and Arizona.
- Job formation total is likely to be lower than in the 1980s, and new jobs will pay less than the old jobs they replace. This will contribute to a continuation of weak demand for office space.
- Competition will increase. New buildings will offer more amenities and services and put great pressure on the already troubled older (10 to 15 years) properties.

- Quality and variety of tenants in suburban buildings will continue to improve.
- There will continue to be a supply of buildings that are not renting well, in many cases, due to a lack of marketing attention.
- Foreign investor interest in quality buildings will continue.

Feasibility

- Rents should stabilize by the year 2000. Demand for longer leases will become intense during the last half of the 1990s.
- Cash flow is unlikely to improve in the short term.
- Tenants will continue to bargain hard on rents and "non-price" items, aided by highly sophisticated analysis programs.
- Environmental costs will increase even as a more balanced approach to regulation evolves.
- Fire sprinkler retrofit will be common.
- Parking will be a key to investment value in the long run.
- Buyers and lenders will insist on more accurate feasibility studies during the next eight to ten years.
- Financial analysis will become more realistic.

Financing

- Office buildings will be difficult to finance for many years.
- Loan-to-value ratios of 70–75 percent will be the norm, as will debt coverage ratios of 1:25 to 1. Due dates will be short.
- There will be less use of mortgage debt to finance acquisitions.
- Commercial banks will be significant national lenders after the current bank consolidation program is complete.
- The variety of deal structures will remain broad.
- The use of participating loans will increase over the next three to five years.

C H A P T E R

3

Industrial Properties

There is a real need, perhaps not fully realized, for baby-boom generation members to protect themselves against a dismal old age; a lot of them have inadequate retirement plans. Many have simply bought a house and are now sitting back waiting for it to make them rich. That may not happen. In any event, it is a dangerous wealth-building strategy because, essentially, houses are not investments and are not meant to be estate builders; the chance that they will remain at a stable value or decline in price is just too great to bet your future on it. Baby boomers need to buy and effectively manage carefully chosen investment real estate that will appreciate over time and, thus, provide for them when social security or other sources prove insufficient. Industrial real estate could be the vehicle that provides a comfortable retirement. Even if the boomers ignore it, industrial real estate will surge in popularity over the next eight to ten years; current conditions, and what are likely to be favorable future market conditions, will lead to its discovery by a lot of new investors.

Of the four major property types, only two show signs of possible strength before the end of this century; industrial is one of them. But not all industrial in all locations.

This chapter covers what you need to know, in good times or bad, to invest profitably in industrial property. You will find information on industrial from multitenant to single-tenant. The chapter begins with the classification system commonly used to identify industrial property types. It then moves to user types and to a short account of the history behind industrial investment. Following that is a section on warehouse/distribution buildings and a segment on industrial parks, including the multitenant business park. Particular attention is paid to the multitenant product, because it is representative of what is happening to our economy and population. Next you will find a section on supply and demand factors important to the industrial investment. The chapter ends with a trends and conclusions review.

Classification System

Most investors use a simple industrial property classification system having two main divisions: multitenant and single-tenant. These simple categories, however, do not describe the full range of industrial property types. A more complete list might include classification as follows:

- By the division of space: multitenant or single-tenant
- By the type of estate: leased or owned
- By type of use: e.g., manufacturing, warehousing, assembly and high-technology properties
- By the number of stories: multilevel and single-level
- By its access to rail: rail-served or non-rail-served
- By type of construction: concrete tilt-up, steel frame, wood frame, metal buildings, masonry buildings, other construction methods
- By the nature of the original tenancy: speculative or build-to-suit
- By tenant size: e.g., a "small tenant park" or a "high cube warehouse"

Industrial property can be classified using one or all of the categories just listed, depending upon your purpose.

As investors, most of us are interested in multitenant or single-tenant buildings that can be used for assembly operations, warehousing or light manufacturing. The buildings will most often range in size from 5,000 to about 150,000 square feet. Occasionally, transactions will be made in the

200,000-square-foot range for single-tenant properties. Multitenant parks can easily total one-half million square feet.

It is apparent even from this brief look at classification systems and tenant types that industrial property is far from a homogeneous segment of the investment real estate market. It may, in fact, be one of the most diverse property types.

Types of Users

Just like building classification systems, industrial tenants can be categorized in a number of ways. One way is by size; divide them into small, medium or large tenants. The most frequently encountered property type is the multitenant, general purpose building designed to accommodate tenants from about 1,000 to 100,000 square feet. No building, of course, can take such a wide range of tenant sizes, so it gives us yet another way to classify buildings—by the size of the tenants. In general, a small tenant will be in the 1000- to 5,000-square-foot range. There are tenants who can use even smaller spaces, and many incubator projects are built to handle them. Some of these small-space developments can be quite profitable, especially during recessionary times when people are losing their jobs and starting their own small businesses.

A medium-sized tenant will range from 5,001 to about 20,000 square feet; large tenants constitute the rest. To some extent, whether a tenant is considered small, medium or large depends upon context. In a warehouse/distribution center, for example, a 50,000-square-foot tenant is not considered large. These size classifications are not hard-and-fast rules; they are simply another way in which people think about industrial.

A Short History of This Product Type

Figure 3.1 is a condensed history of industrial property from 1840 to 1991.

Warehouse/Distribution Properties

Warehouse/distribution properties are often the ugly ducklings of industrial real estate. They seldom win architectural awards; they lack the curb

Figure 3.1   Highlights from the History of Industrial Property

The history of industrial property is not well-documented in easily available publications. I am indebted to the Urban Land Institute for granting permission to paraphrase its text and to use the general historical outline followed in Industrial Development Handbook.

1840	**United States:** Industrial jobs represented 10 percent of total employment; agriculture had 70 percent of total jobs.
1896	**Manchester, England:** Trafford Park Estates, 1,200 acres. World's first planned industrial park and the largest until early 1948.
1902	**Chicago:** Clearing Industrial District. Featured "superblock" planning idea. Expanded by 1,300 acres in 1948.
1910–1916	**Chicago:** Pershing Road Industrial Park. First use of central steam and electricity.
1916	**New York City:** First comprehensive industrial zoning ordinance adopted. Its rank-order zoning theory, which allowed "higher" uses to be built in "lower" zones, created unprotected industrial districts. Ordinance also marked the start of performance standards in industrial zoning.
1920–1922	**England:** Slough Estates, 602 acres. First use of a former military site as an industrial park.
1940	**United States:** Manufacturing jobs equalled 28 percent of total employment; agricultural jobs were at 21 percent.
	Los Angeles: Central Manufacturing District (CMD). First developer was the creator of Chicago's CMD. Later expanded by the Atcheson, Topeka & Santa Fe railroad.
1951	National Industrial Zoning Council adopted "Twelve Principles of Industrial Zoning." Urged prohibition of residential zoning in industrial areas. Led to the abandonment of rank-order zoning. Pioneered the concept that the effect of an industrial use on the environment is more significant than an arbitrary classification into light-use or heavy-use districts.
1954	*Performance Standards in Industrial Zoning,* published by Dennis O'Harrow. Marked the start of many zoning code changes throughout America. Urged objective measurement standards for 11 different nuisances, such as smoke, odor and noise.

Figure 3.1   Highlights from the History of Industrial Property (continued)

1957	**Chicago:** Performance standards for industrial zones adopted.
1960	**New York:** Performance standards for industrial zones adopted.
1960–1967	**San Francisco:** Cabot, Cabot & Forbes developed South San Francisco Industrial Park. One of the first times that open space was consolidated into a parklike area and made available for use by the general public.
1969–1972	Several federal laws passed that forever influenced the siting, design and construction of industrial property. Included National Environmental Policy Act (1969), National Clean Air Act (1970) and Federal Noise Control Act (1972).
1970	Approximately 3,000 industrial parks in the United States.
1988	Industrial sector employed about 26.1 million.
1991	About 8,000 industrial parks in the United States.

appeal of research and development (R&D) buildings and suffer badly if compared to buildings commonly found in the newer multiuse parks. The real beauty of warehouse/distribution properties can usually be found in their income statements. This type of property has consistently provided satisfactory current cash flows and, often, resale profits. Whether it will continue to do so depends upon the long-term trends of supply and demand, which are discussed later.

Warehouse/distribution is the largest use category within the industrial market, representing approximately 60 percent of total use. These properties have been actively sought by wealthy individuals and institutional investors because of their cash flow stability and high return on investment. Good-quality property can be difficult to find, but perhaps because of the narrowness of the investor base, it is usually priced to yield institutional-quality returns.

These properties have never been "popularized" in the way that apartments or office buildings have been. They are not "everyman's" investment. Investors with a small to medium amount of capital seldom participate in the abundant benefits often available from warehouse property. This industrial segment also has generally been avoided by syndicators and other group ownership vehicles because there are too few tax benefits, despite the fact that industrial property needs accelerated depreciation to offset faster-than-average obsolescence. This may be another of the numerous examples that prove there is no logic in the tax law. Foreign investors have had a bias toward office buildings and away from suburban property, so they too have avoided this type of industrial property.

If you want to invest in warehouse property, you've got to like the suburbs; it is essentially a suburban investment. High close-in land prices force it to the outskirts, and as a fortunate by-product of this flight to cheap land, investors often end up holding property in path-of-progress locations. The profits from land price increases are sometimes awesome in absolute terms and virtually always impressive in percentage terms due to low initial land costs. This is not meant to imply that all outlying industrial land increases in value, because it doesn't.

The "land play" phenomenon is also at work in some central city locations that are experiencing a growth in the service segment of their economies. In such situations, warehouse properties can sometimes be put to a higher use for retail, residential and office space.

Industrial Parks

The industrial park is to industrial property what the regional mall is to retail. Those that are composed of leased-only space and sites are the most desired developments. Competition among investors for good parks is stiff, because they are not only scarce but well-suited to institutional portfolios due to their quality and the dollar-size of the investment.

In its 1988 Directory of Membership, the National Association of Industrial and Office Parks defined industrial parks as follows:

An industrial park is the assembly of land, under one continuing control, to provide facilities for business and industry consistent with a master plan and restrictions resulting in the creation of a physical environment achieving the following objectives:

- Consistency with community goals
- Efficient business and industrial operations
- Human scale and values

- Compatibility with natural environment
- Achieving and sustaining highest land values

This definition gives a glimpse of the evolution of industrial parks (today they are quite likely to be called business parks) from pure industrial areas, with no sidewalks and limited, if any, human values such as lighting and landscaping, and few supporting services, to the modern multiuse development that blends industrial with office and retail uses—sometimes on a scale that stops just short of being a new town.

The definition of the industrial park also allows for several divisions into subtypes. Perhaps the most useful park classification system is the one that looks at their general uses:

- Mixed-use parks
- Office parks (these are often classified in with industrial, even though they do not belong there)
- Specialized-use parks, such as high technology parks
- Transportation parks (these are often near airports, railroad or port locations)

Besides considerations of tenant mix and financial strength, which are fully considered during your financial review, the quality of initial development and the operational standards are what discriminate among industrial parks. Location is paramount; superior visibility and access are a must. Beyond that, the characteristics of the site and its amenities are the essence of the investment.

The site should have level or slightly rolling terrain that can be divided into efficient industrial lots. It must be free from environmental problems and not in the path of waste runoff from nearby sites. It should have no flooding problems, and soil conditions should present no special construction problems. And the location must not conflict with neighboring land uses.

Individual sites within the park should accommodate current needs and reasonably anticipate future needs of their users. Parking is but one example. A worker's car already takes more space than the worker does inside the plant, and it is likely to get worse before it gets better. Adequate site size can help to prevent clogged streets that were not designed to handle parking.

Utilities can also make or break your investment. More attention must be given to them today to avoid buying into future problems. One has only to be a casual reader of the local paper to know that many communities have, or will have, serious utility problems. In some well-regarded growth areas, it is the cost and availability of electricity; in others it is, or will be, the availability of sufficient water. You need not saddle yourself with future problems in this area. The availability of utilities over the next 15 to 20 years is not like the earthquake problem; it is foreseeable and avoidable.

The operational management of the industrial park is almost completely within the control of the park owner. It is important to have management policies that are clear and enforceable, and that you enforce them; if you do not, you may lose them. Diligent daily management is a major key to profit.

Multitenant Industrial

Multitenant industrial properties could be one of the best places to invest your real estate capital during the next 10 to 15 years. Many strong population and economic trends suggest that this type of property and the more deluxe version, the multiuse business park, will be best-suited to serve the needs of downsizing older firms and emerging smaller companies. But they have to be the right product in the right place. In some areas this product type is already overbuilt and offers little immediate hope for a speculative profit.

This market segment is widely diversified in its own right; there is an almost equal opportunity to invest wisely or foolishly. Many projects that are small and of poor quality do not interest the long-term investor, although fixer-upper investors and other speculators can make money with them.

The type of multitenant project examined in this chapter is the high-quality, well located, planned development often referred to as a business park, because it accommodates a variety of uses from light manufacturing to small retail and small office use. Total project size will range from 125,000 to 500,000 square feet. They are located on sites that range upwards from ten acres. Building coverage is usually 30–35 percent.

Individual tenant spaces range between 600 and 5,000 square feet; occasionally you will find even larger tenants in these projects. It is not uncommon for the landlord to finance the construction of the tenant's interior improvements and include the cost in the rent.

Because of their appeal to small-space users, multitenant parks are somewhat recession-resistant. Investors, however, should not be lulled into thinking they are recession-proof; no type of real estate enjoys that advantage.

The heyday of this type of product was from 1970 to 1974, which means that many of them are now close to 20 years old. Given this fact and the strong indications that multitenant space will be needed in the next 10 to 15 years, we may well see a mini–building boom in some areas. Competitive pressure on the older parks will increase, but in many cases they will have the advantage of irreplaceable superior locations. This will be true only for those areas in which the tide of business activity is not running strongly toward the new frontiers of the far suburbs.

Institutional investors, particularly insurance companies, have been the big investors for this type of product. This involvement has led the way to many fine investments, as these institutional investors look at their holding period and decide to reap the profit residing in what they feel are aging properties. If the disinflation pressure continues to build in the economy, more such opportunities will appear.

Location is of overriding concern when selecting a multitenant property. Many fine projects exist outside the boundaries of industrial parks, but to maximize your chance for success, do not buy one unless it is in a quality location. Here are the site selection criteria that deliver profits:

- Location is at the entrance to a planned industrial park that exercises reasonable management control over development.
- The park is on a major highway.
- The project is visible from and easily accessible to the highway.
- Being at an on/off ramp is good if no traffic flow inhibitors exist.
- The project must be close to a major metropolitan area that has a diversified economy.

These physical characteristics create and help maintain investment value:

- A good balance between large and small units.
- Set-back, covered front entrances to each unit.
- Individual street number addresses whenever possible.
- Front and rear personnel doors. Rear access through a people door installed in the overhead door is an investment value destroyer.
- Overhead door, preferably a roll-up, rear-loading only.
- Warehouse light switch at both front and rear personnel doors.
- Fifteen to 20 percent prebuilt, carpeted, heated and air-conditioned office space with two restrooms, coffee bar and closet space for coat storage.
- Minimum of three car spaces per 1,000 square feet of rentable space; more parking is better. Most desirable layout: No parking next to the front entrance of any unit. All front parking should be opposite each building next to the perimeter landscaping.
- Eighteen-foot panel height with a 14-foot clear span.
- Fire sprinklers.
- Generous, well-maintained landscaping. Lots of grass, trees and seasonal color. A building coverage ratio of 30–35 percent is best.
- Concrete parking lot. Most projects will not have this, but next to roofs, the parking lot will be your biggest maintenance headache.
- Strict tenant sign controls.
- Architect-designed by a firm experienced in this type of project.

Investment characteristics include the following:

- Fluctuating income primarily due to tenant turnover.
- Short (one-year to five-year) leases to ordinary local tenants. You may get some major credit tenants. Leases generally are net, but some parks may have gross leases.
- Intensive management. Big projects must have on-site management. Vigorous rent collection procedures backed by strong policies is an absolute must. It is not unusual to have rent collection problems with 20–25 percent of the tenants. It is essential that your lease provide that all pro rata charges (taxes, common-area maintenance, etc.) be estimated and collected monthly in advance.
- High maintenance costs due to tenant turnover. Tenant turnover of 30–40 percent annually is not unusual.

Ownership and Yields

Only single-family residential real estate has a higher percentage of owner/occupants than industrial real estate. While no definitive study has been made of the exact division between investor-owned and user-owned industrial real estate, it is estimated at 60 percent investors and 40 percent users. In some ways the big percentage of occupant-owned industrial real estate adversely affects the supply of investment-grade property. Not all of the owner-occupied buildings are permanently unavailable to investors; this is the pool from which many sale/leaseback transactions are made.

Of the property in the hands of investors, much is owned by three types of investors:

1. Life insurance companies
2. Pension funds
3. Wealthy individuals

Wealthy individual investors are attracted to industrial property because it employs large amounts of capital, at better than average returns, over a long period of time. This, of course, is the same reason that insurance companies and pension funds like industrial.

Table 3.1 shows the yields achieved by all major property types over the past 12 years. The data in this table come from reports submitted by real estate fiduciaries on approximately 1,561 institutional-grade properties, of which 523 are warehouse/distribution and 221 are research and development/office. The average property value is about $7 million in the warehouse distribution segment.

Over the past 12 years, the warehouse/distribution and R&D/office segments have turned in a reasonably good performance. Their recent record is, of course, sharply lower than these averages, but Table 3.1 does tend to show why institutional investors have favored industrial investments. Total Return, in Table 3.1, is the combination of current net income and appreciation. Net income, even at the depth of the recession of the early 1990s, was over 7 percent; total return fell, however, as all product types suffered value losses due to the perception that all product types were overbuilt. Vacancy rates in the early 1990s, during the most stressful

Table 3.1 12-Year Annualized Rates of Return By Property Type (1979–1991*)

Property Type	Total Return (Includes Appreciation)
Warehouse/Distribution	10.9%
Research & Development/Office	11.0%
Office	8.5%
Retail	11.3%
Apartments	N/A**

* = Quarter Two, 1991.
** = Return for the past three years (1989–1991) has been 5.7 percent.
Source: The National Council of Real Estate Fiduciaries and the Frank Russell Company, the
NCREIF Real Estate Performance Report, 2nd Quarter, Used by permission.

time real estate has experienced since the 1930s, hovered between 6.9 and 7.5 percent nationally for industrial as a group.

In Table 3.2, you can see, again, that there are usually yield differences among regions of the country. The South, which is expected to do better over the next five years, turned in the weakest performance over the past five.

Financing

Historically, insurance companies have been the largest providers of industrial financing; in most normal years, they will provide more loan dollars than all other sources combined. We have not had so-called "normal" times in financing for a while now, and it is possible that what was normal in the past will not be the standard for the future. The research suggests, however, that there will be adequate financing for the rest of this decade. Table 3.3 shows who the lenders are, how they rank, and how that ranking has changed between 1991 and 1992. The ranking of these loan sources will always change over time, but the sources will remain the same.

Insurance companies are not currently (in late 1992) as active as they have been historically, but evidence points to a change in direction for these lenders, from principally large deals to more small loans with longer maturities. Sellers, who almost always become very active loan sources

Table 3.2 Warehouse/Distribution Properties Total Return by Region: Five
Years and One Year*

Region	Five Years	One Year*
East	9.0%	−3.4%
Midwest	9.1%	0.3%
South	2.8%	−0.8%
West	9.7%	2.0%

* = As of Quarter Two, 1991.
Source: The National Council of Real Estate Fiduciaries and the Frank Russell Company, the
NCREIF Real Estate Performance Report, 2nd Quarter, Used by permission.

during times of recession, will fall back to a relatively minor role as other
lenders regroup and learn how to deal with the new American economic
realities. Table 3.3 data are significant only at the national level; consult
regional and local sources for timely and reliable information for your
own market.

Supply and Demand

Investors are fortunate that the Department of Commerce publishes some
information relative to the new supply of industrial property. You will find
this data in its publication *Value of New Construction Put in Place,* Series
C-30, which is published monthly. Local data is available either from the
building department, the assessor or the planning department in the cities
and counties or townships in your area. Being up to date on additions to
supply is especially important in the industrial area. The permit process
is often easier and construction is certainly simpler than for other types
of real estate. New supply can appear practically overnight. Your study of
total and new supply should include data on permits issued (pending new
supply) and planned (prepermit) construction. Planned construction figures can often be obtained from local industrial real estate specialists and
from some planning departments.

Table 3.4 compares the recent new supply history of industrial property
nationally with that of selected other commercial property; during the
period from 1980 to 1992. It is instructive to note the considerable growth
restraint exhibited by this property type while the office building segment

Table 3.3 Industrial Property Lenders

Type of Lender	Percent of Loans Made	
	1991	1992
Seller	40%	14%
Commercial banks	37	50
Insurance company	10	10
Pension fund	4	3
Loan assumption	3	3
Savings and loan	2	14
Private investor	2	3
Syndication	2	3
TOTAL	100%	100%

Source: National Association of REALTORS®, *Financing Investment Real Estate*, Vol. 4, No. 3, Fall 1991, and Vol. 5, No. 1, Spring 1992 (Chicago), 17, 20.

was being massively overbuilt. It appears, on the national level, that industrial buildings are not the kind of property that gets relentlessly overbuilt. That does not mean it will never be happen, however. There are many local areas that are almost exactly opposite of these national trends.

New construction totals do not define the difference in the total supply each year, because many buildings are removed from the market as they become too old to compete. The relatively orderly pace of new supply additions helps to maintain stability within the industrial property market and is one of the reasons the conservative investor likes quality industrial investments.

The demand picture, while not wildly bullish, is encouraging. Fundamental forces are at work in the economy that will change the nature of industrial space demand. A major shift, from manufacturing to other industrial employment, has already occurred and will continue. *Other industrial employment* is any activity not directly related to manufacturing a product.

Total manufacturing employment may decline by 200,000 to 300,000 jobs per year during the next ten years, while other industrial jobs increase at about 200,000 per year. This may seem to be a zero-growth scenario, but it isn't. The combination of job losses and gains will stimulate a different kind of demand in the nineties than we had in the eighties but

Table 3.4   Industrial and Selected Commercial* Construction: 1980–1992
(in millions of 1987 dollars)

Year	Industrial	% of Total	Yearly Growth Percent	Other Commercial	% Change
1980	19,732	25.0	−15.7	59,240	9.8
1981	22,387	26.9	13.5	62,704	5.9
1982	21,891	25.0	−2.2	65,614	4.6
1983	15,850	19.6	−27.6	65,038	−0.9
1984	16,373	16.9	3.30	80,301	23.5
1985	18,408	16.5	12.4	92,854	15.6
1986	15,470	15.1	−16.0	87,126	−6.2
1987	15,026	14.9	−2.9	85,791	−1.5
1988	15,838	15.4	5.40	87,199	1.6
1989	18,919	17.9	19.5	86,792	−0.5
Average	17,989	19.3	1.0	77,266	5.2
1990	21,441	20.2	13.3	84,626	−2.5
1991	19,951	22.8	−6.9	67,657	−20.3
1992 (P)	19,400	21.8	−2.8	68,900	1.8
Average 1990–92	20,264	21.6	1.2	73,728	−7.2

* = Other commercial included in this tabulation is total private nonresidential construction minus industrial construction.

** = Relationship between totals may not be the same as the figure used due to rounding.

P = Projected; 1992 figure is projected, as is the average for 1990 to 1992.

Source: U.S. Department of Commerce, Bureau of the Census, Construction Division, *Value of New Construction Put in Place* (Washington, 1992).

there will be strong demand for industrial space across the nation, even though it will not be evenly distributed.

Flexible-use/R&D-type space will be in strong demand in many markets due to the employment changes mentioned above and an intense demand from smaller firms. This change will favor many areas in California and other states that have high-tech activity, while hurting areas heavily saturated with traditional manufacturing space.

Other economic and demographic factors, such as continued growth in both imports and exports and a predicted shortage of entry-level employees, are sure to affect the kind of space wanted and its location. The best bet for the next ten years seems to be small, new, highly flexible space in the suburbs.

Trends and Conclusions

Supply

- There is little chance that speculative overbuilding will occur during the next decade.
- National supply/demand balance should remain favorable into the late 1990s. Shifts in the American economy will create areas of surplus.
- Obsolescence will occur at a more rapid rate than for most other types of investment property.

Demand

- Demand is likely to be good overall and may be strong for the type of space favored by smaller firms.
- Smaller, newer buildings in suburban locations will experience the strongest demand.

Investment Considerations

- Industrial property will be "discovered" by many more investors. It could be a very suitable property type for baby-boomer investment holdings.
- Quality and flexibility will be the key to investment success. High-quality, flexible-use buildings and multiuse industrial parks in superior locations are the most likely to prosper over the next ten years.
- Small to medium-size properties will perform better than the high-cube warehouse during this decade.
- Investment opportunities will not be evenly distributed throughout the country. The West and the South should do best; however, there is no guarantee that all properties in the expected growth areas will do well. Some excellent opportunities will still exist in the slower

growth regions. Highly detailed feasibility studies will pay off by helping you to select the right property type in the right area.

- Total returns will be lower for a short period and then rise to levels closer to historic yields. This could create an opportunity for some alert investors. Competition for quality investments will continue to modify returns.
- Some minor tax relief may be given to industrial property in an attempt to stimulate job growth.
- There may be some profitable rehabilitation projects available as institutional holders continue to sell off their older properties.

Utilities

- Availability of water, sewers and electricity may take on critical importance in the next five to ten years, even in major metropolitan areas.

Environment

- It is unlikely that environmental costs will modify much; they may even increase during the first five years of the 1990s.

Financing

- There will be adequate financing for the balance of this decade.

C H A P T E R

4

Shopping Centers and Other Retail Investments

Shopping centers and other retail investments have provided excellent opportunities for well-informed investors for decades. No other real estate captivates investors quite like retail investment. Until the early 1970s, when every retail type became seriously overbuilt, the shopping center was the number-one investment choice. By 1983 they showed strong signs of having regained investor favor, but in 1990 interest in retail waned once more as a recession cut retail sales and vacancies mounted. All through these retail ups and downs, the regional shopping center has been able to hold on to its most-favored position with institutional investors. In fact, the regional's influence touches all levels of retail investing. Some people get into retail investing because of the favorable feelings they've picked up from the high-profile regional centers. Occasionally this "halo effect" imparts strength to a market that should be weakening.

More people now own all or part of a retail center than at any time in our history. What was once only an outrageous fantasy, owning all or part of a major retail property, was made a reality for thousands of small investors with the advent of huge public syndications. But changes in the tax laws, a decline in the growth rate of retail sales and a prolonged recession in the early 1990s turned dreams of retail riches into nightmares for many of these uninformed investors.

Retail investments are easier to find today, but the investment decisions are much more difficult to make than they were during the shopping center boom years of the 1950s and 1960s. There is more market saturation now, capital requirements are higher, and the consequences of a poor decision are greater and more difficult to correct.

This chapter will provide you with the background information you need to judge the feasibility and profitability of a shopping center or other retail investment. It covers the common retail classification systems, new retail formats, the impact of rehabilitation, renovation and additions, the principal demographic and economic factors affecting retail investment, investment characteristics (financial and nonfinancial) and typical deal structures. It concludes with trends and conclusions, including a forecast for the future of this property type.

A Short History

The shopping center industry is a young industry that has been created and matured within the business lifetime of its major practitioners. Its modern history dates from about 1957. The International Council of Shopping Centers was founded that year, when the number of centers nationwide was about 3,000; there are now over 36,000. Today there is about 17 square feet of mall space for every man, woman and child in the United States.

Even though the industry has had a short American history, retailing and retail investments go back to the early history of mankind. During man's tribal and wandering stage, central places existed where the tribes and other groups could gather to hold meetings or conduct ceremonies. These central places evolved into trading posts and bazaars, and later into hamlets, villages, towns and cities.

The original high-traffic retail locations were the town squares that evolved from the centuries-old tradition of central meeting places. Even in primitive societies, these town squares were used for business and social activities when not in use for meetings and ceremonies. Such areas became the social and economic centers of the early towns. It should not be surprising, given this history, that many modern shopping centers have a social and bazaar-like, or festival, atmosphere surrounding them, and that many of them serve as the "downtowns" or central meeting places for their areas. One of the newest retail formats, the factory outlet center (discussed in the next chapter), has many of the central meeting place and festival features of the shopping areas from man's earliest history.

In some cultures, the central square was in front of the town's church. In the United States, the most prominent structure on the square was often the courthouse; it was surrounded by retail activity and small offices on the adjoining streets.

In the 1700s many eastern and midwestern towns were developed around the town square. In almost every American city, precious reminders of those original town squares exist and still support vigorous retail activity. Union Square in San Francisco is reminiscent of such town planning. Figure 4.1 presents some of retailing's historical highlights in chronological order.

Classification System

To examine the full range of retail investment opportunities, it is necessary to divide them into two broad categories: non–shopping center developments and shopping center properties. It is easier to find information on shopping centers than on the non–shopping center format. Much of the retail literature and virtually all of the trade organizations deal solely with the shopping center, even though less than one-half the country's retail sales volume is done through such centers.

The non–shopping center properties range from small mom-and-pop, single-tenant buildings to large major-credit tenant, freestanding facilities. Included also are thousands of street-facing shops along most of our major arteries.

The variety of facilities is large enough to inspire several different classification systems, none of which is completely satisfactory. The most useful is both the simplest and the oldest. It divides all shopping centers into three main types: regional, community and neighborhood. If you add strip retail and freestanding facilities to this list, you will cover virtually every type of retail investment. The simplicity of this system makes it a bit awkward to accommodate the newest retail formats, such as technological centers, factory outlets, warehouse retailing, specialty centers, power centers and a few others, but it is a workable classification method.

Figure 4.1 A Short Retail History: U.S.A.

Early 1700s	American towns begin to develop around a town square.
Early 1800s	First department stores appear and begin to replace the country store.
Late 1800s	Development of the first "streetcar" suburbs. Beginning of specialized downtowns.
Early 1900s	The start of mail-order retailing.
1907	Free parking amenity pioneered by Edward H. Boulton at the Roland Park shopping district in Baltimore, Maryland.
1923	First true shopping center opens: Country Club Plaza, Kansas City, Missouri. Developed by J.C. Nichols.
1929	The first inward-facing shopping center: Highland Park Village, Dallas, Texas. Developed by Hugh Prather, Sr., it is still operating; a charming, successful center.
1930	Self-service retailing pioneered in supermarkets.
1947	Crenshaw Center opens in Los Angeles, California: one of the first regional centers.
1950s	FHA and VA loan programs spur rapid suburbanization. Retail construction boom begins. The first enclosed mall is built in Framingham, Massachusetts. The first regional mall (Northgate Center, Seattle) anchored by a full-service department store is built. It pioneered truck service tunnels.
	The first major discount stores appeared.
1957	The International Council of Shopping Centers is founded.
1960	Self-service retailing expands to department stores. Variety stores begin to disappear. The decade of the open mall begins. Many of the big retail development firms are started. This year also was marked by the first use of the boutique layout by Henri Bendel in New York.
1967	The first food/drug combination store is opened in Pathmark, New Jersey.
1970s	Enclosed malls proliferate and superregional centers emerge. Off-price clothing stores open in New England.

Figure 4.1   A Short Retail History: U.S.A. (continued)

1972	Construction of regional malls peaks. The first factory outlet centers appear.
1980s	A decade of retail market segmentation and of the restructuring of the department store segment. Rapid development of specialty centers. In-fill development and rehabilitation both increase. Rural markets receive new attention as do the long-ignored CBDs. There is a rapid growth of the gas/convenience market format.
1990s	Retail demand falls, space absorption declines, rent increases stalled in many markets. Department store restructuring continues. Start of the "temporary" store phenomenon.

The Regional Shopping Center

The regional center is America's dominant retail institution. About one-third of all retail sales take place there, even though it accounts for less than 7 percent of all retail space. It is the country's premiere investment vehicle and the preferred real estate investment of most large life insurance companies and big pension funds. In the past, some investment demand has also come from real estate investment trusts and syndicators.

Slowing population growth has led some analysts to conclude there is limited opportunity for development of new regional centers but growing opportunity for renovation of or additions to existing centers. Burgeoning areas in the far West and the South will have some demand for new regional centers this decade.

Regional centers are generally enclosed malls that range in size from 300,000 to 2 million square feet; sometimes they are even larger. The average size is about 700,000 square feet. Land area ranges from 30 to 150 acres or more. Lots of parking, usually free, is an absolute must.

The tenant mix of a regional distinguishes it at least as much as its size. It is customarily anchored by one to three full-service department stores and will have a multitude of small satellite tenants. With four or more major tenants, the regional is elevated to "superregional." The trade area for a regional center is ten to fifteen miles; a superregional will have a longer reach than that.

Satellite tenants are not necessarily small, although the trend is toward smaller stores; some mall stores approach 10,000 square feet in size. Typical tenant distribution is general merchandise, 50 percent; clothing and shoe stores, 15 percent; other soft goods, 10 percent; miscellaneous merchants and services, 25 percent.

Lease terms for major tenants range from 20 to 25 years, while the nonanchor mall tenants average ten years, and some even have leases as short as three to five years. Virtually all leases are triple net (NNN), with all expenses passed through to the tenant.

Regional centers seem to take three to five years to reach their best performance and will need rehabilitation after ten years. Santa Monica Place, in Santa Monica, California, for example, was refurbished in 1991 after 11 years of operation at a cost of about $15 million dollars. That was small change compared to the $120 million spent on the Brea Mall, in Brea, California, after a similar period.

The Community Center

Community centers, whether older or newly developed, have been one of retail's hottest property types. As retailing gets more competitive, retailers want to locate as close as possible to their customers in facilities that are smaller, easier for their customers to reach, and faster and less costly to build and operate. The community center and its smaller counterpart, the neighborhood center, are in the mainstream of this trend. They have been the fastest-growing segment of the retail investment market.

Community center size ranges from 150,000 to 300,000 square feet. They are usually unenclosed, but occasionally one is developed as an enclosed mall. They will use from 10 to 30 acres of land. Parking is generally free.

The amount of parking is critical to the success of *any* center, not just regional or community centers. The amount needed is about the same for all centers. Here is what you should find as a minimum: Regional centers, 5.7 spaces per 1,000 square feet of gross leasable area (GLA); community centers, 5.6 spaces per 1,000; and neighborhood centers, 5.5 per 1,000. Some centers will have much more parking than this, which often indicates an expansion possibility.

Community centers are anchored by a variety of tenant types; the variety store, a discount retailer, a superdrug, a major home-improvement center, a supermarket and a junior department store are typical anchors. These centers are never anchored by a full-service major department store.

The typical tenant mix is anchor merchant, 20 percent of the space; clothing and shoe specialty stores, 30 percent; other goods and services, 50 percent.

Leases, for the anchor tenants, run from 15 to 25 years; for the smaller tenants, they range from one to five years. There will be a lot of three-year leases. Triple-net lease terms are common in the newer centers. Be sure to check the lease terms in older centers carefully, as many of them have gross or modified-gross leases providing that the landlord pay all or part of the real estate operating expenses.

The community center's trade area extends from four to six miles and includes about 150,000 to 200,000 people.

These centers, if well-chosen, have good long-term investment prospects. Investors should consider that they are quite vulnerable to regional center competition. They seem to reach their peak volumes in three to four years and remain competitive for 10 to 15 years. The good ones respond well to renovation. Many centers built in the late 1970s and early 1980s are now excellent rehabilitation candidates.

The Neighborhood Center

Neighborhood centers are the retail type closest to the customer. They provide the goods and services needed by people in the immediate area. Recent and continuing changes in the American lifestyle favor both the community and the neighborhood center, particularly the demand of the two-income family for quick, convenient shopping. The neighborhood center is a broad retail format that can include anchorless strip centers, small convenience centers or a center with one or two anchor tenants.

They range from 50,000 to 200,000 square feet in size on a land area of from four to ten acres. A lot of highly visible free parking is a competitive necessity.

These centers are typically anchored by a supermarket and/or a large drugstore, or a food/drug combination. The major tenant can be from 30,000 to 60,000 square feet and often comprises 30 percent of the center's footage. Satellite tenants are made up of convenience goods and service providers such as florists, banks, optometrists, dry cleaners, barber and beauty shops, coffee shops and small restaurants, jewelers, liquor stores and other tenants of this type. The center will customarily have 15 to 20 tenants. Empty stores, trade schools, government tenants, too many service providers and too few sellers of merchandise are signs of weakness.

The trade area is from one to two miles, serving a population of 2,500 to 40,000.

Both strip commercial and convenience centers fit into the neighborhood center category. Strip centers are those small groups of street-facing stores that you see along our major surface streets. They are frequently at intersections and may range in size from 5,000 to 25,000 square feet. Investors should avoid (or very carefully evaluate) centers that are on traffic-choked corners. Many of these sites were formerly service stations. These developments are difficult to access (even though visibility is great), and quite often they experience costly tenant failures and extreme turnover.

The newer strip centers and convenience centers usually have highly visible on-site front parking, although older stores will frequently rely on public parking lots, street parking or rear parking. In most cases strip commercial has no major anchor tenant.

The convenience center is distinguished by the presence of a convenience market or a combination gasoline sales and food market. Easy in-and-out access is essential, although many of the marginal ones do not have it. Don't be overly impressed by a "big name" on the tenant's sign. The biggest and the best go bankrupt today.

Neighborhood centers are numerous and fairly easy to acquire. Before committing to such an investment, it is important to understand the major tenant's lease (as well as all other leases) and to completely consider the future value of the location, the amount and visibility of the parking, ingress and egress, and the adequacy of the net income. You should be able to make 10–12 percent on your invested funds. Otherwise, keep looking.

Other Retail Formats

Other retail formats, some of which were developed over the past 10–12 years, are the specialty center, off-price and factory outlet stores, high-fashion retailing, warehouse food stores, catalog showrooms, nonstore retailing, the trade or technology mart, mixed-use developments and small stores by big retailers. Many of the so-called "new" formats are not so much new in concept as they are in emphasis.

Off-price and factory outlet stores have been on the retail scene for decades. Warehouse food stores were pioneered in France years ago and have not been unknown in the United States. Nor is the specialty or theme center new in the sense that it suddenly emerged without any warning. If anything was new at the time each of these retail types became popular, it was the demographic and economic factors that collided and made promotion of these highly segmented market approaches feasible.

Specialty Centers

The specialty center is composed entirely of stores that retail closely related goods and services. It is built around a concept or theme and has been described by Lewis Bolan and Leanne Lachman as "a thematic, anchorless collection of small boutiques and food-service establishments" (Lewis Bolan and Leanne M. Lachman, "What's in the Picture for Retail Investment in the 1980s?" Real Estate Research Corporation [Chicago, 1981]).

Their market is often heavily tourist-based. When competition intensifies, small theme centers proliferate; it is likely we will see more of them appear in the next several years. Specialty centers also include food parks, specialized business service centers, hobby centers and groups of high-fashion retailers. They are a phenomenon of the late 1960s and early 1970s that is still vigorous today. These centers have been one of the competitive forces eroding the marketing power of the traditional department store.

The size range for specialty developments is from 50,000 to 70,000 square feet, although many are larger. Lease terms will be from one to ten years; most are less than ten years.

Typical tenants include unique local merchants, such as gourmet food shops, sellers of handcrafted items, small specialty shops selling quality goods at fairly high prices, and food purveyors. Tenants often include some well-known national merchants who cannot get into the regional mall or who want lower rent and better customer access than they can get there.

Festival Retailing

Festival retailing is a term used to describe one type of specialty center; it is more of an atmosphere than a retail format. Many specialty centers try to create a sense of excitement or high ambience in an attempt to make shopping an experience. Some of them have made creative use of historic buildings, such as Faneuil Hall in Boston and Ghirardelli Square in San Francisco. Others take advantage of some unique historical or environmental feature.

Festival specialty centers need a large trade area to support them; many get only 50 to 60 percent of their volume from the local population. Unless the tourist or convention business is large, it is unusual to see more than one large festival center in a trade area.

They are a risky, highly selective retail investment. Their long-term prospects swing from poor to excellent; they are especially sensitive to economic change. It is, essentially, a stagnant retail type. Most major markets have all the festival centers they need. The more straightforward, local-consumer, soft-goods specialty center that is located near a major mall has a better chance of exhibiting staying power if the management is extremely nimble and able to react quickly to change.

Off-Price Retailers

One of the hottest development types in the 1980s (and continuing into the 1990s) is discount retailing. Warehouse stores and the factory outlet center are the leading examples of this retail segment. These stores cater to value-conscious buyers.

The warehouse store is an expanded version of one or two major departments in a traditional department store, while factory outlet centers are often more like specialty centers containing manufacturer outlet stores that offer high-fashion, brand-name goods. The future of off-price retailing looks strong; discount shopping has become the acceptable way to shop. The warehouse store, for example, showed a 28 percent increase in volume in 1990 over 1989, and the number of factory outlet centers is increasing steadily toward a saturation point.

Warehouse Markets

Warehouse markets are the off-price operators for food retailing. They have proliferated across the country by providing a large selection of food and nonfood items on a cash-and-carry basis. The customers sometimes pay to "belong" to the warehouse store, but the nonmembership store is gaining in popularity. Average store size is 60,000 to 100,000 square feet; some are larger in the bigger population centers. Most use freestanding locations. The prognosis is quite good for the continued health of this type of investment. It is often difficult, however, to find one for sale at a sensible price; capitalization rates of 5 or 6 percent have been reported. Such rates are too low, especially when many of the leases are not NNN; there are other opportunities to invest in retail that will return more just as safely.

Nonstore Retailing

Nonstore retailing has made substantial gains in the past ten years and now must be counted as a significant retailing marketing force. To the extent that such retailers take business away from the normal retail operators, they represent a lessening in demand for retail space. Substantial capital is required, however, to start and maintain a catalog retailing operation. For this and other reasons, it does not seem to be a major threat to conventional retailing.

The Technology Mart

The technology mart is a retail format struggling to come to life. It copies the basic format of the furniture, gift or apparel mart and is one of the newest retailing ideas. The Infomart, in Dallas, with over 1 million square feet, is an outstanding example of this type of retailing; it has struggled to fill its space. It seems unlikely that a wave of technology marts will sweep over the country. Because of its highly speculative nature, investors need to get more than a 10 percent current return.

Mixed-Use Centers

The mixed-use center combines retail with other land uses, such as office buildings, hotels, residential, entertainment and cultural facilities. Very occasionally a mixed-use development will include an industrial element. The era of their greatest popularity was the mid-1980s; they seemed to emerge in response to aggressive building restrictions in some of the major metropolitan areas and to lender concern about overbuilding office space.

Current interest in mixed-use projects by equity investors and lenders is so strong as to be faddish. Some lenders feel there is more security in huge projects by well-known developers. They have not been right about that, but they keep trying.

In major markets that have a strong tourist and close-in residential base and where the demand for office space is substantial and growing, mixed-use developments have a strong investor appeal. But bigger is not always better from an investor's perspective. Thousands of mesmerized investors have lost money on these big projects.

The best cities for such developments are Boston; Washington, D.C.; Chicago; San Francisco; and others of that caliber. Because these projects have a long lead time, you have to be able to forecast market conditions many years into the future. The supply/demand balance must be right when the project opens, and that could be five years or more from the day you start working on it.

Examples of this type of development can be found in most metropolitan areas. Here are a few:

Water Tower Place	Chicago
Trump Tower	New York
Plaza of the Americas	Dallas
The Galleria	Houston
World Trade Center	New York
Citicorp Center	New York, Los Angeles
Rincon Center	San Francisco

Power Centers, Big Tenants/Small Stores, Temporary Stores

Three other formats are worth noting briefly. One is the power center; the other two are the big retailer/smaller store and the temporary store.

Power centers are made up of 60–80 percent major, or anchor, tenants, with the balance of the tenancy being food, other services, and some unique local merchants. The centers are commonly built on lower-priced land near a regional or superregional mall. The intent of the location is to put them in an interceptor position to the traffic-generating mall. The power center ranges in size from 200,000 to 700,000 square feet. With so many major tenants, the base rent per square foot is low for those stores that are investor-owned; because of the tremendous drawing power of a combination of strong tenants, however, percentage rent levels can be significant.

Big retailers began moving into smaller markets in 1984–85. Sears, for example, opened a 14,000-square-foot store in Alma, Michigan, in 1985. Sears executives hailed it as a first step into markets with less than 100,000 in population. Other retailers have since opened small operations in suburban markets.

The temporary store is just what its name implies. These stores are not open year-round but are leased year-round. It is common for them to be open only on high-traffic days or during the busiest seasons. They sell popular goods at a discount and are often in somewhat out-of-the-way locations. Those who own retail locations that the market seems to have passed over may find tenants from among this group.

Supply and Demand Factors

No other land use is as sensitive to demographic and economic factors. The principal demographic elements of importance to retail fall into two main groups: the amount and distribution of our population, and changes in population characteristics. Examples of changes in the makeup of our population are smaller family size, more two-income families, more older families and some lifestyle changes. A review of what these changes may mean to retailing and the retail investor are shown in Figure 4.2.

Population statistics forecast a weakening of the retail boom as early as 1992. Our population is now growing at a slower rate than it did in any of the past four decades. Many areas, as pointed out in Chapter 1, are losing population or have stagnant growth. The Southeast and the far West still exhibit some encouraging trends. On balance, the population statistics suggest less than vigorous growth for retailing. This makes careful selection of the retail investment even more important.

Figure 4.2   Selected Population Characteristics and Their Implications
for Retailing

Smaller Family Size

- May favor revitalization of some Central Business Districts by stimulating "gentrification."
- When the number of households is increasing, retailers like home furnishing stores prosper. But smaller family size means smaller purchases of furniture, etc., by any one family. Today, approximately one-third of all households are single-person. Population trends suggest that furniture stores and similar retailers will have a difficult time in the 1990s.
- More dollars will be spent on adult or family-type needs.
- Should benefit auto retailers and automotive parts stores.
- May have a negative effect on retailers of children's goods and services.
- Will benefit home security businesses.

More Two-Income Families

- There will be a greater need for convenience centers and neighborhood and community centers.
- Catalog retailing will prosper.
- Downtown retailing will do better.
- More dollars will be spent on housing.
- May stimulate customer service changes, such as delivery of goods at nonconventional times.
- More dollars will be spent on entertainment, travel and education.

The Aging of America

- May mean more self-service retailing as pool of younger workers grows smaller.
- Favors full-service restaurants over fast-food outlets.
- Drugstores, high-fashion retailers and outlets that sell quality goods and services should do well.
- Will affect education, forcing the closing of many schools and lessening the value of school-dependent sites. Areas experiencing high immigration will be unaffected.
- Favors retailing that is tourist-dependent.
- More sophisticated consumers will demand more value for money spent. Favors factory outlet stores, off-price retailing, warehouse stores, catalog showrooms and well-run appliance service operations.

Figure 4.2   Selected Population Characteristics and Their Implications for Retailing (continued)

Lifestyle Changes

- Greater emphasis on health will affect food stores, exercise facilities, recreation and personal improvement centers. Will cause repositioning of the kinds of stores found in regional malls.
- Steady demand for tourist experiences will favor hotel retailing, specialty shops, mixed-use centers and participative recreational facilities, particularly golf.
- The desire to make dollars go further will favor the renting of goods used only occasionally. This need also will favor off-price retailing.
- Home-improvement centers will do well.
- Consumer credit volume may fall or be slow to rise.
- There will be a continued emphasis on the natural as opposed to the artificial. Favors yogurt shops, handcrafted item sellers, garments made from natural fibers.
- Interest in preservation will grow stronger. Favors the specialty center, antique stores and the renovation of existing facilities.

Retailing needs population density and high disposable income as well as rising family incomes to flourish. Income trends for the balance of this decade do not provide the investor with as much comfort as he or she would like. Median family income has not increased since 1973, even though it showed some spark of renewed life in the late 1980s. The harsh truth is that over the past 19 or 20 years, American living standards have declined; this is not the kind of environment that makes retailing red-hot. But there are active retail areas. The most active will be where the people are; those are highlighted, by region, in Chapter 1.

Population statistics also suggest that the go-go days of the regional center developer are just about over. The data also shows that the high-density, mature areas of the Northeast and Midwest should present many rehabilitation chances in the 1990s. There will also be some new centers built in these areas to replace those that have been razed.

The total square footage of retail built peaked in the 1980s; we will not see that kind of new construction activity for at least ten more years, maybe longer. But you will see new construction. The developments that get financed will be the community, neighborhood and convenience center; factory outlet stores and other off-price developments; and some specialty centers.

The retail market is maturing—and when that happens to a product type, the demographic influences on supply and demand assume increased importance. As the importance of such data has increased, the supply of it has also grown. It is now possible to get information on lifestyle characteristics by region and local area, including consumer interests, activities and lifestyle changes. You can get a lot of the facts you need from the Census Bureau, either locally or in Washington, D.C. (they are both only a telephone call away), and you can subscribe to trade publications that offer such data together with valuable insights into its meaning.

Economic Factors

All is not doom and gloom. Retail sales have been growing, both in absolute terms and by comparison with the CPI. In 10 of the last 13 years, retail sales have outperformed the consumer price index. Sales increased 79.2 percent from 1980 to 1990, while the cost of living rose 58.6 percent. Table 4.1 details the recent history of the Consumer Price Index and Retail Sales. These income trends are at least as important as the population growth statistics.

Retail sales were not as robust from 1986 to 1990 (up an average of 5.9 percent annually) as they were from 1981 to 1985 (up 6.2 percent). Based on these figures, the growth in retail space that occurred from 1987 to 1990 was not fully justified, and seems to have been stimulated more by the supply of money than by the supply of customers. It is all hindsight now, but the figures were there awaiting your interpretation while the oversupply was being created.

The observation that it is people with money to spend who create real estate value is true for all real estate, but it is especially true for retail. From the perspective of that aphorism, the future for retail property does not look too rosy. According to the U.S. Department of Commerce, in the period 1967 to 1990 the upward march of median family income, per capita income and per capita disposable income has been slow.

Median family income grew from $31,043 in 1967 to $35,353 in 1990, a growth rate of only 0.58 percent per year. Per capita income grew from $9,642 to $14,387, or 2.05 percent per year, and per capita disposable income went from $6,730 to $11,509, or 2.96 percent per year. After

Table 4.1   Retail Sales and the Consumer Price Index: 1980–1992

Year	Retail Sales*	Percent Change	Consumer Price Index**	Percent Change
1980	$.793	NA	82.4	13.5
1981	.857	8.1	90.9	10.3
1982	.877	2.1	96.5	6.2
1983	.848	8.1	99.6	3.2
1984	1.014	7.0	103.9	4.3
1985	1.072	5.7	107.6	3.6
1986	1.124	4.9	109.6	1.9
1987	1.199	6.7	113.6	3.6
1988	1.280	6.8	118.3	4.1
1989	1.358	6.1	124.0	4.8
1990	1.440	6.0	130.7	5.4
1991	1.465	1.7	136.2	4.2
1992	1.500(Est.)	2.4	141.3 (9 mos)	2.5

*Retail sales figures are in trillions of dollars and exclude automobile sales.
**CPI figures are for all urban consumers, all items, U.S. city average on a 1982–84 = 100 base.
The percent change is average to average.
Sources: U.S. Department of Commerce, Bureau of the Census, Revised Monthly Retail Sales and Inventory, BR-91-R (Washington). U.S. Department of Labor, Bureau of Labor Statistics (Washington, October 1992).

inflation adjustments, it is apparent that the American consumer has less money to spend in real terms.

The 24-year time period should be enough to convince reasonable people that these income figures are a persistent trend and not just some economic statistical "blip." Given such data, it is difficult to see how retail sales can show any significant increases. Without higher retail sales volumes, rents will not rise; without higher rents, values will not move upwards except to reflect inflation. The figures also seem to suggest that another retail construction boom will not occur anytime soon.

This does not mean that retail investment values will not appreciate in some markets. Incomes and population are not distributed evenly, so some areas will do well even while other areas stagnate or decline.

Investment Characteristics

Judging the worth of a retail property is no more complex than evaluating other income property. The usual method used is the income approach to value; the net income divided by the purchase price yields a capitalization, or "cap," rate. Cap rates normally fluctuate within a narrow range except during periods of high investment demand or exceptionally poor economic times. For the largest, most desirable regional malls, the cap rate range has been between 5 and 6 percent, with the majority closer to the 5 percent number. In spite of their uniqueness and other attractions, it is inevitable that their prices will fall.

Most "real world" centers (the kind you can really buy) have cap rates ranging from 7 percent for the highest-quality center to 13 percent or more for the smaller, less desirable properties. Cash-on-cash returns of 8 to 10 percent are achievable, and total returns (the internal rate) of 15 to 20 percent are possible. As the meaning of the demographic and economic trends becomes clearer, investors may demand even higher returns.

Fully indexed or very short leases combined with percentage rents make retail almost as responsive to changing price levels as hotels and motels. The type of lease and the amount of return, however, are not the whole story.

Investors need to look at the location, tenant mix, tenant credit strength, income level (base rent plus percentage rent), total expenses and all the terms of each lease, and to fully consider the fact that retail will need substantial remodeling every eight to ten years.

Particular attention also must be paid to the amount and frequency of rent escalations and expense pass-throughs; some of the common lease provisions are shown in Figure 4.3.

Basic Elements of Income and Expense

There are five basic elements of income and expense:

1. Base rent
2. Percentage rent
3. Common-area maintenance (CAM)
4. Expense prorations—Tenant pass-throughs of taxes, insurance, maintenance, etc.
5. Merchant association dues

Figure 4.3 Common Retail Lease Provisions

Term of Lease:	Major tenant leases run from 10 to 20 years. Minor tenant leases run from one to ten years.
Option To Renew:	Often accomplished with a right of first refusal clause. Rent usually specified to be at the currently prevailing rent at the time of the exercise of the option.
Cancellation:	A clause that allows the cancellation of the lease at the tenant's option upon the occurrence of a specified event.
Percentage Rent:	Provides for the tenant to pay additional rent calculated as a percentage of defined gross sales volume once gross sales exceed the level specified.
Common Area:	A clause that provides for tenant payment, as additional rent, for a pro rata share of common-area expenses, such as parking lot and walkway maintenance and cleaning costs. Usually paid monthly.
Merchant Association:	Provides for membership in the tenant organization devoted to increasing customer traffic and for a sharing of the costs associated with those efforts.

Retail income is received in two ways: from base (or contract rent) and from percentage rent based on the tenant's defined gross sales over the base rent minimum. It would be unusual for a tenant to pay percentage rent only (that is, have no base rent). However, percentage-only leases have been used during slow economic times to rent long-vacant space.

Investors always give more weight (assign a lower cap rate) to the base rent. Some investors will pay little or nothing for percentage income, reasoning that new competition will soon make it disappear. In those cases where percentage rent is judged to have value, it is almost always given a lower value (assigned a higher cap rate) than the contract, or base, rent.

The rental income per square foot of gross leasable area in a community center will range from $5 to $6 per square foot in an average market; in hot markets it will be $10 to $12 per square foot, sometimes more. Neighborhood centers will generate from $6 to $7.50 per square foot, with those in the better areas getting $10 to $14.

Total expenses range from $1.50 to $2 per square foot for an average community center to $4 to $5 for centers in the better areas. Neighborhood center expenses average from $1.75 to $2.50 per square foot, with the better ones showing costs of approximately $3.50 to $5. These are national averages based on data generated by the International Council of Shopping Centers. You will need to develop reliable local data, of course, but these figures tend to indicate that the neighborhood center can be a strong performer.

A simplified chart of accounts looks like this:

1. Gross Scheduled Income
   A. Store rents
   B. Common-area maintenance income
   C. Reimbursed expenses income
      a) Property taxes and other taxes
      b) Insurance
      c) Utilities (from on-site or off-site)
      d) Miscellaneous income
   Less: Vacancy and collection loss
   Equals: Adjusted Gross Income
2. Operating Expenses
   A. All taxes
   B. Insurance
   C. Utilities (including cost of on-site plant)
   D. Maintenance
      a) Building structure
      b) Common areas
      c) Management
         −On-site
         −Off-site (administrative)
         −Leasing commissions
   E. Miscellaneous expenses
   Equals: Net Income before Debt Service
3. Debt Service
   Equals: Net Income after Debt Service

Figure 4.4   Retail Loan Sources

Life Insurance Companies

One of the best loan and equity sources for larger projects. During normal times the life companies provide about 20 percent of all major retail financing. Good source for joint venture participation. Also interested in participating loans, convertible loans and the full range of nonparticipation loans. Prefer deal sizes from $5 million, with no upper limit. Most loans will be amortized over 20 to 30 years, with due dates from five to ten years.

Pension Funds

Actively involved in retail financing since the early 1980s. Generally want low-risk projects. Their underwriting standards are similar to the life insurance companies. Some funds (most often union funds) do construction financing. Deal size starts at $5 million. Access to pension funds is generally through their adviser or a mortgage banker or broker.

Commercial Banks

Banks have been the largest source of construction loans. They also will make intermediate-term (five- to ten-year maturity) permanent loans. Have not done participation loans. They are a major source of financing for community and neighborhood centers. Often structure loan interest to float against some common index. Banks all but withdrew from the commercial real estate loan market in the early 1990s, but they will be a major factor in such lending during the balance of the decade.

Savings and Loans

The S&Ls were once a major factor in financing strip retail as well as some community centers. It is unlikely they will be a viable source for commercial real estate loans until the association failures of the 1980s and 1990s are but a dim memory.

Foreign Capital

This has been a major source of real estate financing for more than ten years. The main lenders have been from Japan, Germany, the Netherlands, France, Canada, Hong Kong, Taiwan, South America and the Middle East. Your best access is through local branches of the foreign banks and through mortgage bankers and brokers. Foreign lending in the United States is likely to decline in the near term.

Figure 4.4   Retail Loan Sources (continued)

Government-Assisted Financing

A variety of programs are usually available. Look for Urban Development Action Grants, interest subsidies, industrial revenue bonds, loan guarantee programs and a host of local redevelopment programs. Access through commercial banks and mortgage bankers and brokers.

Deal Structures and Financing

Retail projects need financing at four different stages of their life cycle:

1. *The Predevelopment Stage.* At this point front-end money is needed to assess feasibility, find major tenants and do preliminary architectural and engineering work. The usual funding source is the developer and, in some cases, a redevelopment agency.
2. *The Construction Stage.* Temporary loans will be needed to finance construction.
3. *The Finished Product Stage.* A permanent loan will be needed to pay off the construction loan and, possibly, recover some of the developer's equity.
4. *The Investment Stage.* Funds are needed for equity.

Figure 4.4 shows the principal lending sources and their criteria.

For the past 50 years, until the credit crunch of 1990–92, quality retail property has been easy to finance; even some of the marginal strip centers have been able to find financing with little trouble. Funds are much harder to find today, as you will see detailed in Chapter 11. If you are thinking of developing a retail project, you will find that up to 35 percent hard equity is required for every project regardless of the strength of the developer or the tenants. As always, you will have to have firm commitments from your major tenants and, in some cases, much of the satellite space leased before you will get a construction loan.

The fact that retail, to a greater extent than other real estate types, has been demand-driven rather than money-driven has tended to keep the surplus under some control. But surpluses do develop as recessions rock the economy.

The most common deal structures over the next four or five years will be joint ventures and participation financing. It would not be surprising to see participation deals at 35–45 percent of the loan market.

Trends and Conclusions

The research for this chapter uncovered more than 100 retail trends. The major ones are listed below, grouped by topic, for your convenience.

Demographic and Economic Trends

- Slower population growth means fewer regional centers will be built in the 1990s.
- Limited population growth also means that existing well-located centers will hold their value and, possibly, show some value increase.
- Retail sales slowdown will be followed by a period of slow growth. The "go-go" days of retail are over for the foreseeable future.
- Consumer desire to continue to lead the good life favors retail formats such as off-price, factory outlet, discounters and nonstore retailing.
- If home prices begin and sustain a price decline, retail sales will fall as consumers' sense of being wealthy disappears.

Government Regulation

- Local regulation of the retail development process will increase.
- The environmental movement will continue to add to construction costs by sponsoring more regulation.
- There is a slight possibility that the high cost of environmental protection will spawn a backlash resulting in more realistic and less costly regulation.

The Developer

- A new breed of developer, one that is equipped to deal with big government and small loans, will continue to mature.
- The developer will become a big investor and a stronger asset manager.

- Many developers will evolve into build-to-order specialists.
- Retailers will be a major factor in the development business.

Regional Malls

- Regional malls will become an investment type with limited new growth potential.
- Old trade areas will become more important than new markets.
- Rehabilitation of existing centers will boom.
- Most development activity will be in the South and far West.
- Small regional centers in smaller markets will be attractive to investors.
- Strong local merchants will be more welcome in some of the regional malls. Smaller store size will be encouraged.
- Regional and superregional malls will continue to be a favorite investment of insurance companies and pension funds, but more of them will be for sale than during the 1980s.
- Consolidations and failures among large department stores will continue. Other large retailers may be affected.

Mixed-Use Development

- Mixed-use will continue to be attractive to the bigger investor, but the development pace will be slower than the recent past.

Other Shopping Centers

- Much more renovation, recycling and additions to existing centers.
- More specialty centers in the smaller markets.
- Continued growth of specialty centers near the regional malls.
- Neighborhood centers will outperform all other centers on a per-foot-sales basis.
- Creating a unique shopping environment will become more important.
- Food and entertainment elements will become more important.
- The move toward community centers by many larger retailers will continue.

Financing and Deal Structures

- Higher equity requirements will persist.
- Scarcity of loan funds is likely to stretch well into 1993.
- All underwriting standards will be tightened and stay that way. Loan-to-value ratios will be lower and debt coverage ratios will be higher.
- Fundamental lack of demand will mean that fewer centers get built.
- Preleasing will be more important.
- Participation loans will be more popular with lenders.

Construction

- Value of new construction (annually) will decline from 1989 levels until at least 1993.
- Theme centers will be a popular retail format.
- New construction, when it does start up, will be the greatest in the South and far West.

Miscellaneous

- Parking ratios will decline slightly and parking structures will contain more retail and entertainment facilities.
- Investment returns will increase. Sale price increases, if any, will be modest.

The shopping center industry is changing from one of intensive development to one of intensive management, according to Edwin Homer, former president of the International Council of Shopping Centers. During this century, this product type is likely to offer more viable investment choices than the office building; however, continued weakness in the growth of personal and family income, household formations and population growth, combined with possibly less vigorous home price trends, creates strong reasons for the investor to be cautious and to invest only after thorough demographic and financial analysis of the proposed acquisition.

PART
II

Specialized Commercial Real Estate Investments

CHAPTER
5

Factory Outlet Centers

Factory outlet centers are an emerging real estate retail segment that is still a long way from maturity. They are a subdivision of the retail investment that has continued to grow even during the slow-growth period from 1990 to 1993. Perhaps because they offer more value to the consumer, they have had a special appeal as hard-pressed shoppers try to stretch the buying power of limited dollars. In spite of their fairly bullish prospects, they demand a unique type of high-risk investor because of their locations, the nature of their income stream and their generally short leases.

In this chapter you will find most of what you need to know before investing in this promising product type. It begins with a definition and ends with a short history, industry trends and our conclusions. In between, you will find facts on location, design, construction costs, tenant mix, income and expense guidelines, developers and their projects, and a section on how these centers are marketed to the consumer.

Factory outlet centers belong to a group rather attractively described as "value retailing." Within this retail subdivision are discount and off-price developments such as K-Mart or Wal-Mart, hypermarkets such as

Carrefour, and membership stores like Price Club, Price Savers and others.

In their purest form, factory outlet centers are made up of merchants (and minor supporting services) who sell goods manufactured by the factories that operate the stores in the center. They are sometimes called manufacturers' outlets.

Factory outlet centers are often confused with the more numerous and familiar off-price or discount centers; they are not the same. The principal difference lies in how the goods are acquired. Discount merchants buy in large quantities at very low prices from a wide variety of manufacturers and jobbers. They then sell at prices well below those charged by traditional retailers in facilities that are comfortable but not the equal of the regional mall. Factory outlet merchants manufacture the goods they sell, and, by selling direct from low-rent stores located outside the main retail areas, hope to offer a shopping adventure and prices that are lower than those of most retailers. As retail competition becomes more intense, the price differential between the factory outlet center and traditional retailers is narrowing.

The shortest useful definition of a factory outlet center is: "A retail center in which the majority of tenants sell, at reduced prices, branded goods manufactured in their own factories." Such a concise description ignores many of the nuances.

Industry Statistics

A look at some of the industry's statistics helps to explain the size and importance of this type of retailing; Figure 5.1 and Table 5.1 display that information.

The projects listed as "announced" cover planned openings in 1992 and 1993. The estimate for the volume of business done is derived from a thorough survey of the literature; a study of the town of Boaz, Alabama, the site of many factory outlets; a number of interviews with industry leaders; and the calculations shown in Table 5.2. The Boaz study points out how effective an individual investor can be in making his or her own independent investigation of an industry's volume claims. All income claims should be verified, regardless of the product type.

In the more than 50 references that were reviewed and in numerous telephone interviews with industry leaders, there was only one estimate

Figure 5.1   Factory Outlet Center Industry Statistics

Number of existing centers	200 (+/−)
Announced centers, 1992 and 1993	120
Percent of announced centers that get built	33 ⅓
Total square footage of existing centers	35 million
Average number of centers opened per year (1982–1991)	24
Average square footage of existing centers	177,000
Average tenant size (square feet)	4,500
Existing centers by type: Strip:	48%
Enclosed mall:	42%
Village style:	9%
Total Annual Dollar Volume	$4 to $5 billion
Annual U.S. dollar volume nondurable goods:	$812 billion (Est.)
Number of manufacturers selling through factory outlet centers	200 (+/−)
New vs. adaptive-use ratio:	new, 71%; rehabilitation projects, 29%

Sources: *Value Retail News,* St. Petersburg, Florida.
U.S. Department of Commerce, Survey of Current Business.
Shopping Centers Today, ICSC, New York.
Grubb & Ellis Research Services.

of annual industry volume that exceeded $8.75 billion; all others were in the $3.5 billion to $4 billion range. These numbers and the Boaz study are referred to in greater detail later in the chapter.

Community Impact

There are frequent references in the literature regarding the beneficial effect of factory outlet centers on the communities in which they locate. These claims are of interest to investors, because very often they are the basis upon which local politicians make the decision to allow this kind of investment to be built. Investors are sometimes in on the "ground floor" of an investment as initial capital providers, so it is important that they be aware of the basis of all claims made and be able to test their validity against a reasonable standard. The developer's assertion of financial

Table 5.1 Estimates of the Total Annual Volume of Factory Outlet Centers in the United States

Dollars per Square Foot	Estimated Volume (35 million square feet)
$100	$3.50 Billion
$150	$5.25 Billion
$200	$7.00 Billion
$250	$8.75 Billion

benefits to the target community are meant to smooth the way for approval of the project, but they can also be used in the decision-making process of the initial investors if the claims are valid.

The small community of Boaz, Alabama, is representative of a half-dozen or more similar towns affected by factory outlet development. What we found in studying Boaz provided much more information than we originally expected.

Boaz is a community of approximately 7,500 people. The first factory outlet center was built there in 1982; it was 113,000 square feet. Thereafter, additional centers were built rather regularly, and today Boaz has approximately 485,000 square feet of such space, according to *Value Retail News*. Other sources claim there is between 650,000 and 700,000 square feet in town.

The study, which covered a ten-year period, focused on sales tax receipts and the square footage of factory outlet space in Boaz. Table 5.2 shows what we found; the findings vary from the conventional wisdom regarding factory outlet centers. It is possible, of course, to disagree with the findings of this study based upon its methodology. For those who may be so inclined, the approach we used is explained below.

Total retail dollar volume was estimated from sales tax revenue and the percentage rate charged, both of which were cross-verified with three sources. Tax revenue for the calendar year 1982 was $668,000, which represented 2 percent of retail sales. Thus $668,000 ÷ .02 = $33,400,000. The total sales tax charged in Boaz is 7 percent, but only 2 percent of that number (which is the number shown in column two) goes to the city. Boaz had few, or no, factory outlet retailers in 1980, 1981 and much of 1982. Accordingly, these years were used as the base level of retail activity—that is, the retail volume without factory outlet stores. This base year

Table 5.2 Impact of Factory Outlet Retailing on Boaz, Alabama: 1989–1990
($ and sq. ft. in thousands)

Year	Sales Tax Revenue	Base Sales Tax Revenue	Retail Volume	Factory Outlet Volume	F/O Sq. Ft.	F/O $ Sq. Ft.
1980	$508	n/a	$27,900	n/a	n/a	n/a
1981	$621	n/a	$31,050	n/a	n/a	n/a
1982*	$668	$613	$33,400	$2,750*	113	$24
1983	$1,128	$638	$56,400	$24,500	113	$217
1984	$1,275	$663	$63,750	$30,600	163	$88
1985	$1,498	$684	$74,900	$40,450	263	$154
1986	$1,908	$717	$95,400	$59,550	373	$160
1987	$2,203	$746	$110,150	$72,850	485	$150
1988	$2,279	$776	$113,950	$75,150	485	$155
1989	$3,351	$806	$167,550	$127,150	485	$262**

* = Partial year
** = If 700,000 square feet were used, this number would be $182.
Sources: Department of Revenue, State of Alabama, Mayor's Office and City Clerk,
City of Boaz, Alabama.
Value Retail News, St. Petersburg, Florida.

activity was estimated to be $613,000 in sales tax revenue, which in-creased at 4 percent annually. In 1986, for example, the base number had grown to $717,000, and the calculation for factory outlet volume was $1,908,000 (column 2) minus $717,000 (column 3) equals $1,191,000 divided by .02, which equals $59,550,000 (column 5). The square footage calculation is Column 5 + Column 6 = Column 7.

There was some disagreement among our sources as to the amount of factory outlet space in Boaz on December 31, 1989. It seems likely that there was more than 485,000 square feet, but that number was used because it was the *Value Retail News* figure and, hence, represented consistency with all the other estimates of footage used in the study. Using a larger number would have lowered the dollar volume per square foot.

One of the ways a community might expect to benefit from factory outlet stores would be in more income for its residents, but this does not seem to have happened in any dramatic way. The per capita income of Boaz has increased steadily from 1980 (see Table 5.3). In the ten years between 1980 and 1989, per capita income increased 65 percent, to about $8,100. The impact of a fivefold increase in retail sales volume might have

Table 5.3   Per Capita Income, Boaz, Alabama

Year	Amount
1980	$5,300
1983	$6,731
1985	$7,600
1989	$8,100

Sources: Department of Revenue, State of Alabama, Mayor's Office, City of Boaz
U.S. Department of Commerce, Bureau of the Census, Income Statistics Division.

been expected to have a greater influence on the incomes of Boaz residents, but at least half the workers in their factory outlet stores (like most of the customers) live out of town.

The study, which is as valid today as when it was completed in early 1990, shows that the dollar volume per square foot claims made for factory outlet centers are often overstated, and that the value of such developments to a community may be principally in increased sales and real estate tax revenues rather than in real income improvements for residents.

Location

The location of a factory outlet center is just about everything. They are usually found in remote locations, which makes the decision to invest particularly difficult for both equity and debt investors.

The criteria for a good location are few and simple; finding sites that fully satisfy those criteria is not so simple. The "perfect" location has three characteristics:

1. It is on a major highway with a minimum traffic count of 50,000 cars and is within 50 miles of a large population center.
2. The site is highly visible and easy to enter and exit.
3. It is at, or on the way to, a successful tourist attraction or second-home location.

There are hundreds of undeveloped sites that *seem* to satisfy these three conditions. Indeed, if all a developer had to do was find such sites, the number of factory outlet stores would soon double.

However, many potential locations on major highways fail to qualify because the composition of the traffic is not right; a high traffic count that is made up of commuters does not help a center succeed.

Competition

A location must not interfere with a potential tenant's retail customers in nearby cities. Most centers are many miles from town just so a manufacturer does not compete with its urban customers. How close is too close? The distance varies with the strength of the site, but it is shrinking as factory outlet centers continue to demonstrate retailing power. In 1983 it was 29 miles; by 1988 it had shrunk to 18.9 miles; today it is 15 miles, sometimes less. The minimum distance from nonoutlet retailing, expressed in driving time, is 20 minutes.

Destination Centers

New locations are often pioneered by smaller developers who take the risk just to get started in this area of development. Larger developers seem to prefer to build projects at proven sites. Destination locations are often created by this "copy-cat" development strategy. A destination center is one where several outlets have clustered. It is not unusual to find 100 or more stores within four or five blocks. Boaz, Orlando, Florida; and Reading, Pennsylvania; are all destination centers.

The tourist trade is extremely important to most factory outlet centers. In some markets the local residents claim that only the tourists shop at the factory outlets, but the facts, as shown by sales volume, belie such assertions. The best sites are those that can deliver year-round activity by generating business in almost equal parts from the local, regional and tourist segments. Developments that are heavily dependent on tourist business often suffer three to four months of off-season slowness.

The importance of tourism is further demonstrated by the many states in which such centers are among the top tourist attractions. The Belz factory outlet center in Orlando, Florida, is said to draw almost 4 million tourists annually. The tiny town of Boaz will attract 74,000 shoppers (about ten times its population) on a good weekend.

The manufacturer-tenants of such centers like tourist locations because tourist traffic is "good" traffic. A person on vacation is usually in a happy, spending mood and seldom postpones a purchase "until tomorrow." On a short vacation, which is becoming more common, there is no shopping "tomorrow."

Added to their high propensity to spend is the fact that there are so many tourist customers. Every major holiday puts millions of potential factory outlet customers on the road. The U.S. Travel Data Center provides some insight into the size of this market. On the 4th of July in 1988, almost 34 million tourists took an auto trip of 100 miles or more. That is about 14 percent of our population. Labor Day of that year there were 24 million tourists on the highways. Millions of tourists on the road during national holidays is a trend that is expected to continue.

American vacation habits are changing, but what this may mean to factory outlet developments is not yet known. One of the strongest trends is the move toward shorter vacations (three or four days). Some think this may work against factory outlets, because there is so much time pressure during such a short holiday. Others say the trend means more people are traveling more frequently, which increases the customer base exposed to factory outlet centers. Many developers believe they can exploit this "quickie vacation" trend by locating centers at or near major resorts.

Some of the most popular factory outlet tourist sites are Orlando, Florida; Potomac Mills Center in Virginia; Saratoga, New York; Monterey, California; Niagara Falls, New York; and Hot Springs, Arkansas.

Nontourist Locations

One of the major difficulties faced by factory outlet centers in their efforts to attract equity and debt investors is that many analysts do not understand that not all outlets are tourist-oriented. Many sites can and do exploit the surrounding market area. Even when that area is lightly populated, it can deliver year-round volume. Shoppers in rural areas are used to traveling long distances to shop. A site with a permanent population of from 1 million to 3 million within 50 miles can frequently do well.

You do not have to be located near a tourist center to succeed. Boaz, Alabama, certainly isn't a tourist destination, nor is it on the way to any. Secaucus, New Jersey (about 20 minutes from New York on a very good traffic day), was formerly noted for its pig farms and garbage dumps. It is now home to the Meadowlands and millions of square feet of office, industrial and retail space. It is a major factory outlet center. Being in the shadows of Manhattan's skyscrapers hasn't hurt it.

The "Big Five" locations (irrespective of tourism) are: Reading, Pennsylvania; Orlando, Florida; Boaz, Alabama; Fall River, Massachusetts; and Kittery, Maine.

Evaluating the Center

This product type is quite new and is not yet well understood by analysts or investors. The locations are out in the country; the tenants appear solid, but their leases are often short and sometimes provide an early out; and center income is heavily dependent on percentage rent and the quality of the center's marketing effort. Many potential investors wonder "Is this retail type here to stay?" and, if it is, "Will it get overbuilt like just about everything else?" To make the right judgments, you have to know a lot about factory outlet centers.

Most analysts are quite good at looking at the numbers, but many have little or no feel for the softer, nonfinancial considerations. Some do not understand a retail development as a living economic entity; it is doubtful that many of them see factory outlet centers as shoppers see them. Few analysts seem to understand how far an American in search of a bargain will drive to find it.

Site Plan and Design

If the location and tenant mix are right, the drawing power of a center is immense. The challenge is to create a site plan and project design that maximizes the power of a good location and good tenants; the goal is to enhance the customer-pulling power of the project. It is surprising how often the site plan and design fail to do that.

Visibility, Access and "Out" Parcels

Project visibility and ease of ingress and egress are primary design considerations. Developers should, but seldom do, resist the temptation to sell off "out parcels" or "pads" at the entryways or corners of the site. It may appear, as you look at a development pro forma, that selling these highly visible parcels is a fast way to big profits, but in many—perhaps even most—cases, the development of these gateway parcels by fast-food operators, gas stations and the like will have several undesirable results that will negatively affect your highest-volume tenants, who provide you with the bulk of your operating income.

Out-parcel development can create traffic congestion; make entering and leaving the center more difficult; eat up valuable parking; and destroy the center's visibility. It can hurt rather than help a center. Unfortunately, by the time long-term investors consider a factory outlet center, the out parcels have already been exploited, and in spite of their potential for long-term negative effects on investment value, the out-parcel tenants are credited with increasing the income to stratospheric levels. Be careful.

Basic Design Schemes

The basic building layouts may be described as linear, L, X, U, cross-shaped, or the closed box, where center parking is surrounded by stores. Early in the history of the factory outlet center, the style of centers was about evenly divided between strip developments (unenclosed) and the enclosed mall. The high-atmosphere, village-style center currently accounts for about 5 percent of American factory outlet centers. One of the reasons the enclosed mall quickly gained a large share of the total was the ease of adapting older buildings, such as old factories that once produced such varied goods as pajamas, hosiery, women's clothing, shoes, textiles, pottery, pianos, pasta or tires, as well as printing plants and old soft drink–bottling facilities. New construction of enclosed malls (excluding adaptive use) has accounted for about 15 percent of the total new supply.

Regardless of the basic layout, it is critical that a shopper be able to park close to the stores and be able to see them all from his or her parking space. The enclosed mall and the village-style centers often successfully violate this planning principle.

Often, in a pioneering location, the size of the site might be somewhat larger than needed for all phases of the planned project. If a site turns out to be really good, however, you can be sure that other developers will appear. The chance to profit from this second-generation development is increased if you control the surrounding land.

Tenants and Tenant Mix

The statement "If the location is right, the tenants will be right" is a retail truism. But good tenants and a good tenant mix are not automatic no matter how good the site is. Almost two-thirds of all announced centers never get built simply because they cannot attract enough strong tenants. The main reason has to do with manufacturer-tenants' concerns about competing with their retail accounts. One location, in Southern California's Riverside County, seemed a natural for a strong factory outlet development, but announcement of four regional malls planned for the area killed any hope for factory outlet success.

Hundreds of manufacturers have opened stores in factory outlet centers. Anyone who may still hold the opinion that the modern factory outlet is a marginal, tacky, temporary business akin to the surplus store will dispel such feelings by reviewing even a partial list of typical tenants or by simply visiting a few of the newer centers.

Anchor Tenants

As with virtually all significant retail projects, factory outlet developments must have advance tenant commitments before financing can be arranged. Unlike the community center, factory outlets don't have an anchor tenant in the traditional sense—one or two dominant, traffic-generating merchants, such as a discount store, major market, or drugstore. There is evidence, however, that major tenants are taking large amounts of space in some factory outlet centers, and these large space users may look like the anchor tenants most investors are used to seeing. In a factory outlet center, 40,000 square feet is a huge tenant; a tenant of that size might not be a major anchor in some nonfactory outlet centers.

Tenant Mix

A successful center will have a tenant mix that is led by name-brand women's apparel. Women's fashions are the number-one traffic generator. A "hot" center will have a tenant mix that looks like this:

- Women's clothing
- Children's clothing
- Menswear

- Shoes (men's, women's, children's)
- Housewares, home appliances
- Gifts
- Leather goods
- Electronics
- Toys
- Food service (sometimes includes a sports bar)

A large center will also have support services, such as gift-wrapping, packing and shipping, information booths or stands, tour bus driver's lounge, and lots of big, well-lit restrooms with baby-changing facilities. Some developments will also have a children's playland.

Most tenants, regardless of their name power, are small users of space. The average store size is 4,500 square feet, but it is not unusual to lease much smaller spaces. Figure 5.2 lists some of the common tenants; those tenants who use a larger-than-average amount of space are indicated with an asterisk.

Income and Expenses

Rental income is generally a combination of a flat sum (base monthly rent) plus a percentage of gross business. The definition of gross business will be found in the tenant lease. Most factory outlets differ from community or regional centers in that a much larger percentage of total income is derived from percentage rent rather than from base rent. This makes them riskier from an investor's perspective. Total income can be quite high, with successful centers earning $200–$300 per square foot.

Rents are usually net of expenses, with the tenants responsible for all operating costs such as utilities, common-area maintenance, real estate taxes, etc. Tenants are particularly sensitive to the amount of the common-area maintenance charge; the trade literature has been full of references to disputes over this item and to tenant demands that all charges be fully justified.

There is not yet much authoritative information on operating costs. What is available suggests that total expenses per square foot per year run from $3 to $5. Common-area charges range from $1 to $1.50 per square foot annually; sales promotion will cost from $.60 to $1.25. The expense

Figure 5.2   Partial List of Typical Factory Outlet Tenants

Tenant	Product Line
Gruppon GFT	Designer menswear
Calvin Klein	Men's sportswear
Gucci	Accessories and apparel
Tahari	Sportswear
Joan & David	Designer shoes
Nike	Athletic shoes
G.H. Bass	Shoes
Dexter Shoes	Shoes
Burlington Coat Factory*	Outerwear, family clothing
Anne Klein	Women's clothing
Carolina Pottery*	Tableware
Westpoint Pepperill	Fabrics, bedding, towels
London Fog	Outerwear
Liz Claiborne	Women's clothing
Polo/Ralph Lauren	Men's & women's clothing
Van Heusen Company	Shirts and sweaters
Royal Doulton	Tableware, housewares
Old Time Pottery*	Tableware
V.F. Industries*	Lingerie, hosiery, Lee Jeans
Pfaltzgraff	Housewares
Ikea	Swedish furniture
The Ribbon Outlet	Fabric, yarns, notions
Harve Bernard	Women's clothing
Leatherloft	Leather goods
L.L. Bean	Outerwear
Russell	Cotton goods
Mikasa	China
Black & Decker	Appliances, tools
Bogner	Ski apparel
Aileen	Women's wear
American Tourister	Luggage
Corning	Housewares
Oneida	Silverplate
Towle Silversmiths	Silverplate
The Paper Factory	Papergoods, cards, gifts
Fieldcrest Cannon	Linens

* = Larger tenants

items covered in total operating expenses include real estate taxes, insurance, building maintenance, parking lot cleaning and repair, all common-area maintenance charges including heating and air-conditioning costs, plus a charge for general administrative costs to operate the center. The total amount of all chargeable costs will vary with the skill and experience of the management, the age of the property and the region of the country.

The great consumer attraction of a factory outlet center is the ability to buy quality goods at bargain prices. Low total occupancy costs, the tenants argue, help make this possible. A great shopping environment created by a well-planned, vigorously merchandised center is what creates volume, according to the landlords. Whatever the real answer, the tenant's orientation is toward low total rent, which they feel is justified by the out-of-the-way, low-cost locations; low construction costs; and their high-volume, low-profit marketing strategy. Base rents will range from $9 to $11 per square foot (net). It is important to consider the quantity, quality and durability of the income. Short leases (seven years or less) cause these centers to score low on the durability measure.

You must also give careful consideration to the location by comparing its value as a "going concern" with its value if the center closes. Most land costs $8 to $12 per square foot after all the off-site improvements are completed. In the case of a to-be-built center, you will want to look at what other merchants have already decided to locate near the proposed site. The presence of a fast-food operator, like McDonalds, or a high-volume gasoline station might indicate that this location is a natural stopping point for travelers. All other location criteria, set forth earlier, must be given full consideration. It is also wise to remember that competing centers may be attracted to the location. Table 5.2, the Boaz, Alabama, study, shows the economic effects of this in both the short and long term.

Construction Costs

Low base rents are partly a reflection of the cost of construction. Both site costs and less-than-elaborate architecture contribute to low total building costs. Pure construction costs range from $35 to $40 per square foot, while total costs (including land and all soft and hard costs) will range from $52 to $60. Costs will increase along with other costs, and with the addition of better finish in the public areas and generally better design.

Merchandising the Center

The day-to-day marketing of a factory outlet center has a critical influence on its success. One of the most difficult judgments an investor must make is the one involving the strength of the center's marketing effort. You can't depend on a center to generate its own traffic. Tenant mix is part of the judgment process. There are some who think a factory outlet center is contaminated in some way if it mixes direct factory sellers with some off-price/discount merchants. In many cases, however, you need non-manufacturing merchants to round out what is being offered to the consumer. Without a well-balanced selection of sellers, the center will be difficult to promote because it will have too narrow an appeal. Very small centers (under 100,000 square feet) might get by with a manufacturers-only tenant mix, but no super center (750,000 square feet and up) could ever do that.

Here are the elements of good marketing:

Signage

Highway billboards.   These signs must be big—the bigger the better. They should be on both sides of the main highway and all logical connecting roads.

Great tenants make a great sign; tenant names should be featured more prominently than the name of the center.

Driving directions and other copy must be simple and easy to read. All copy, and the sign, should be "fresh." New copy every six months is typical. Time and temperature displays are acceptable on the highway signs.

Off-highway directional signs.   These must be simple, easy to find and easy to read. There should be enough of them to prevent driver confusion and to allow them to work even if one or two are temporarily down.

On-site signage.   These include identifying signs for the center and parking lot signs (if lot is large) to help customers locate their cars after a day of shopping.

Tenant signs should be visible from the parking lot and from the street approach.

An information center is important both for the center itself and to provide directions to nearby local attractions.

Print Advertising

Brochures.   The center should have an attractive color brochure to be used in mail campaigns, to put in any nearby visitor's information centers, and for use at local tourist centers. It is also used as a "take-with" so shoppers can show it to their friends.

A map of the center should be displayed if a shopper cannot see the entire center by standing in one place.

Newspapers and travel magazines.   These include local newspaper ads to attract local and regional customer base and travel magazine ads to tap tourist trade.

Direct Marketing

- To tour bus companies
- To travel agents

Radio and Television

- Promotional spots on the local clear-channel radio station
- Local television advertising and a public relations effort to get exposure on local news and information shows

Special Promotions

- Use of traffic stoppers such as clowns, old fire engines, antique cars, etc.
- Special demonstrations of products sold by the center's merchants
- Annual or semiannual sales event

Lease Terms and Conditions

There is no "standard" factory outlet lease format such as you may be used to seeing when dealing with regional malls, community centers, or office buildings and industrial property. Lease terms run from three to seven years, with the five-year lease being the most common. There is often a clause requiring that a certain percentage of the stores (50–75 percent is common) be operated by factory-direct merchants. There is sometimes a clause that prohibits off-price retailers in the center. Percentage rent clauses are in practically all of the leases; common-area maintenance clauses are in all net leases, and most leases are net.

Will Factory Outlets Get Overbuilt?

The more cynical among us are likely to shout a vigorous YES! in response to that question. But factory outlet retailing has some built-in restraints that may prevent severe overbuilding. Among them are the following:

- You must have a large percentage of the center leased to responsible tenants before you can get the financing to build.
- Manufacturers will not (as yet) get too close in miles or minutes to their best retailer customers.
- Financing is tough to get, even with good tenants, due to the out-of-the-way locations and still unproven performance of factory outlets.
- Potential investors (purchasers of the finished product) are still wary of this product type.

These factors seem to indicate that, while factory outlets will continue to expand, growth will not get out of control.

Analysis Difficulty

Boaz, Alabama, presents an interesting contrast between the "truth" one can easily obtain by reading current articles in trade publications, or scanning newspaper ads, or talking with developers active in building factory outlets, and the "truth" not so easily obtained from sources that are not so easily accessed. Boaz also points out the difficulties you are likely to encounter in any attempt to do a thorough evaluation.

The study of Boaz was undertaken to examine the claims made as to the benefits of factory outlet development on a small town's economy; it ended by failing to support annual sales volume reports of $200 or more per square foot. The basis for skepticism is the amount of sales tax revenue collected in this jurisdiction; it just does not support specific claims made by developers active in Boaz. There is always the possibility, of course, that the sales tax receipt figures are wrong, but in the Boaz study these were cross-checked and verified three times. It is also possible that the square footage numbers are wrong; if they are, there is a remarkable consistency of error over time.

The lesson for the careful investor from this study and from the data in Table 5.2 is that claims of hefty square foot sales volumes should be tested by getting signed volume statements in the case of an existing center, or statements of volume in similar locations (from proposed tenants) in the case of a proposed center.

Developers and Their Projects

Factory outlet centers have established themselves as a unique development type even though many investors remain skeptical. Those who build such centers do not, for the most part, build off-price centers, and those who do off-price do not often get involved in factory outlet—at least, not during "normal" times.

There are about 100 active factory outlet developers nationwide; about 12 of them account for the bulk of the activity. The two largest are Popularly Enterprises (Memphis, Tenn.) and Company Stores Development Company (Brentwood, Tenn.). Third place is held by VF Factory Outlets of Reading, Pennsylvania.

Other major developers, not necessarily in exact rank order, are: Benderson Development Company (Buffalo, N.Y.), WCI Investments/Johnson Development (Myrtle Beach, S.C.), The Chelsea Group (Flemington, N.J.), The Horizon Group (Muskegon, Mich.), Manufacturer's Retail Outlets (Huntsville, Ala.), West Point Pepperill (West Point, Va.), Stacey K. Tanger Company (Greensboro, N.C.), Balcor Development Company (Skokie, Ill.), and Wiley Creek Development Company (Exeter, N.H.). This list of developers is subject to rapid change due to the exigencies of the economy and other factors.

Popularly Enterprises projects are located in Orlando and Tampa, Florida; St. Louis, Missouri; and Pigeon Forge and Memphis, Tennessee. The Chelsea Group, which has done more village-style centers than anyone else, has projects in Monterey, California (The Cannery);

Flemington, New Jersey (Liberty Village); Lawrence, Kansas (Lawrence River Front Plaza); Malta, New York (Saratoga Village); and several other locations.

You can find a Company Stores development in one of the following cities: Atlanta, Georgia (Outlets Ltd.); Louisville, Kentucky (Outlets Ltd. Mall); Cincinnati, Ohio (Outlets Ltd. Mall); and Williamsburg, Virginia (also an Outlets Ltd. Mall).

Wiley Creek Development Company's projects may be seen in Vacaville, California (The Factory Stores at Nut Tree); Kent Island, Maryland (Eastern Shore Factory Stores); Conway, New Hampshire (Conway Crossing Outlet Center); and Lake George, New York (The Log Jam Factory Stores).

The examples cited above are but a small sample of the more than 200 existing factory outlet centers in the United States. One of the most complete sources for a list of developers and their projects is the annual edition of the *Value Retail News* book called *The Book on Value Retailing*; some of our developer data came from that source.

History

The history of factory outlet developments, as we know them today, is quite short. The earliest centers opened in 1972. Factory outlet stores, the ancestors of our current centers, have been around for at least 150 years, however. Figure 5.3 is a condensed version of what has been an exciting new retail product's history.

Trends and Conclusions

Perhaps the most persistent trend of all is that of factory outlet stores and centers to upgrade their facilities and the quality of their locations. This could continue until they eventually look pretty much like any large discount center or community center. If such an evolution occurs, factory outlet centers will be left with little to distinguish themselves save the presence of manufacturers as tenants. They will then become just another lump in the bland retail porridge that is mixed, in large part, by lenders and equity investors rather than by creative retailers and their customers.

Figure 5.3   A Short History of Factory Outlet Retailing in the United States

Late 1800s	Many Northeast factories open outlet stores to sell surplus or damaged goods to their employees.
1950s	First major discount stores (K-Mart, Woolco, etc.) appear. These help to set the stage for value retailing.
1970s	Recessions provide impetus for start of factory outlet developments; Vanity Fair opens its first outlet in Reading, Pennsylvania.
1972	First true factory outlet center opens in Reading, Pennsylvania. City is currently credited with being the capital of factory outlet retailing in the United States.
1972–1976	Many manufacturers open factory outlet stores.
1974	"Shopping Spree in Pennsylvania Dutch Country," a pioneering brochure, is published.
1977	Lynn Ellsworth, Brentwood, Tennessee, set a new industry standard with a completely new construction factory outlet center.
1978	Kemmons Wilson develops the cross-shaped design. First such plan was opened in Memphis, Tennessee, in 1979.
1980	Modern era of factory outlet retailing begins.
1981	Twenty-six factory outlet centers in the United States.
1982–1988	Sales volume grew at 11.5 percent annually.
1983	Average distance to competing retailers was 29 miles.
	More than 150 factory outlet stores in Reading, Pennsylvania.
1984	*Off Price News* changes its name to *Value Retail News* to encompass more of the discount retailing activity.
1988	Average distance to competing (nonfactory outlet) retailers is 18.9 miles.
1989	198 factory outlet centers open in the United States; 95 more are in the planning stage. More than 300 outlet retailers in Reading, Pennsylvania, doing about 17 percent of the national factory outlet volume.

Figure 5.3 A Short History of Factory Outlet Retailing in the United States (continued)

1990	The Citadel factory outlet center opens in Los Angeles on the site of a former tire manufacturing plant. Development is within 10 miles of the Central Business District.
1991	226 factory outlet centers in the United States; annual volume estimated at $5.2 billion.
1992	Factory outlet volume improves during long recession.

At least they will then be easier to finance and sell. These are the other trends uncovered by the research for this chapter:

- Sources and costs of financing will be somewhat uncertain until the overall reputation of investment real estate is improved and investor concerns about the long-term viability of this product type are answered.
- The distance between factory outlet centers and major urban retail activity will continue to decline.
- The American consumer's love for a bargain plus continuing downward pressure on their disposable income will continue to support the factory outlet trend.
- Centers will become more elaborate, cost more to build and have higher rent.
- Travel trends, on balance, favor this product type.
- Entertainment, as a traffic-builder and shopper-retention device, will become more popular.
- The number of centers will continue to grow but at a less vigorous pace than the average of the past ten years.
- The average size of a new center will be about 150,000 square feet.
- The enclosed mall design will gain in popularity.
- The number of manufacturers selling through factory outlet centers will increase.
- Food service will become more important and more elaborate.
- Factory outlet centers with strong anchor tenants will become more common.
- Lease terms will lengthen in response to financing difficulties and tenant successes.

- Total development costs will rise as projects are built "closer in" on higher-priced land.
- Institutional lenders will become more active in financing and buying factory outlet centers.
- Major tenants are not likely to emerge as a big factory outlet development force.
- The presence of a factory outlet center within a mixed-use development will increase.

Factory outlet centers, even though they are somewhat risky due to their short history and difficult-to-understand locations, have been one of the brightest development and investment opportunities available during uncertain times. In spite of the tendency to overbuild everything, it is less likely that this segment will suffer from substantial surplus because of financing restraints and a higher-than-normal investment risk.

CHAPTER

6

Hotels, Motels and Resorts

During the past decade, hotel construction boomed while occupancy rates declined, and as a result, hotels, motels and resorts are not at the top of many investors' "must buy" lists. This does not mean that good things have not happened in the past ten years, nor does it mean that there are no prospects for profitable lodging industry investment in the future. The oversupply created during the 1980s has set the table for an investment feast in the 1990s.

This chapter provides a broad overview of the U.S. hotel industry from an investor's perspective. It begins with a look at some of the outstanding events of the past decade, then moves on to a short history of the hotel industry before reviewing the supply and demand factors an astute investor needs to consider. Immediately following that are segments on the characteristics of a lodging industry investment and operating result guidelines. You will also find sections dealing with three important market segments: the resort, the all-suite hotel and economy lodging. This is followed by a look at feasibility reports and valuation techniques, plus financing and deal structures. The chapter ends with a review of foreign investment activity and the usual section on trends and conclusions.

A Decade of Change

The past decade was a period of tremendous change for hotels and for virtually all areas of American life. The decade began with interest rates soaring past 20 percent and inflation at 9 percent or more, and ended with much cheaper money and with inflation at approximately 4 percent; it had fallen to 2 percent by the end of 1992. We experienced a long recession early on and ended the decade with a record-setting period of prosperity. The nineties began as the eighties did—in recession.

During the past decade the globalization of quality commercial real estate became a fact of investment life. Foreign competition in the financing and purchasing of hotels became intense by the mid-1980s. Figure 6.4 (in the Foreign Investment section) details some of the foreign investment activity.

In 1986, tax reform spelled the end of the syndication boom and the beginning of unusually hard times for many types of real estate. For hotels, it marked the end of "easy" development deals. As if the 1986 tax law were not a severe enough blow, the stock market, only one year later, had one of the worst price declines in its history. The markets recovered from this trauma to end the decade at prices significantly higher than at the start of the eighties, and they continued to soar during the first two years of the nineties.

In the 1980s we also saw the rise and fall of junk bond financing, mega-leveraged buyouts, massive insider trading scandals, and savings and loan failures of such extraordinary magnitude as to almost defy characterization. The impact of these events on real estate was not fully felt until the early nineties; the effect on hotel development and investment sales was seen as early as 1989. Overbuilding, low average occupancy levels and difficulty, of the sort not seen since the depression years, in funding new projects or selling existing ones are but three of the results. Some think that these troubles are leading the way to market price adjustments that will create some favorable investment opportunities.

A Brief History of Lodging

People have been providing temporary lodging to others almost since time began. Our brief history in Figure 6.1 does not reach back quite so far, but

Figure 6.1   The Lodging Industry: Historical Highlights

1760	First English taverns.
1794	First U.S. hotel (73 rooms): Tontine City Tavern in New York City.
1829	First bellboy: Tremont House, Boston.
1831	First presidential nominating convention (Henry Clay was nominated): Barnums City Hotel, Baltimore.
1833	First baggage elevator: Holt's Hotel, New York City.
1840s	American Plan developed. The Parker House in Chicago (built in 1855) was an early American Plan hotel.
1859	First great modern hotel and the first passenger elevator: Fifth Avenue Hotel, New York City.
1892–1927	First in-room use of telephones: Hotel Netherland, New York City (1894). Five of America's grand hotels open: The Brown Palace in Denver (1892); the St. Francis in San Francisco (1904); The Copley Plaza in Boston (1912); The Broadmoor in Colorado Springs (1918); and the Hay Adams in Washington, D.C. (1927).
	World's largest hotel (from 1927 to 1962), the Stevens, now called the Conrad Hilton, opens in Chicago.
	First use of the word *motel* (1915, in California).
	Pebble Beach Golf Course and Resort construction starts (1919).
1920s	Greenbrier Resort (West Virginia) is developed; Camelback area of Phoenix starts to develop.
1950s	First use of curtain wall construction: the Hartford Statler designed by William Tabler. Kemmons Wilson opens first Holiday Inn in Memphis: room rents—$4 single, $6 double.
1961	First limited-service all-suite hotel (Lexington Hotel Suite Concept) opened by Mr. and Mrs. Zulon Wilkins, Sr.
1962	First budget motel: Motel 6, Santa Barbara. Room rate: $6.
1963	Kahala Hilton resort built at a cost of $33,000 per room.
1967	Atrium lobby design introduced in John Portman's Hyatt Regency Hotel in Atlanta.
1969	First all-suite hotel developed by Robert Wooley: Granada Royale, Phoenix.
1970	Resort hotels begin to fully exploit the occupancy potential of large group meetings.

Figure 6.1 The Lodging Industry: Historical Highlights (continued)

1971	Walt Disney World opens in Orlando. Hotel building boom begins in local area.
1976	Industry was overbuilt nationwide.
1978	Japanese investors begin buying high-quality U.S. hotels. Prices start to rise in spite of occupancy doldrums carrying over from 1976 and 1977.
1980s	Development of mega-resorts accelerates. Resort segment of industry begins to explore chain affiliations. Resale prices stable for all types of hotels. Twenty-two branches of foreign banks in New York City mark start of most recent wave of foreign interest in U.S. real estate.
1983	All-suite concept spreads widely.
1984	Foreign investor interest in American hotels reaches new high. Resale prices climb rapidly.
1986	U.S. tax law changes severely affect sale and financing of lodging facilities.
1987	Lender foreclosures on U.S. hotels set modern record.
	Mauna Kea hotel in Hawaii sells for $1 million per room.
Late 1980s	Hotel building boom ends.
1989	Resale prices for lodging facilities set new highs. Bel Air Hotel (Los Angeles) sold for $1.2 million per room.
	More than 350 foreign banks have offices in New York City.
1991	Hotel occupancy levels drop below 60 percent in many prime markets. Lack of financing keeps clamp on resale prices and new construction.

even an abbreviated chronicle helps to point out where the industry has been and, perhaps, give some clues as to where it may be going.

Supply and Demand

The hotel business is one of America's leading industries. There are approximately 3 million hotel rooms available nationwide; the industry has an annual volume in excess of $50 billion. The average rate of revenue

Table 6.1 Hotel Construction in the United States: 1974–1991
(constant 1987 dollars in billions)

Year	1974	1975	1976	1977	1978	1979	1980	1981	1982
$	3.7	2.3	1.9	1.8	2.5	3.4	4.2	4.9	5.2
Year	1983	1984	1985	1986	1987	1988	1989	1990	1991
$	6.4	8.0	8.5	8.4	8.1	7.2	7.8	8.7	5.6

Source: U.S. Department of Commerce, Economics and Statistics Administration, Bureau of the Census, *Value of New Construction Put in Place*, C30-9105 and C30-9207.

growth since 1973 has been approximately 14 percent a year. In spite of the impressive growth in industry size since the early seventies, it is not recession-proof. The recession of 1980 and 1981–1982 hurt the industry badly; there were 47 straight months of declining occupancy, followed by a strong recovery starting in August of 1983. During the recession of the early nineties, occupancy rates fell below 60 percent in a significant number of markets.

The hotel industry is still in a fragile condition, making it necessary for investors to approach any lodging investment with extreme caution. This overall fragility does not mean that every segment of this highly segmented business is in trouble. Nor does it mean that conditions are not right for selective purchases. Current industry conditions may be the best argument for investing now.

Market segmentation is a fact of hotel life. This is an industry that has gone crazy with a proliferation of specialized lodging segments, such as economy, budget, hard budget, all-suite, extended stay and many others. The segmentation phenomenon is, in fact, adding to the industry's woes rather than alleviating them by increasing the oversupply and putting heavy pressure on traditional full-service mid-market hotels.

Investor and Guest Demand

There is a general agreement among lenders and other investors that the industry is overbuilt. Table 6.1 details the dollar value of hotel construction from 1974 to 1991. As of July 1992, that figure was $1.7 billion, leading to a full-year estimate of $3 billion. The steep decline in new construction since 1990 will help improve occupancy levels.

The lack of strong tax incentives since 1986 has contributed to a decline in construction that may, in due time, allow the industry to achieve a better balance between supply and demand. This is not expected before the late nineties.

Investor demand for trophy properties peaked in 1988, pushed to stratospheric new prices by foreign investors.

Partly as a result of the buying frenzy surrounding the premier hotels, average facilities also experienced strong investor demand from 1985 to 1989, even as they were struggling to keep occupancy from plunging below 60 percent. Prices for nontrophy properties, on a per-room basis, rose 230 percent from 1984 to the end of 1988. Now that the full effect of overbuilding is evident and the memory of a severe recession is still fresh, per-room prices have softened considerably. Bargain-priced offerings have already appeared in the B and C grade properties.

This is not the first time that hotel resale prices have declined because of overbuilding and the effects of a depressed economy. In 1976–1977 average resale prices dropped approximately 30 percent, but prices began to move up again in 1978, although that rise was interrupted by the 1980–1982 recessions. Some analysts expect the present flatness in hotel sale prices to end and start to move up after 1996.

Investors who buy into markets where overbuilding and severe recession coincide can suffer huge losses. In Texas and Colorado, for example, the energy crisis plus overbuilding led to foreclosure sales in the late 1980s and early 1990s. Hotels that cost $80,000 to $100,000 per room to build were sold at $25,000 to $30,000 per room. Most of those "bargains" needed considerable renovation, but even with those costs added the total cost per room was below replacement costs. If contrarian investors and others with a long-range perspective are looking for such values today, they will find them.

Demand from investors is lukewarm at best today; demand from guests is even weaker in many markets. Occupancy, on a national basis, is in the low 60 percent range, with many areas struggling to get up to that level. But occupancy has been strengthening since 1991, and there is reason to believe it may return to the 65 percent level and begin to stabilize. When hotel occupancy falls below 65 percent it is difficult to make money. Given the tendency for occupancy to fall to 60 percent or lower during difficult financial times, investors may have to reexamine the somewhat traditional use of 65 percent as the stabilized pro forma level of occupancy.

Table 6.2 Hotel Occupancy Levels by Regions: 1988–1991 (in percent)

Region	1988	1989	1990	1991
United States	62.8	63.8	64.9	65.4
New England	62.3	57.9	70.4	71.6
Mid-Atlantic	66.4	64.9	71.3	70.9
South Atlantic	64.7	66.7	61.9	61.9
East North Central	59.8	59.0	63.0	62.6
West North Central	58.1	58.8	63.7	65.9
West South Central	55.1	57.5	62.6	63.4
Mountain	61.9	63.3	64.5	65.2
Pacific	69.1	69.7	66.8	67.3

Source: Smith Travel Research, *Lodging Outlook*, December 1991. Used by permission.

The occupancy figures referenced above are national averages. They are useful as an indicator of where the business is and where it may be headed. But this is a highly diverse industry that is affected by regional and local economic and locational differences. No investment decision should be made without examining the occupancy and average daily rate history of the local market and the property being considered. Table 6.2 shows occupancy levels by regions since 1988. There are wide differences between regions, just as there will be between local markets. The regional data, however, support the earlier conclusion that an assumption of a 65 percent baseline occupancy level is not supported by market trends.

In spite of the difficulty the industry has had in maintaining occupancy, average daily rates (ADRs) have increased significantly in the past 20 years. Since 1973, when the average ADR nationally was $22.05, room rates have increased at 12.25 percent annually. The average ADR is $75 today. ADRs have made significant increases when compared against inflation over the past 20 years, outperforming it annually. Recent performance, however, has not been as good as the 20-year average. Many markets have had small, or no, ADR increases in the past two years, and nothing but modest increases are seen for at least the next three to five years.

Average daily rates are used by some investors, in a rule-of-thumb fashion, to quickly estimate the value of a hotel property. The ADR should, according to this estimating method, be 1/1000th of the acquisition or development cost per room. If a project costs $250,000 per room, then the ADR should be $250. Very few hotels perform to that rule of thumb today.

Room demand profiles are not strong. The generally overbuilt condition of the market works against rapid ADR growth. Competition for guests is intense, and marketing and other costs are rising. In such an environment, profits will be hard to generate if acquisition costs do not fall.

Investment Characteristics

A number of different systems are used to classify hotels. They are grouped by the price they charge for a room into low-, mid-, high- and higher-priced facilities. They are also described by the level of service they provide, such as full-service, limited service and convention hotels. The type of guest is also the basis for a classifying system. Guests are divided into the business traveler, the resort or vacation traveler, and the convention traveler. The length of stay is also used; guests are described as transient (short stays), resident (long stays), or apartment or permanent guests. The resort hotel would fit into the resident hotel classification if classified by the length of guest stays.

The lodging industry has further divided itself into two main groups: facilities that cater to luxury-minded guests and those that serve the economy-minded guest. This two-segment division of the industry may seem extreme, but it serves to highlight the fact that market segmentation is a strong reality in hotel investment life. Segmentation is encouraged, in part, by the fact that many of the new segments are doing better financially than more traditional facilities.

Hotel investments seldom return quick profits; investors need to take a long view. The internal rate of return (IRR), using a ten-year holding period, should be 19 percent to 22 percent. That return is heavily weighted to resale profit—and with resale prices falling, it won't be easy to achieve such IRRs this century.

The first four to five years of a hotel's operation mean very little; it takes many of them longer than that to break even. In economic boom times, some hotels seem to be developed for the sole purpose of generating a development fee and a one-time resale profit for the developer rather than because supply/demand studies show a real need for them.

Hotels are a relatively high-risk investment, and the returns they earn have reflected this characteristic. Cash-on-cash returns range from 8 percent to 25 percent. In normal times, substantial resale profits from a successful development venture can be expected within five to seven years. The recent history of resort hotels shows that it is possible to make some excellent profits by investing in existing (not necessarily new) hotels. Figure 6.3 (in the Foreign Investment section) contains some examples of profits made by well-timed sales.

The days of the very low equity deal (except for distressed properties) are over. It takes an investment of at least 25 percent to 35 percent of the total cost to acquire a hotel today. Prices range from $1.8 million to $8 million for a 300-room facility.

Developers, insurance companies and wealthy individuals, both domestic and foreign, are the most common investors in both new and existing hotels.

Hotels are as much a business as they are a real estate investment, and because of this, they offer some additional tax benefits. The serious negative effects that have flowed from the 1986 Tax Reform Act may, in the long run, become advantageous to hotel investors if the reduction in hotel construction lasts long enough.

Institutional investors have long viewed hotels as an inflation hedge. Their hotel investments, often in the form of debt, generally provide for a substantial participation in net operating income increases and in resale profit. This reliance upon hotels as an inflation hedge has been well placed; they have been almost perfect in that respect.

Lodging facilities have some other distinctive investment characteristics that may make the more conservative investor uneasy. They have a short economic life. Functional and economic obsolescence is high. It is a rare hotel that can operate for more than ten years without significant rehabilitation. It is even rarer to find one that is highly profitable in its tenth year.

Easy money leads to quick overbuilding. The supply of hotel rooms is unusually sensitive to the availability of affordable credit, and for good or ill, periods of abundant credit seem to occur with some regularity in the United States.

Hotels are a labor-intensive, retail-type business in which wages and benefits can amount to 40 percent of gross revenue. It is also a business that requires substantial amounts of working capital. Unlike most other

Table 6.3   Hotel Revenues and Expenses by Major Categories (1990)

Revenues	%	Expenses	%
Room rentals	63.1	Salaries, etc.	32.4
Food sales	22.7	Operations	24.5
Beverage sales	6.7	Cost of sales	8.4
Telephone sales	2.0	Energy costs	3.6
Other departments	3.2	All taxes	3.3
Other income	2.3	Other expenses	28.0
Total	100	Total	100

Source: Pannell Kerr Forster, *Trends in the Hotel Industry USA Edition,* 1991 ed., 46.

types of real estate investment, hotels require capital for furniture, fixtures and equipment (FF&E), which can amount to 25 percent of a property's total value.

Hotels are particularly sensitive to the quality of their location. The cost of a good site is usually 20–25 percent of total facility cost. But the cost of a location is a one-time expense in most cases. Operating management is not.

The decision on who is going to operate the hotel is both critical and recurring. On-site management can make or break your investment. Without superior management you will not be able to get financing, nor will you be able to generate the revenue needed to service your debt, pay expenses and make a profit.

Operating Results

Investors, except for a few exceptions during periods of buying frenzy, have always placed heavy emphasis upon net operating income (NOI) when determining hotel value. Pannell Kerr Forster (PKF), in its *USA Trends Report* (1990), suggests that NOIs range from 17.6 percent to 22.3 percent depending upon the type and size of the facility. It should be noted that NOI results vary, within hotel categories, based upon the size of the facility and the services offered. Transient hotels with 1,000 rooms or more showed a higher NOI (20.7 percent), as did resort hotels with 250 or more rooms (23.7 percent). Motels without restaurants showed an

Table 6.4   Average Room Rates: 1990 and 1991

Type of Property	1990	1991
Luxury	$86.31	$87.24
Upscale	$59.81	$59.99
Basic	$46.95	$45.81
Economy Upper	$51.17	$50.28
Economy Moderate	$31.29	$32.65

Source: Smith Travel Research, *Lodging Outlook,* December 1991.

exceptional 40.5 percent NOI. The figures quoted are from PKF's 1990 report.

Revenue and expense guidelines.   The most profitable activity and the largest revenue source is room rentals; the largest expense is payroll, but this figure declined from 40.8 percent in 1989. Table 6.3 shows the sources and distribution of revenue and expense from an 1,100-hotel sample. Table 6.4 shows average daily room rates for five types of properties for 1990 and 1991.

Management fees run from 2 percent to 8 percent depending upon the nature of the management contract. Property maintenance will be 3 percent to 4 percent of gross revenue. Interest expense is about 6.5 percent of revenue, and depreciation will be approximately 6 percent.

The high cost of labor leads hotels to invest heavily in in-house service facilities to help raise profits. The extent to which a hotel, particularly an older one, has committed to labor-saving devices is one of the indications of profit potential.

Investors have access to an immense amount of published data on hotels from trade publications, newspapers and accounting firms that serve the industry. The easy access to such data makes it possible to get enough information to make critical judgments without being a hotel expert. To avoid being misled, it is crucial that you consult a variety of sources to get a complete picture. A valuable information source is *The Uniform System of Accounts for Hotels;* first published in 1925, it is now in its 8th (1986) edition. You can get it from the Hotel Association of New York.

Rental rates and occupancy. These factors provide the basis for a rule-of-thumb estimate of per-room value. A room cost of $60,000 should support an average daily rate of $60 ($60,000 × .001). This rule has a built-in assumption of 70 percent occupancy and 55 percent gross profit on room rentals; however, we have already seen that these assumptions may not be accurate today. Occupancy rates are also sometimes used to calculate what size facility to build. If average occupancy is forecast to be 80 percent and the market will support 400 rooms, you might build a 500-room facility, which, at 80 percent, would capture the entire market and give you some room to grow.

Room rates (ADRs) are moving slowly upward in spite of the decline in average occupancy that has occurred over the past few years. Luxury hotel occupancy does not appear to be rate-sensitive, but budget and economy hotel occupancy is quite responsive to room rate.

Over half of American hotels have posted room rates between $30 and $59.99. The prognosis for room rates increasing faster than inflation is not good unless the inflation rate stays below 5 percent. It is difficult to increase room rates quickly today due to the heavy competition in virtually every market area and marketing segment. The battle to achieve a breakeven, or slightly profitable operation is intense and is likely to be a long one.

Over time, occupancy of 60–65 percent is common. Until the last recession, average occupancy nationwide fell between those numbers for 25 years. A return on investment of 10–14 percent is possible at historic occupancy rates. Investors should probably not look for a much higher return from any hotel investment over time because of the relative ease with which new supply can be created. Competition tends to remain intense, forcing supply to a level that stabilizes rates at a point just high enough to provide a modest investment return.

About 73 percent of the average hotel's business takes place in four days each week. It's a 200-day-a-year business; weekend occupancy is usually quite low and often at reduced rates.

Many of the specialized concepts, such as all-suite, have reported first-year occupancies far in excess of the historical 60–65 percent rate. It is difficult, however, to find the bottom-line results, in their annual reports, of these high initial-year occupancy rates. First-year results are often much different from stabilized, long-term numbers.

Room sizes, space allocations, furniture, fixtures and equipment guidelines. Room sizes fit into multiples of the standard 12-foot to

14-foot carpet widths, with room depths ranging between 25 and 30 feet. Average room size runs from 300 to 420 square feet. The minimum size for a double bedroom is about 180 square feet. The size of the room varies according to the type and quality of the lodging facility. All-suite units tend to be the largest.

Bathrooms are generally double-stacked (built back-to-back and directly in line with those above and below) and will range from 100 to 130 square feet.

Typical per-room construction costs will range from $18,000 for an economy project to $100,000 and up for a luxury hotel. Newspaper accounts of construction costs are often overstated by 25 percent to 33⅓ percent.

Figure 6.2 will help you to judge the adequacy of back-of-the-house and other guest support facilities. Storage space varies with the size of the hotel, although it is quite common for new hotels to have too little of it. The optimum is about 25 to 30 square feet per guest room; the common allocation is about half of that in a 100-room hotel and about eight square feet per room in a 1,000-room facility.

The total cost of FF&E will range from $5,000 to $18,000 per room; franchises and large chains can often do better than this due to their buying power. It is necessary to have about 133 percent of the expected daily use of china and silver on hand, plus approximately 110 percent of the total needed for all other service equipment.

The useful life of FF&E items is short. It ranges from 2 to 6 years for carpeting, 5 to 15 years for lobby and guest room furniture, and 8 to 25 years for kitchen equipment.

Resorts, All-Suites and Economy Hotels

The resort market has done well, even during the recession of the early nineties, and should continue to do well throughout the 1990s. Resorts represent about 20 percent of the hotel room supply and slightly more than 20 percent of industry revenue. There are about 4,300 resorts nationwide with 560,000 rooms. They have shown an average occupancy slightly higher than the total industry average.

U.S. population is no longer growing rapidly, but changes in the composition of our population strongly favor the resort segment of the

Figure 6.2   Space Allocations: Selected Functions

Type of Space	Allocation
Food Facilities	
Coffee Shop	12–15 square feet per seat
Dining Room	18–30 square feet per seat
Specialty Restaurant	23–35 square feet per seat
Quiet Bar	15–20 square feet per seat
Entertainment Bar	20–25 square feet per seat
Banquet/Ballroom	10–20 square feet per seat
Kitchen: Coffee Shop	45% of restaurant area
Kitchen: All Dining Rooms	60% of all food-serving areas
Lobby	4,000 to 5,000 square feet
Administration	
100-Room Facility	5 square feet per guest room
1,000-Room Facility	35 square feet per guest room
Parking	
Per Guest Unit	1 space
Per Restaurant	1 space for each five seats
Per Employee	1 space for each three
Service and Loading	3 space minimum

Source: Warren, Gorham & Lamont, *How To Provide a Hotel in a Development and Benefit Both,*
(Boston/New York: 1979).
Donald Lundberg, *The Hotel and Restaurant Business* (New York: Van Nostrand Reinhold).

hotel industry. Table 6.5 shows the expected changes in the makeup of the population during the 1990s.

One example of how these changes affect resorts can be found by examining the baby-boom segment. Those born between 1946 and 1964 number about 80 million out of a population of about 250 million. Many of the "boomers" will be entering middle age during the decade of the nineties; they will be at the peak of their earning power. This is also the group that swells the ranks of the two-income families. Further, most of them, at least those who are earning $50,000 or more per year, are working 50 hours (often more) per week. The baby boomers have the money for vacations but not a whole lot of time to take them. Short, but expensive,

Table 6.5   U.S. Population by Age Brackets: 1900–2000 (percent of change)

Age Group	Percent Change
0–17	3.32
18–24	–5.64
25–44	3.78
45–54	47.58
55–64	14.23
65–74	.75
75–84	19.51
85 Plus	40.33
Total Population 248,710,000	Total Population 268,266,000
Median Age 32.9 years	Median Age 36.4 years

Source: U.S. Department of Commerce, Economics and Statistics Administration, Bureau of the Census, "Census Bureau Completes Distribution of 1990 Census Information from Summary Tape File 1A," Release CB91-217 (1991).
U.S. Department of Commerce, Economics and Statistics Administration, Bureau of the Census, "Current Population Reports, Population Estimates and Projections," Series P-24, No. 1018 (1988).

resort minivacations fit their lifestyle. American resorts are perfectly suited to cater to this market.

Until the severe credit crunch hit the hotel business in 1989, the supply of American resorts had been growing rapidly. Because competition was increasing, the size of new resorts and their luxury level escalated. This caused the cost of developing a new resort to skyrocket. Resorts that used to cost $80,000 to $85,000 per room as recently as 1980–1983 now cost $300,000 per room; some are even higher. We have entered the era of the Super Resort. In 1988 the Phoenician Resort, on 130 acres in Scottsdale, Arizona, cost a record-setting $485,000 per room to develop. Competition has brought on the day of mega-resorts designed with a carefully crafted fantasy environment, and they cost big dollars to create. It is possible, however, that their construction costs have peaked as the economic slowdown returns investors to reality.

A look at the recent history (see Figure 6.3) of resort development provides some insight into the progress of costs and amenities and the profit potential of a winning project.

Resorts market make-believe to their guests. Even in Hawaii—perhaps especially in Hawaii, where many resorts are built at the water's edge on

Figure 6.3 The Recent History of Resort Development

1980	**Hyatt Regency, Maui.** 800 rooms, 18-acre site. Features lavish gardens, rock-formed pools, waterfalls. Original art on display. Cost $83,000 per room to complete. Sold to VMS (a syndicator) in 1985 for $240,000 per room. Bought by Kokusai Motorcars Corporation in 1987 for $392,000 per room. Many hotel analysts think that the 1985 transaction marked the start of the late 1980s resort hotel construction boom.
1982	**Marriott Resort, Maui.** Sold (the first time) for a profit estimated to be 291 percent on the equity invested to build it.
1987	**Disney Resorts, Orlando, Florida.** Four resorts open: • Grand Floridian, 900 rooms • Caribbean Ranch Resort, 2,000 rooms • Convention Kingdom Hotel, 1,800 rooms • Disney Beach and Yacht Club, 3,500 rooms
1988	**Hyatt Regency Waikoloa, Hawaii.** 1,244 rooms. Total cost $360 million, or $290,000 per room.
1988	**Phoenician, Scottsdale, Arizona.** 130 acres. $485,000 per room.

sites that were volcanic deserts—the guests are surrounded by man-made Edens. Lush tropical gardens, pools and waterfalls, plus hundreds of acres of golf courses, cater to the guest's fantasy of Hawaii.

Guests are demanding elaborate fantasy environments, and they seem willing to pay for them. The average daily rate at resorts is an industry-high $81, and many of them charge $300 or more.

The trend toward super resorts has inspired some operators to acquire or develop a product that is just the opposite: the "boutique" (small) resort. Facilities with 150 rooms or less have been in high demand, by both guests and investors, if they have a select, special-interest clientele (golf, tennis, water recreation, etc.) and project an air of exclusivity. Most such facilities operate as independents (non-chain-affiliated), and many investors think this adds an element of snob appeal to their allure.

The all-suite hotel has been another bright spot in the hotel market. All-suites represent about 3.5–4 percent of the market; some observers think they will grow to a 10 percent market share by the year 2000. The concept is growing—not because of a rapidly expanding market for hotel rooms but from occupancy losses in other hotel segments. It is the hotel equivalent of building a better mousetrap and selling it for the same price—or less.

All-suite facilities in the Central Business District are targeted at the customers of midpriced, full-service hotels. By providing a two-room suite with 600 square feet, sometimes more, at ADRs of $85 to $100, they are capturing an increasing share of the value-conscious guest market. It is almost impossible for the conventional, older hotel with smaller rooms to compete with the new all-suite projects, although some (in very good markets) have done it with rehabilitation and room rates of $75 to $100 per day.

Even though the large size of the typical suite is one of its most powerful marketing appeals, the trend in suite size is downward as major chains enter the market. Some of the newer all-suite projects have suites of less than 500 square feet. Whether this reduction will lessen demand or create a premium value for the older all-suite hotels remains to be seen.

Occupancy rates are higher in a successful all-suite hotel than in almost any other type of lodging facility (except resorts). But are they high enough to support the high cost of building them? Based on previous levels of construction activity, many lenders and equity investors thought so. Average all-suite occupancy was 67.8 percent in 1991, which is the latest available figure, but occupancy varies considerably with the region of the country and the strength of the location. The national trend has been downward since 1988.

All-suites, like resorts, cost more per room to build than their current ADRs will support. A CBD all-suite can cost $200,000 per room. This is a cost that cannot be justified, in today's competitive market, by the 1/1000th-of-cost-equals-rent formula. Nevertheless, high occupancy is being achieved (in some cases), which, optimistic operators claim, justifies the high cost of construction. This cost vs. room rent ratio is a strong signal to investors to exercise caution when considering this type of hotel.

The healthiest segments within the all-suite category have been family travel, female guests and three-day weekend business. As the concept grows in consumer awareness, it is expected that an increasing number of male business travelers will discover the comfort and value offered by this product type.

All-suites have attracted some of the biggest franchise and management names in the hotel industry: Marriott (Residence Inn) and Holiday Inn (Embassy Suites) are two of them. There is no shortage of other well-known participants, such as Sheraton, Hilton, Hyatt and Radisson. Other familiar names are Quality International, Howard Johnson, Comfort Suites, Guest Quarters and Pickett Suites. In the extended-stay area, Homewood (Holiday Inn), Residence Inns (Marriott) and the Oakwood Corporate Apartments are three of the most well known.

Economy and budget hotels were a fast-growing market segment in the late eighties, due in part to the relatively low cost of building them, which made it possible for small to midsize local developers to get into the hotel business. There are more than 5,500 budget, economy or limited-service facilities in the United States; their total room count is approximately 550,000 rooms, or about 18 percent of the total room supply. Annual growth, in number of rooms, got into double-digit numbers in 1986 and 1987 but has since slowed to about 4 percent per year. Growth is not expected to reach the levels of 1986 or 1987 due to the overbuilt condition in the industry, the difficulty in finding good sites, scarcity of financing, and the fact that there are fewer properties left that can be converted to the standards of the more than 500 budget and economy franchisers.

To qualify as an economy facility, the daily room rate must be $40 or less. The price range stretches from less than $29 to approximately $40 per day. Facilities with rate ranges between $33 and $40 are averaging 74 percent ($33) and 71 percent ($40) occupancy on a national basis.

Days Inn was a long-time leading operator in the economy market segment, but many of its facilities were upgraded to ADRs above those that fit into this segment. Comfort Inns and Hampton Inns have been among the fastest growing. Other familiar names in the economy lodging field are Super 8, Travelodge, Econolodge, Motel 6, La Quinta, Red Roof Inn, Rodeway Inn, Holiday Inn Express and Budgetel Inns.

Economy and budget facilities generally have no meeting rooms, no pool, and no restaurant or food service.

Total development costs come closer to being supported by actual room rents than any other type of hotel project. Development costs range from $32,000 to $62,000 per room for an economy project. A budget motel, depending upon the land cost, will range from $18,000 to $22,000 per room. The contrast between these costs and the projected costs for the full-service Regent Hotel in New York City ($750,000 per room) marks both ends of today's lodging development costs. What investors can be induced to pay, however, is often much, much more than bare development cost.

Because all segments of the industry are overbuilt, everyone is fighting to grab a profitable share of a stagnant to slowly growing market. You may expect to see much heavier advertising budgets in the economy/budget segment.

Conditions have been right for some time now for numerous consolidations in this segment. It is very likely that by the end of this decade, there will be far fewer than 500 franchisers.

Feasibility Reports

The bridge between the idea of a hotel and its reality is the feasibility report. No project can attract debt or equity financing without a strong feasibility study. As competition increases, both lenders and equity investors are demanding more complete and costly studies. A more complete report can cost as much as three times the price of a standard report.

Being able to evaluate a consultant's report is one of the keys to making a sound lodging industry investment. Yet most investors don't know how to distinguish between a thorough, accurate, sophisticated report and one that is too simple to be useful. Because of this ignorance, they are often willing to accept just about any kind of market research as valuable. In truth, much of it is junk.

The popular concept of a feasibility report is that it is a marketability study supported by financial analysis. They are much more than that. Feasibility reports cover four main areas:

1. The Market—This section looks at current and future demand.
2. Marketability—This section covers occupancy, pricing, and amenities.
3. Financial Feasibility—This part deals with income, expense and return on investment.
4. Valuation—This is the appraisal.

A good report will contain a complete presentation on both current and anticipated competition, a marketing segmentation study, a market share forecast, a review of all potential locations, data on office space construction and occupancy, and a presentation on the local food and beverage competition. The report should cover a period of five to ten years; the very best ones will show three possibilities: aggressive, probable and conservative.

You should be able to test the validity of a report's assumptions and conclusions by comparing them to what you learn from studying easily accessible independent data. A vigorous examination of the feasibility report leading to your own separate opinion is essential.

In such a heavily overbuilt product type, all of the justifying feasibility reports simply can't have been right. Watch for these critical indicators:

- Employment levels in the local market—past, present and projected; diversity of economic activity is especially important
- Airline travel volume—both amount and type of traveler
- Disposable personal income trend
- Office building activity—construction and occupancy level
- General economic activity trend
- Travel expenditure level
- Energy prices—they affect the amount of auto and airline travel.
- Corporate profits—when they are good, so is hotel occupancy.
- Population migration patterns
- Money supply and interest rate trends
- Teleconferencing use—such conferences often substitute for travel.

Interest rates, taken alone, may not be a good indicator of hotel feasibility. The industry seems to have adapted to high rates rather quickly in the past. Rates as an indicator of the supply of funds might be useful, although it should be remembered that the supply of loan funds for real estate construction in the early nineties was low to nonexistent despite low interest rates.

Valuation

In most respects, a hotel investment is much like any other income-producing piece of real estate. There are income and expense streams that must be calculated and examined, and there is an appropriate capitalization rate that can be applied to the net operating income. Currently, the cap rates range from 8 percent to 15 percent, with the most common being 11–12 percent. The net income used is the income before interest and depreciation costs.

The valuation of a hotel seems to be a somewhat uncertain business. It is not uncommon for a wide range of opinion to exist as to a facility's value. In one recently reported case, two experts came to opinions of value that ranged from a low of $2.5 million to a high of $4 million.

All three of the common appraisal methods are used in hotel evaluation. The easiest method to understand, and the most frequently used, is the income approach to value. Most valuations include a ten-year operating projection.

With today's room rates and the near-term to midterm prospects for the economy, a forecast that relies on a 5 percent to 6 percent annual growth rate (to achieve a 16–18 percent internal rate of return) is open to serious question.

Financing and Deal Structures

In a normal financing market, getting a loan is basically a process of negotiating the project's assumptions with the lender. Often the developer expends a great deal of energy trying to sell the lender assumptions that are more optimistic than the lender, or the lender's consultant, is willing to buy. The feasibility report is important to this process. If the lender understands and agrees with the report's favorable assumptions, getting the loan will be routine. If the report is unfavorable, it will be almost impossible to sell the lender, or any other investor, on the idea of ignoring it.

Some track-record developers (during good times) can get loans funded using only the marketability section of a feasibility report plus jointly developed (lender/developer) financial forecasts.

Lenders are interested in three basic considerations: the concept, the quality of the sponsors and the management. The five keys to financing are:

1. The intrinsics of the project
2. Its market potential
3. The financial strength and reputation of its sponsors
4. The operating and marketing management
5. The current state of the money market

It will help, when applying for a loan, if you have an affiliation with a national chain or strong franchise; about two-thirds of all new hotels have such an affiliation. In the absence of such a connection you will need, at the least, access to a strong reservation system. Other routes to a loan include a lease or joint venture with a national operator. The willingness to accept a participation loan may also be helpful. In "credit crunch" times, the ability to pledge additional collateral (or an exceptional net worth) will also help.

The most common sources of hotel financing are life insurance companies, commercial banks, some savings banks, credit companies, pension funds, financial conglomerates, and mortgage bankers or brokers who represent lenders or who know which lenders are active. From time to time, federal, state and local programs are available to provide loans or loan guarantees. There are many ways to put a deal together, but there is no hotel financing "cookie cutter." The usual process is to get a construction loan from one lender and a permanent loan from another. In the past, some commercial banks offered a combination of a construction and a mini-perm with a seven-year to ten-year maturity. Such one-stop shopping is difficult to find today.

Land sale/leasebacks have been used as part of a hotel's financing. The attraction of this structure is that the developer gets 100 percent financing on the land. It also puts 100 percent of the downside risk on the developer. One of the problems, when financing becomes difficult to get, is the danger of creating overly complicated financing structures that add significant costs to the project without creating real value.

Here, in broad terms, is what you will find in the loan market:

- **Loan amounts**—First mortgage loans will range from 60 percent to 80 percent of the total development budget. An equity of 25–35 percent is common today.
- **Loan maturities**—Ten to 15 years with a 25- to 30-year amortization.
- **Loan rate**—Nine percent to 10.5 percent on first loans. When rates are high, most loans accrue interest. Participation loans are popular with lenders.
- **Construction loans**—It is usual to have two lenders—one for the construction loan and one for the permanent loan. The permanent loan commitment is required before the construction loan will be funded.

Other financing techniques include the following:

- Developer equity syndication
- Subordinated ground lease
- Credit financing using the credit of the lessee
- Condominium and time-share structures
- Equipment loans
- Part of the equity or working capital provided by the operating manager
- Joint ventures
- Convertible loans
- Variable-rate loans
- Fixed-rate bullet loans
- Public syndication of equity or debt

Debt coverage ratios are calculated using the first stabilized year of operation (year 3, 4, or 5). The cash flow figure reflects deduction of all operating expenses, property taxes, insurance and replacement reserves.

Lender and Developer Concerns

Lenders have always viewed hotels as long-term, fairly high-risk loans. They are concerned by the overbuilt condition in the industry, which they believe will lead to stiff occupancy and rate competition. They often see themselves as being on the brink of getting into the hotel business, and it is a business they did not do well in during the 1930s and the 1970s. From time to time, however, the more aggressive lenders try to enter the business on the development side.

Developers worry about the increasing tendency of lenders to want to participate in the cash flow. They are also concerned about the lack of good financing and the decreasing opportunities to build new projects, especially the small to midsize deal. The problem of raising equity, in the negative environment created by the oversupply in the industry, is one that thousands of developers have failed to solve—and, hence, they have gone out of business.

Figure 6.4   Hotel Sales in the United States: 1985–1992 Selected Purchases by Foreign Investors

Year	Hotel	Buyer	Dollars (in millions)
1985	Beverly Wilshire	Regent Interests (Hong Kong)	125
1985	Essex House (New York)	Japanese Government	N/A
1985	Halekulani (Honolulu)	Mitsui Fudosan	16
1985	Nikko (Chicago)	Japan Airlines	35
1985	Makani Kai (Honolulu)	Individual Investors (Japan)	2.5
1985	Waikiki Beach (Honolulu)	Individual Investors (Japan)	50.3
1986	Aladdin (Las Vegas)	Ysuda Ginja	54
1986	Westin (Indianapolis)	Kumagai Gumi	59.5
1987	Naniloa (Hilo)	Nakano Group	11
1987	Waikiki Beach (Honolulu, see 1985)	Azuba Building Co.	86.7
1987	Westin Hotels & Resorts (the chain)	Aoki Corporation	1.53 Billion
1987	Dunes Hotel & Casino (Las Vegas)	Masao Nangasku	158
1988	Inter-Continental Hotel Group (the chain)	Seibu Saison Group	2.15 Billion
1988	Mauna Kea (Hawaii)	Prince Hotels (Japan)	310
1988	Hyatt Regency (Waikiki)	Kitaro Watanabe*	245
1988	Hyatt Regency (Maui)	Kokusai Jidosha	319
1988	Turtle Bay Hilton (Oahu)	Asahi Jyuken	127.5

 * Also bought four other Hawaiian hotels in 1988.
** Also owned by Japanese investors: The Breckinridge (Colo.) (Victoria, Inc.); Steamboat (Colo.) (Kamori Kanko): Stratton, Vt. (Victoria, Inc.).
Source: U.S. Department of Commerce, International Trade Administration and various news reports, 1985 to 1991.

Figure 6.4   Hotel Sales in the United States: 1985–1992 Selected Purchases
by Foreign Investors (continued)

Year	Hotel	Buyer	Dollars (in millions)
1988	Hyatt Regency (Oakland)	C&L Financial Corp. (Hong Kong)	N/A
1988	La Costa Hotel & Resort (Calif.)	Sports Shinko (Japan)	250
1988	Bel Air (Los Angeles)	Sekitei Keihatsu	110
1989	Hyatt Grand Champions Resort (Indian Wells, Calif.)	Maruko (Japan) (sold by the Resolution Trust Corp.)	65
1989	Biltmore Hotel Complex (Los Angeles)	TAT (Japan)	219
1989	Le Meridien (San Diego)	Chiyoda Finance, Inc.	75–80
1989	Ramada, Inc. (franchisor)	SAS Airlines: 40%	500
1989	Los Angeles Hilton	Korean Air Lines	168
1989	Registry (Universal City, Calif.)	Tuntex (Taiwan)	N/A
1990	Dana Point Resort (Calif.)	Masuiwaya Calif. Corp.	104
1990	Pebble Beach Golf Course & Resort (Calif.)	Minoru Isutani (Ben Hogan Properties)	800
1990	Portman (San Francisco)	Pan Pacific Hotels (Tokyu Group)	N/A
1990	Motel 6 (the chain)	Accor (French)	1.3 Billion
1990	Heavenly Valley Ski Resort (Calif.)	Kamari Kanko Co.**	80–100
1991	Phoenician Resort (Phoenix)	Kuwait Government	N/A
1992	Pebble Beach Golf Course & Resort	Taiheiyo Club Inc. (Lone Cypress Co.)	500

Foreign Investment Activity

Foreign investors have been active in the U.S. hotel market for the past 20 years. The most active in recent years have been from Japan. Japanese interest first surfaced in 1978 with some minor acquisitions. In 1983 the Japanese began buying luxury hotels and resorts in earnest. The story of price appreciation at the top end of the market from 1983 to 1989 was the story of price aggressiveness by the Japanese. The Japanese have not been the only foreign buyers of hotels, but since the mid-1980s they have been the strongest market force in both buying and financing of this product type. Figure 6.4 shows some highlights of foreign hotel investment activity from 1985 to 1992. In 1988 five of the non-Japanese investors were from Hong Kong.

The peak period for Japanese investment in U.S. real estate was 1988, when they spent about $16 billion on all types of property; by 1991 their expenditures had dropped to about $5 billion. This precipitous decline is bound to have a negative effect on resale prices. Just as foreign investment in U.S. real estate did not suddenly begin in 1985, so too has Japanese interest been a longstanding one; many of their early acquisitions were notable. In 1962 Kokusai Kogyo bought the venerable Moana Hotel in Honolulu, and in 1974 the Sheraton Waikiki was sold to Kenji Osano for $105 million.

There is a multitude of reasons for foreign interest in U.S. hotels. In some cases, owning a hotel that is known worldwide gives the investor added prestige in his or her home country. Foreign airlines such as Korean Air (the Los Angeles Hilton, the Sheraton in Anchorage and a hotel in Honolulu), All Nippon Airlines (Le Meridien in San Francisco and others), Japan Airlines (Nikko Hotels) and Scandinavian Air Systems (40 percent of the Intercontinental chain) buy hotels to complete their service package. All of these airlines are able to exploit their reservation system and customer base, just as United Airlines once did, to add occupancy to the hotels they own.

Foreigners sometimes value the hotel's real estate element much more aggressively than domestic investors. Seeing an ADR differential between rates in their home countries and in the United States, they often feel that the average daily rates are too low here and, hence, are bound to rise. This kind of thinking has justified (at least partly) the high price they have been willing to pay for an outstanding hotel.

Trends and Conclusions

These are the trends most likely to be noted during the next seven to eight years:

Development

- New-construction level will remain low until the late 1990s.
- The midprice market will attract less development (when compared to the past five years) over the next five years.
- Persistent overbuilt market condition will lead to a continuing loss of small to midsized developers. They will return when the money does.
- Major developers, looking for things to do and often without any hotel development experience, will "crowd out" smaller builders.
- There will be a strong interest in small markets as developers do everything they can to "shoehorn" a deal into a very tight market.
- Architectural style changes will continue. Newer hotels will look more like mansions and less like office buildings.
- Razing of older hotels will increase; at the same time, the rehabilitation and renovation of hotels will grow steadily, particularly in the North and Northeast.
- The majority of new hotels will be in the economy and budget market segments.
- Super resorts, at superior locations, will be able to attract investors.
- Land prices for the best sites will remain high.

Financing

- Difficulty in raising debt or equity capital will continue until occupancy stabilizes above 65 percent.
- Participation loans and joint ventures with lenders will become more numerous.
- Financing sources will be fewer, more traditional and more conservative in their approach to hotel transactions. There will be adequate capital for those few projects that can meet rigorous underwriting standards.

Labor Costs

- Wages and benefits costs will move upward as hotels find they need more and better-quality help to provide the higher standard of guest service that will be demanded.
- Demographic trends suggest there may be a shortage of labor during the latter part of the 1990s.

Average Daily Rates

- ADR increases will be quite low in many markets. They may fail to match even a low level of inflation in some markets.
- Resorts are favored by the long-term trend toward shorter, high-experience vacationing. ADRs will outperform the hotel market generally and could double in the next seven years.

Occupancy

- Overbuilt condition nationally suggests that occupancy average in many markets may not rise above the low 60 percent level in the next three to five years.

Market Segments

- The all-suite market will grow in the nineties. It could reach a 10 percent market share by the year 2000.
- The extended-stay format will become slightly more popular.
- The budget and economy market segments could become quickly overbuilt when easier financing is available.
- The biggest guest age group will be those 25 to 44 years old.

Demand

- Travel and tourism will continue to grow worldwide until they are near the top in most lists of the world's largest businesses by the year 2000.
- The United States' share of world tourism, however, is likely to continue to decline.

- Convention hotels will suffer from the continued decline in the group meeting business.
- The role of market research will become more important as demand fragments and competition becomes more intense.
- Heavy advertising and other big marketing programs will be common throughout the 1990s.
- The trend toward consolidation and growth through acquisition will continue as hotel chains try to develop into the size and geographic distribution needed to support big marketing programs.

Foreign Investment

- The frantic pace of foreign acquisition that developed in the eighties will not be seen in the nineties, but foreign interest in quality U.S. hotel properties will not disappear.

Conclusion

The industry is overbuilt, oversegmented and oversupplied with persistently increasing costs. It is undersupplied with guests and competent employees and in love with big marketing efforts designed to solve its occupancy problems.

Words such as *speculative* and *risky* are appropriate when discussing hotels. While it is possible to make immense profits, it is far more likely that the average investor will suffer losses. Since 1985, countless "new" hotels have foundered; the Resolution Trust Corporation undoubtedly has the best list of such failures. You don't need its entire list, however, to be sobered by the fact that many properties on it have fallen 50 percent or more in market value in only seven years. Extreme caution is the best course to follow if you are considering any kind of hotel investment.

The first half of this decade may not be rich with easy development opportunities, but careful investors (those who are the second or third buyers of a facility) will profit from buying, selling and repositioning existing properties. Development will be infrequent, but even now, in the early nineties, developers who can find and control a superior site will find their efforts generously rewarded. However, it will be a selective and chancy development market for the rest of this decade, and perhaps for as far as any of us can see into the future.

CHAPTER
7

The Golf Course Investment

In these days of oversupply in most types of investment real estate, golf courses are one of the bright exceptions.

There is little doubt that golf is in the midst of another surge in popularity—the third it has experienced in this century. Golf plus real estate began to be a formula for profit in the 1960s. In 1989, over one-half of all new courses built in the United States were part of a real estate development. A short history of golf is shown in Figure 7.1.

This chapter has four major sections. Section one covers the supply and demand issues; section two covers feasibility and financing; section three is design, construction and due diligence; and section four highlights the major trends in golf courses as an investment.

Types of Courses

There is no standardized, universally accepted scheme for classifying golf courses and facilities from an investor's perspective. We divide them into public or private courses based solely on whether a person can play the course without being a member or a guest. Public courses are further divided based on public or private ownership. To avoid total confusion, all government-owned courses are referred to as municipal courses, while the privately owned public courses are called daily-fee courses or facilities.

To complicate the classification system a little more, all courses or facilities regardless of ownership can be differentiated by size, such as 9-hole, 18-hole or more than 18 holes. In this chapter, anything less than 18 holes is called a course; 18 holes or more is called a facility. Among players and course operators, a further breakdown into regulation and nonregulation length is used, as are the ideas of par 3 and executive course. Yardage and acreage ranges for each type of course are shown in the Feasibility and Financing section.

Supply and Demand

In this section you will find information on industry size; past, present and projected supply; course openings from 1989 to 1992; the top courses in the United States; the best areas in which to buy or build; and supply constraints. On the demand side, you will find facts on the demographics of golf, golf participation levels from 1974 to 2000 and why demand is growing.

The imperatives of supply and demand appear to be so favorable that many investors may be tempted to ignore a thorough examination of the factors behind these vital issues and move quickly to feasibility and financing questions. That would be an error, but not an uncommon one, given the oversupply we have in practically every type of real estate. In spite of what appears to be a generally favorable supply/demand picture, investors need to be cautious; a prolonged recession can cool off the hottest demand profile. Production is sometimes overstimulated because of the tendency of real estate developers to create golf courses and use them as housing sales amenities even when effective demand is weak.

Industry Size

Golf is a multibillion-dollar business that is relentlessly promoted by organizations such as the National Golf Foundation (NGF), the U.S. Golf Association, the National Sporting Goods Association, the Association of

Table 7.1   Distribution of Golf Revenues: 1989 (in billions)

Item	Amount
Fees and other course expenditures	$ 2.1
Travel and accommodations	$ 7.0
Tournaments: admissions and sponsorships	$ 0.3
Home purchases in golf course developments	$ 3.8
Miscellaneous	$ 0.9
TOTAL	$20.0

Source: *Business Week,* March 27, 1989: 76–79.

Golf Course Architects and many others. This incessant and vigorous promotion has added to investment values by fanning demand to a white heat.

Approximately 24.8 million people play golf, according to the National Golf Foundation, and they spend more than $20 billion per year doing it. These numbers are expected to increase to 30.1 million golfers spending $30 billion by the year 2000. Not all the money spent on golf, however, is spent at the golf course. Table 7.1 shows how the $20 billion dollars spent in 1989 was divided.

Supply: Past, Present and Projected

No other country has a golf market equal to that of the United States, although Japan has an intensity of demand, as a percent of population, that is even stronger.

To serve its current demand, the United States has approximately 14,136 golf courses, and the supply is increasing an average of 200 new courses or course additions per year. Significant additions to supply are not unusual. In this century, which about covers the history of golf in the United States, the game has enjoyed three periods of high demand that have led to large increases in the supply of courses. In the period 1923 to 1929, the industry built 600 new courses per year; from 1960 to 1970, the pace of construction was 350 courses annually. Over the past 100 years

Figure 7.1   A Short History of Golf

1552	St. Andrews golf course opens in Scotland.
1890	Approximately 1,200 golf courses in the United States; there are over 13,000 today. Average increase of 118 courses per year from 1890 to 1990.
Late 19th century	First modern practice range evolves from old "shag" fields.
1923 to 1929	The Golden Age of U.S. golf: about 600 new courses built annually.
1950	A watershed year. Prior to this date most players played on private courses. Today most golfers play on public courses.
1956	A landmark year in the popularization of golf: CBS televises the Master's Tournament for the first time.
1960 to 1970	Supply of golf courses grew at about 5 percent per year, demand at approximately 10 percent. First post–WW II indications that real estate developers were starting to capitalize on the demand for golf course homes.
1989	Almost one-half of all new courses were built to serve a real estate development.
1991	Golf enjoys its third major popularity boom in this century.
1992	Early signs that pace of course development has slowed.

(1890 to 1990), supply has increased at an average of 118 courses per year. Figure 7.1 sets out a short history of golf.

In the most recent 30 years, the number of courses has more than doubled, while the number of golfers has gone up by about five times. Table 7.2 shows how the growth of supply and demand compare for the period 1960 to 1990. The National Golf Foundation (NGF) feels that it is reasonable to expect the number of golf courses to increase by 200 per year until the year 2000 while the number of players increases to about 30 million. All demand predictions should be viewed in conjunction with expected changes in economic conditions.

In 1991 course openings averaged nearly one a day. There were 351 new courses or course additions in 1991—the highest number since 1972.

Table 7.2   Golf Courses and Golfers: 1960–1990

	1960	1970	1980	1990
Number of courses (in thousands)	6,400	10,200	12,000	14,000
Number of golfers (in millions)	5.0	11.2	15.1	24.7
Average annual growth rate for golf courses	NA	6.3%	2.7%	1.7%
Average annual growth rate for golfers	NA	4.5%	1.6%	6.7%

Source: National Golf Foundation (Jupiter, Fla.: June 1990).
Note: The National Golf Foundation changed the basis for estimating the number of golfers (by including all golfers 12 years old and older) beginning in 1986. This table shows the number of golfers before that change.

Of these, 116 were built in support of a real estate development. Twenty were resort courses and 18 were some combination of real estate development and resort course. Of the 351 courses, 236 were completely new and 115 were additions to existing courses. In spite of this active 1991 pace, evidence points to a slowdown in new course openings because of a lack of financing.

There is ample opportunity to invest in golf courses based upon the distribution of courses by type and the playing habits of golfers, more than 70 percent of whom play on public courses. Nationally, 46 percent of golf facilities are daily-fee, 16 percent are municipal and 38 percent are private clubs.

The Top Courses in the United States

William Davis, in cooperation with *Golf Digest/Tennis Inc.,* has written a book called *100 Greatest Golf Courses—And Then Some.* You may wish to consult it to experience the pure joy of seeing some of the country's best courses, or if you do not have a clear idea of what a great golf course looks like.

It may seem, while looking at a list of the top 10 or 20 courses, that nothing of much account has been built since the 1920s. That is not true.

Beautiful, wonderfully challenging yet playable courses are being designed and built today just as they were throughout the 1980s and earlier. Any tour of modern courses will quickly establish that many of these new courses will one day work their way onto someone's top 100 list.

Promising Areas

Ten states accounted for 52 percent of the 236 new course openings in 1991. The top 12 states for 1991 and 1992 are shown in Table 7.3.

The most promising areas for new courses are those that will support move-up housing. In 1991, California, with about 863 golf courses, had 100 in the planning stage; Florida had 111; and Virginia had 55. Twelve other states (New York, Pennsylvania, Illinois, Indiana, Ohio, Wisconsin, Georgia, Maryland, North Carolina, Texas, Oregon and Washington) all had more than 30 courses in planning, reported the NGF in its publication *Golf Facilities in the U.S., 1992 Edition.*

Supply Constraints

Limits on the production of an adequate new supply of courses could come from at least two directions—environmental considerations and housing demand. Environmental problems are the least troublesome right now. Zoning and environmental costs will add about $100,000 to current 18-hole construction costs.

Golf courses, touted by Robert Trent Jones as the "lungs" of America's communities, are not immune to severe criticism from environmentalists and others for their "elitist" single-purpose use of scarce land and their profligate use of even scarcer water. Concern has also been expressed that using public land for a golf course (even one that is built at private cost) is pandering to the recreational needs of a very small segment (9 percent to 10 percent) of the total community, while what is really needed is multipurpose use of the scarce land.

A shortage of water may turn out to be the most serious threat to the production of new courses and the maintenance of existing courses. An average course will use 1.5 inches of water per acre per week in areas with "normal" rainfall of at least 30 inches. That is over 180 million gallons of water if an 18-hole regulation course is irrigated for 30 weeks a year. In drier climes with longer playing seasons, a course can use more

Table 7.3   Golf Courses Built and Under Construction: 1990 and 1991
(selected states)

State	Under Construction 1990	Opened 1991
Florida	46	35
Michigan	23	20
South Carolina	25	20
North Carolina	20	14
Illinois	21	17
Texas	16	9
Indiana	11	11
Georgia	18	17
Arizona	NA	2
Virginia	12	9
Ohio	17	12
California	31	21
TOTAL	241	187

Source: *Golf Market Today,* National Golf Foundation (March/April 1992).

than 200 million gallons of water per year. The long-term, persistent shortage of water will eventually mean fewer courses and substantial design changes for both old and new courses. In some areas, it could mean a return to the way the game was played 400 years ago, on courses with very few fully watered fairways. It seems clear that water conservation will act to raise operating costs slightly and to modify new additions to supply.

Production of golf courses by public entities could decline significantly. A shortage of funds at most levels of government suggests that municipal courses may not play as large a role in total supply as they traditionally have, even though there may be a temporary increase in the number of new municipal courses. Private investor opportunities will increase as a result.

The aforementioned close relationship between new housing and golf course production presents some investment problems. Many real estate developers strongly believe that golf sells houses; therefore, courses are sometimes built to spur demand for housing and not because of a demand for golf. As a result, oversupply is a continuous threat. Fortunately, during recessionary and tight-money times, additions to new supply are likely to decline—just as supply is apt to grow quickly during housing (and resort) "boom" times. By late 1992, construction of new courses had fallen off dramatically in response to the recession that began in 1990.

Developers, financiers and investors often argue that a golf course is of substantial benefit to a community because of the open space it provides. The kind of "open" space provided, however, is often of the "look but don't touch" variety. In addition, many courses are effectively walled off from any public access, meaning the open space is not only unreachable, it is unseen by the majority of the community. Further, in some areas the open space is created at a very high cost in terms of loss of natural vegetation; this has been true virtually throughout the history of U.S. golf. In 1923, when the magnificent Winged Foot West course was built in New York State, developers cut down over 6,500 trees. Such "clear-cutting" tactics may not be possible in the future. The environmental movement's concern with preserving open space in a natural condition will influence both the design of golf courses and the number of new ones that get built.

A few critics have also argued that the open space gained from a golf course comes at a price of very high densities granted on adjacent land. Considering the numerous environmental concerns, investors in new courses should not expect an easy journey to zoning approval. Investors in older courses can expect to see many changes in the way courses are operated, which will increase operating expenses.

Almost half of all new courses opened in 1991 were associated with a real estate development. Investment demand has been strong, especially for quality courses, but the intensity of investment demand may lessen as real estate in general is affected by weakening demand. It would not be surprising to see prices for existing courses (especially the marginal ones) fall 30–40 percent; when this happens, a rare buying opportunity will exist. Table 7.4 shows the distribution of courses by type in 1991.

Based on current data, the prospects for golf course construction and successful operation of existing courses is quite good over the next ten years.

The constraints on new supply, if demand continues to be strong, should have a favorable effect on investment values in the long run.

Table 7.4   U.S. Golf Courses by Type

Type of Course	Percent
Daily Fee	46%
Municipal	16%
Private Clubs	38%

Source: National Golf Foundation (Jupiter, Fla.: 1991).

The Demographics of Golf

Golf is a growth activity, partly because population characteristics favor the growth of the game. Our population is aging and turning toward less demanding lifetime recreational activities. As golf has become less elitist, it has embraced a bigger share of the population; many of these new adherents of the game are blue-collar workers and lower-middle-management employees. A significant number of them, according to some demographers, have more time to play because of the rising popularity of flex time and the trend toward shorter but more frequent vacations. An increase in the number of workers taking early retirement is also adding to golf demand.

Some observers point to the fact that U.S. incomes have remained relatively high (more people have jobs and they have more money to spend) as one more reason golf demand is rising. Recessions tend to obscure this trend.

Not everyone agrees with that observation, however. On April 21, 1990, David M. Gordon, writing in the *Los Angeles Times,* addressed the issue. Dr. Gordon is a professor of economics at the New School for Social Research in New York. Here, in part, is what he had to say as he compared the then-current economic boom to the boom that occurred from 1961 to 1969:

Real median family income grew by 29.4 percent from 1961 to 1969 but only 9.8 percent from 1982 to 1988, which is the last year for which data is available. Real spendable hourly earnings for production and nonsupervisory employees, which is a good measure of the hourly take-home pay for the vast majority of wage and salary employees, rose

Table 7.5   Golfers by Age Group: 1992

Age Group	Percent	Number (in millions)
12 to 17	7.4	1,835
18 to 29	26.7	6,621
30 to 39	26.1	6,472
40 to 49	17.5	4,339
50 to 59	9.1	2,256
60 to 64	4.2	1,041
65 and over	9.0	2,232

Source: National Golf Foundation, *Golf Participation in the U.S./1992 Edition* (Jupiter, Fla.).

employees, rose by 9.6 percent from 1961 to 1969 but did not increase at all, remaining exactly the same, between 1982 and 1988.

Dr. Gordon's views are reinforced somewhat by Martin Feldstein, the former chairman of the President's Council of Economic Advisors, who stated in *The Wall Street Journal,* on May 18, 1990, "Since 1975, real wages per worker have fallen more than 10 percent...." At the very least, these comments suggest quite a careful look at income assumptions if you believe that income levels affect the demand for golf.

Finally, the tendency of our population toward residential mobility seems to be one of the reasons real estate development golf courses are able to do well.

Golf is not as elitist as it once was, but according to NGF statistics it is still a man's game; about 75 percent of the players are men and 46.5 percent are in clerical, sales or blue collar occupations. More than half the people playing are in the 18–39 age group, while about 22 per cent are over 50. Table 7.5 shows the complete breakdown.

Golf Participation Levels

Interest in golf has been increasing steadily since the 1950s, when the combination of television and Arnold Palmer gave it its first big push. The participation figures since 1984 are interesting and are even more so when you compare the rates of participation in three popular activities. Golf

Table 7.6   Golf, Tennis, Running/Jogging Participation Rates (in millions)

Activity	Year					
	1984	1985	1986	1987	1988	1989
Golf	16.5	18.0	20.0	22.0	23.4	24.7
Tennis	19.5	19.0	17.0	17.0	17.3	18.8
Running/ Jogging	29.0	27.0	23.0	24.8	22.9	24.8

Source: National Golf Foundation (Jupiter, Fla.: June 1990).
National Sporting Goods Association (Mt. Prospect, Ill.: June 1990).

participation is up about 50 percent since 1984, while tennis and running/jogging have fallen off in popularity. The industry expects the number of golfers to increase to 30 million by the year 2000. Table 7.6 sets forth the changes.

Feasibility and Financing

The task of a feasibility study is to pinpoint the market area, evaluate the level and type of demand, suggest revenue potential, and estimate the operating costs and net income to be expected. Even when demand is so strong that success is apparent to everyone but a hermit, a feasibility study is still essential.

It is difficult to evaluate the validity of a feasibility study without two essential ingredients:

1. A knowledge of the broad picture of supply and demand
2. An awareness of what a feasibility study is supposed to cover

These studies are as varied in content as the abilities of the people who research and write them. There is, however, a general outline that should be useful for investors and others. This is what a feasibility study should contain:

1. Part One: General Information
2. Part Two: Income and Expense Forecasts
3. Part Three: Financing Alternatives

Part One: General Information

Here in summary form is what should be covered in part one of a feasibility study.

1. Demand
   - Market area, primary and secondary; will include a 5- to 20-mile radius
   - Market Characteristics
     - Population—size and characteristics: current and trends
     - The economy, employment total, diversity of activity, per capita income, average wage
     - current data and trends; other economic data may be included, depending upon the competitive situation
     - Competition—existing, under construction, planned
   - Type of course the market will support—public, private, municipal

A lot of detail on population and economic activity is normal, as is an exhaustive study of every aspect of competing courses' features and revenue base. Considerable information should be provided on the number of rounds played, greens fees, golf cart rental fees and policy, supporting services offered and other recreational features of the course or facility.

2. Land
   - Availability and cost; list of comparable sales
   - Location analysis of available sites; access to the market
   - Site preparation costs: clearing, drainage, grading; will include aerial photos and contour maps of site
   - Utilities: availability and cost
   - Zoning considerations (particularly the attitude of local authorities toward golf course development)
   - Special problems: hazardous waste, historic sites, archeological sites; aerial photos common

Virtually any one item on this checklist can destroy the feasibility of a location, so you will usually find a lot of detailed information in this section. Knowing how to evaluate the data is one key to long-term success.

Table 7.7   Annual Dues Charged for 18-Hole Courses

$ Amount	Percent
Up to $200	9.9
$201 to $500	10.5
$501 to $1,000	26.2
$1,001 to $2,000	36.2
Above $2,000	17.2

Source: National Golf Foundation (Jupiter, Fla.: 1986).

It is common to have, either as a part of the study or in a separate report, the preliminary opinions, recommendations and cost estimates of a golf course architect. The range of cost for this item is $10,000 to $50,000 plus expenses.

Part Two: Income and Expense

Part two deals with the operating characteristics of the proposed course. The following items should be covered:

1. General Information
   - Climate and length of season
   - Competing recreational uses
2. Income
   - Typical sources are initiation fees, dues, greens fees, golf cart rentals, practice range, instruction, merchandise sales, food service and miscellaneous.

The dues-paying membership base ranges from 300 to 500 members at most clubs. The following data are offered as a guide in evaluating the adequacy of the major income items.

Initiation fees and dues.   Initiation fees range from about $4,000 to $10,000 and are often much higher. At equity clubs (members own the land and buildings) the fee can range upward from $50,000.

The annual charge for dues ranges from just under $200 to more than $2,000. Table 7.7 shows dues for 18-hole courses. These data (1986 is the last year it was published) are presented only as a general guideline;

Table 7.8 Median Operating Costs: 1988 18-Hole Course

Type of Club	Private	Municipal	Daily Fee
Annual Cost	$206,914	$180,952	$120,714
Cost per Hole	$ 11,495	$ 10,052	$ 6,706

Source: National Golf Foundation (1989).

contact your consultant or the NGF for current data applicable to your area. Average dues for all private facilities in 1991 were $1,445.

Greens fees (18 holes). The current range is $12 to $22 per person. The average revenue per round at daily-fee clubs ranges from $6 to $9 per round when season ticket sales are considered. Investors should not be surprised to find that some local courses are still charging $4 to $8 per round. On the upside, however, some trophy courses can charge $200 or more per round. In June of 1990 (the off-season), it cost $125 (cart included) to play the Stadium course at PGA West near Palm Springs, California. Charges of $60 to $75 are common at high-quality newer courses in Southern California and elsewhere. Investors might want to keep in mind that the amount of the fees is not the average golfer's biggest concern; the overall maintenance of the course is much more important than the cost to play it. It would also be wise to recognize that greens fees decline during severe recessions.

Golf cart fees. The range is $5 to $9 per person, with the $9 charge becoming the norm. The use of golf carts is mandatory on many courses, both to speed up play and to increase revenues.

Operating Expenses

Common costs are payroll (including taxes and benefits), all other taxes, water, other utility costs, fertilizer and chemical costs, equipment maintenance, course supplies, sand, seed, etc. Table 7.8 shows the level of these costs in 1988, which is the most current data available from this source.

The American Society of Golf Course Architects offers guidelines for the annual cost of operating an 18-hole real estate development golf course (see Table 7.9). Most costs will vary with the length of the playing season, water costs, and the amount of hand maintenance necessitated by the course's design.

Table 7.9   Development Costs: 1990 (Real Estate Development Courses, 18 holes)

Item	Typical Cost
Payroll	$190,000
Labor, taxes, benefits	$ 40,000
Water costs	$ 30,000
Fertilizer	$ 20,000
Chemicals	$ 25,000
Equipment, maintenance, course supplies	$ 70,000
Total	$375,000

Source: American Society of Golf Course Architects (Chicago: April 1990).

Net Operating Income (NOI)

When the course has been operated long enough to stabilize net income, it is common to generate NOI of between 15 percent and 20 percent on invested capital; if you are particularly fortunate, you may earn up to 25 percent.

Courses are usually valued by capitalizing current NOI at some appropriate interest rate. Land value is of incidental importance unless it exceeds the capitalized value of the course, in which case the course has outlived its economic usefulness as a golf course.

Financing: Sources and Amount

Savings and loans are no longer active in financing golf courses, although some of the stronger ones might be interested in a real estate development course because of the home loans. There is no longer government-assisted financing, such as the Farmers Home Administration, which fueled the nine-hole course construction boom of the 1960s.

Most of the courses being built today are part of a real estate development and are being financed as a part of the land development loan package. There are few private, nonmember courses being financed.

Private membership courses can still be built and financed in the old-fashioned way—for cash—from members' initiation fees, private bonds or limited short-term financing. Expansion of or improvements to existing courses are financed from retained cash, membership dues and special assessments.

Municipal courses, often financed by some type of bond, are of interest to private investors only if they have some private-sector involvement, such as a development contract, a long-term operating arrangement or a sale to the government entity.

Daily-fee courses may be financed as follows:

- With 100 percent equity by an individual or small private group. In some cases, a course may find funds as part of a limited partnership financing offering.
- With a loan from a bank or insurance company.
- From the seller of the land or of the course.

Some courses follow a life cycle that is partly influenced by financing considerations. The cycle looks like this:

- Starts out as a regulation-length, nine-hole, daily-fee course.
- Expands to an 18-hole course.
- Becomes a private, nonequity membership course.
- Becomes a private, equity membership course.

The amount of debt is widely variable depending upon the type of course and its setting. It is not unusual for a real estate development course to attract 100 percent financing for the cost of course development plus enough to carry the operating deficit for two years. The operating deficit, however, may persist for three to five years. No-equity loans are not the rule today; investors should plan on down payments of at least 20–30 percent, whether they have seller-carried or institutional financing.

Permanent loans, irrespective of their source, are divided between conventional, fully amortized loans and participating loans. All types of financing, except seller-carried, become more difficult to arrange during poor economic times.

Design, Construction and Due Diligence

Whether you build your own or buy an existing course, a basic understanding of course design is useful.

If you are a golfer, you no doubt already have some notion of what constitutes a great golf course, and these ideas will influence your investment decision. Nongolfers may not have any firm ideas about what makes a course a pleasure to play and might find it useful to look at some that the experts decree are among the great ones. Your course architect or consultant can give you a list of local and regional courses to visit.

If you feel like traveling a little farther, look at the courses in Hawaii. Some of the nation's best courses are in the islands. One of the newest is the Bass Brothers' course (designed by Robert Trent Jones) at Waikoloa, which is reported to have cost $16 million to build. If time is short and you want to see a wide array of course design without too much travel, visit the Palm Springs/Palm Desert area of Southern California, where you can see, in one or two days, everything from a Scottish-type course to the most lavish parkland course.

The mention of Scottish and parkland courses reminds us, again, that there is no general agreement on how to describe courses from the point of view of their basic landscaping plan. A Scottish course is quite often situated close to the ocean or other major body of water and is devoid of such common landscaping elements as big trees, although it will have strategically placed clumps of bushes and seasonal color. Such courses do not irrigate as much as most U.S. golfers are used to. In this respect, at least, they are less likely to draw fire from environmentalists.

A parkland course is the U.S.A's traditional course: it looks the way a course should look when you conjure one up in your imagination. But that "tradition" is decidedly North American, because the oldest golf courses, in the birthplace of golf, are generally not landscaped as courses here are. Because "traditional" could be misleading (about as misleading as "trophy," "signature" and "championship"), some golf analysts encourage the use of "parkland" in its place.

If the water and utility cost and land availability trends continue on their present course, it is likely that future courses will look more Scottish than parklike.

Whatever the underlying landscaping style, strong course design is as important as the essential feasibility study. It is through design that the demand, uncovered by the feasibility study, is satisfied.

Construction

An understanding of how a course is put together and of what the various elements cost is helpful in making a sound judgment on whether to build or buy. One way to look at a golf course is to see it as having three major elements:

1. The land and the course built on it
2. The maintenance facilities
3. The social facilities

While sometimes available at no cost, land is usually one of the major development costs for courses near a big city. Land costs range from about $3,000 per acre to $100,000 dollars or more. A $40,000-per-acre land cost would not be unusual in a well-located suburban location.

More important than its initial cost, perhaps, is the character of the land. Golf courses can be built on any type of land—even land that is as flat as a table and is located in a desertlike climate; the new Tustin Ranch course, on the Irvine Ranch in Southern California, is proof of that. However, it is often much less costly to build on a site that has been more generously provided for by nature. Here are some site characteristics to consider:

- The site must be of adequate size. Table 7.10 provides information on the acreage needed for various types of courses.
- A north-south orientation is most desirable to avoid early morning and late afternoon sun problems.
- Soil should be sandy loam. Heavy clay is expensive to fertilize and drain.
- The shape of the site should be regular.
- The most desirable sites are next to a major natural water element, such as the ocean, a large lake or a river.
- Sites that are on wetlands or next to airports or major highways are not as desirable as sites without these location burdens.
- The site should not be too heavily wooded. Woodlands are expensive to clear, and the process may raise strong local opposition.

Table 7.10 Approximate Acreage Required for Various Golf Courses

Item	Length	Par	Acreage
18-hole regulation	5,200 to 7,300 yards	66+	100 to 150
9-hole regulation	2,600 to 3,600 yards	33+	45 to 75
18-hole executive	4,000 to 5,200 yards	58 to 66	80 to 125
18-hole par 3	Less than 4,000 yards	54	40 to 90

Source: National Golf Foundation (Jupiter, Fla.: July 1990).

- Avoid historic or archeological sites. A recent (1991) planned expansion of a course in Canada resulted in protests that led to the death of one person during a gun battle with Indians claiming historic rights to the site.
- The site should be clear of any toxic material and should not be in the path of hazardous waste runoff.

The way a course is designed and built has a huge influence on its future operating costs. It is quite possible to design and build courses that are aesthetically pleasing, fun to play, challenging and still reasonable to maintain. When you look at a course, or the plans for one, here are some of the things you need to know.

The tees.   Almost all courses have multiple-position tees (four positions, sometimes more) today to accommodate a wide range of playing skills. Tees must be large enough to accommodate the volume of play handled by the course. Most tee areas for quality courses are at least 7,500 square feet and some are a bit larger. The range for all courses is 5,000 to 7,500 square feet.

The fairways.   These need to be pleasing to the eye, playable and safe. There should be enough trees (or fairway width) to create safe playing conditions without unduly interfering with an ordinary golfer's play. Trees, shrubbery, bunkers, mounds and water elements should be placed to challenge good golfers to make strategic shots. Look for standing water on the course, which may indicate poor drainage or irrigation practices.

Cart paths.   Most modern courses are built with continuous pathways for golf carts. Older courses may not have golf cart paths, or may only have paths that access the tees and greens. Paths tend to speed up play and lower the maintenance costs for the golf carts. The most desirable paths are concrete and at least ten feet wide.

The greens.   You will seldom encounter greens that are too large. The average green is 6,500 square feet. Many are improperly built, which leads to constant high maintenance costs and eventually costly rebuilding. Look for poor drainage, inappropriate size and poor trapping (there are often too many traps and many that are poorly designed with steep sides that are expensive to maintain). It can cost $15,000 to $20,000 to build a green and $35,000 or more to rebuild it. Also, look for poor placement of tees or greens, which may be causing problems for the neighboring users of real estate.

The irrigation system.   This is one of the most important elements of a course. The most water-efficient systems are those with valve-in-head sprinklers that are computer-controlled from weather station information. A "wall-to-wall" system (100 percent coverage) can cost up to $900,000 for a regulation 18-hole course. This includes all pumps and storage ponds. There is a tendency to overlook the importance of the irrigation system, because water has always been so cheap and plentiful.

To do a proper job of analyzing the investment merit of any course, you will need an "as built" plan of the course that shows the full site—every tee, green, fairway, service road, cart path, bridge, shelter and all structures. Maps should be in a 1″ = 100′ scale. Separate plans will show all landscaping and the irrigation system.

The Maintenance Facilities

The maintenance building is, according to many who write about golf course operation, the most important building on the course. This building—not the clubhouse—is where your profit or loss is made.

Some of the most interesting and enjoyable courses have been designed with as much of an eye on maintenance costs as on playing challenge, beauty and all the other attributes of a popular course.

The cost range for an adequate maintenance building is $125,000 to $300,000. Total cost will depend upon the size of the building and the type of construction. The size range for the main building is 2,500 to 15,000 square feet. Common building dimensions are 40′ × 70′ and 90′ × 150′. It is not unusual to have a separate storage area for fertilizers and chemicals.

The Social Facilities

The clubhouse is often the focal point of the course. This structure frequently has considerable aesthetic appeal and can be the source of serious financial trouble for courses both public and private.

Most clubhouses contain a pro shop, locker rooms, meeting areas or rooms, food service areas (kitchens, dining rooms, snack bars, cocktail lounges) and golf cart storage (and possibly service area).

You will need room to store and service from 27 to 70 golf carts, depending upon the size of the course. Each golf cart will need 75 to 80 square feet of storage area.

If there are other recreational facilities, such as tennis courts, swimming pool, gymnasium, etc., they should be considered in conjunction with your review of the clubhouse. You will often find putting greens and a practice range close to the clubhouse.

Virtually any amount of money can be spent to create a clubhouse, but the cost range is from $45 per square foot to about $100. Clubhouses range in size from a modest 2,000 or 3,000 square feet to 50,000 square feet and more.

The National Golf Foundation has publications that deal with area requirements for the different parts of this building. The question to ask, from an investment perspective: Is it appropriately sized, and does it—or can it—operate at a profit?

The Cost To Build

The American Society of Golf Course Architects suggests that most 18-hole courses can be built for somewhere between $1.5 million and $5 million (not including grow-in and preopening maintenance). This estimate includes basic golf course construction: clearing; grading; construction of tees, greens and bunkers; seeding; irrigation system; shelters; bridges; cart paths; and service roads. In addition, plan to spend $300,000 to $400,000 for maintenance equipment and another $125,000 to $300,000 for the maintenance building.

The National Golf Foundation provided these figures in one of its 1988 publications:

Basic construction costs	$600,000	to	$1,000,000
Shelters, bridges, cart paths	48,000	to	240,000
Irrigation system (includes pump station)	240,000	to	960,000
Service road	24,000	to	42,000
Maintenance building	96,000	to	180,000
Maintenance Equipment	180,000	to	300,000
Totals	$1,188,000	to	$2,722,000

Due Diligence

We have stressed the importance of using a golf course architect when designing and building a course, even though some courses are built without the services of a member of the American Society of Golf Course Architects. If you are considering a major investment in an existing course, you might want to consult with an architect for an advisory opinion on what, if anything, needs to be done to maximize the course's potential. The cost of an architect's services to design and supervise the building of a new course can range from $100,000 to $1 million, depending upon whom you get. Their fees for a preliminary opinion range from $10,000 to $50,000 plus expenses.

Trends and Conclusions

Some people who know the game well think that golf will change more in the United States in the next ten years than it has in the last 100 years. The catalyst for change? The environmental movement. New courses, they forecast, will be designed to conserve water, fuel and power. Further, the courses will be miserly with the use of land.

Existing courses will increase in value, but not without paying the price, in many cases, of modernizing their irrigation systems and reducing the amount of irrigated area. None of this will happen until economic incentives and environmental pressures force the changes, but it will happen. Here are 16 other trends to watch for:

Supply and Demand

- In spite of high demand, there is no certainty that more courses will be built in the nineties than in the eighties.
- The number of new courses will fluctuate with the strength of housing demand.
- More government-owned courses will be turned over to private ownership as government revenue sources continue to be tight.
- Golf will increase in popularity as other sports, such as running, jogging, aerobics and tennis, decline somewhat in popularity.
- Golf will be heavily promoted as an almost ideal form of lifetime recreation.
- Pace of supply increase will slow. This will help strengthen investment values.
- Emphasis over the next five years will be on acquisition and management.
- Equity requirements will range from 30–50 percent for a financed course.

Demographics

- More women will take up golf.
- Aging of the population favors golf; it is the only major sport in which the participants spend more money as they age.

Operations

- The industry will develop a standardized chart of accounts to bring some uniformity to the way facilities and courses report operating results. This will help increase investor confidence in golf courses.
- Costs will continue to rise, but net operating income will increase steadily over the next ten years.
- Professional management firms and franchisors will become increasingly important.
- Average greens fees will rise above $20 within three years.

Course Design

- Fewer full-size courses will be built.
- More of the older-style, limited-landscaping courses will be built as a host of environmental concerns affect the industry.
- Publicly financed courses (government-owned) may have to be a part of a larger recreational complex or environmental preserve to gain public support.

CHAPTER
8
Self-Storage Facilities

A self-storage facility is a real estate development consisting of one or more buildings that are divided into small, private, lockable spaces ranging in size from 25 to 400 square feet. The spaces are rented for the temporary storage of household or business goods.

This product type has been overbuilt for at least the past seven years. Vacancies have been high and cash flows have been hard to maintain in many projects. Some poorly planned and poorly managed projects have gone through foreclosure; doubtless others will go this route. Given this bleak recent history, it would be easy to conclude that self-storage projects hold little promise for individual or institutional investors. The research, however, leads to a different conclusion.

The industry went through ten years of supercharged growth from 1977 to 1987, which added millions of square feet to the supply. Now, as the industry settles into its mature phase, the stage is set for good profits from buying, selling and properly operating well-designed self-storage facilities. The near future will be characterized by the selling and exchanging of existing developments rather than by the building of many new ones.

The private storage industry has prospered in the past due to a remarkable ability to raise capital by attracting thousands of small, relatively inexperienced investors through private and public syndications. That source of capital is not easily available today.

If you are asked to consider investing in a new development or a "time-tested" existing project, this chapter will be most useful. The chapter covers industry size, supply and demand factors, feasibility studies, general comments on financing, some financial analysis, investment characteristics and design considerations. It ends, as usual, with a segment on trends and conclusions.

Industry Size

Is this a legitimate, well-established real estate investment market segment or is it just some "boutique," get-rich-quick, cash-cow scheme? It is hard to know at first glance. No authoritative data exist on the size of the self-storage industry. Our research suggests that there are between 18,000 and 20,000 projects in the United States with an average size of 30,000 to 40,000 square feet. The dollar investment is sizable, with construction costs, including land, ranging from $20 to $25 per square foot for older developments built on low-cost land to $35 to $45 for newer projects in areas where land costs are relatively high. Rents per square foot per month range from $.50 to $1.35, depending on unit size and the competitive environment.

Sales have not been numerous, making it difficult to establish a capitalization rate upon which to calculate value based on net income. Cap rates of 11–13 percent are frequently mentioned as achievable in a resale of a well-run property showing stable occupancy of 80 percent or better. Cap rates of 9 percent or less are also encountered as asking prices, but it is questionable if many sales are made at such a low rate.

Table 8.1 uses all of this data, and more, to create a snapshot of industry size. We have extended average project size to 50,000 square feet simply to encompass what must surely be the upper end of industry size, at least for older projects. Newer facilities, some of which are multistory, often have 60,000 square feet or more, but these are fairly new developments that do not make up the bulk of the industry.

If industry propensity-to-rent figures mean anything, there is a range of demand from 1.7 square feet to 4.0 square feet per capita. With U.S.

Table 8.1 The Self-Storage Industry Size Estimate

TABLE 1—ESTIMATE OF INDUSTRY SIZE

A Average Project Size in Square Feet	B Number of Projects in the U.S.		C (AxB) Total Square Feet (In Millions)		D (DxC) Total Value Based on Construction Cost Including Land (In Billions) — Cost Per Square Foot				E (ExC) Gross Scheduled Revenue at 80% Occupancy (Annually In Billions)		F (FxC) Cap Rate Capitalized Value Using 45% Net Income		
	Low	High	Low	High	$20.00	$25.00	$35.00	$45.00	Low[1]	High[2]	Cap Rate	Low Net $3.24[3]	High Net $4.32[4]
30,000	18,000	20,000	540	600	10.8 to 12.0	13.5 to 15.0	18.9 to 21.0	24.3 to 27.0	3.1	4.6	11%	15.9	23.5
											12%	14.6	21.6
											13%	13.5	19.9
40,000	18,000	20,000	720	800	14.4 to 16.0	18.0 to 20.0	25.2 to 28.0	32.4 to 36.0	4.2	6.1	11%	21.2	31.4
											12%	19.2	28.8
											13%	17.9	26.7
50,000	18,000	20,000	900	1,000	18.0 to 20.0	22.5 to 25.0	31.5 to 35.0	40.5 to 45.0	5.2	6.9	11%	26.5	39.3
											12%	24.3	36.0
											13%	22.4	33.2

1) .60 x .80 x 12 = $5.76   2) .80 x .80 x 12 = $7.68   3) .60 x 12 x .45 = $3.24   4) .80 x 12 x .45 = $4.32

Investor Outlook, November 1988

Source: Grubb & Ellis Research Services. Used by permission.

population at about 250 million, this suggests a potential market size of from 425 million to 1 billion square feet. At our current population, if supply rises above a billion square feet nationally, competitive pressures will lower rents and raise cap rates.

While Table 8.1 encompasses every current view on industry size, the actual current size range of the industry is 540 million to 600 million square feet.

Feasibility Studies

You may invest in the self-storage market at the development phase or at the going-concern stage. At the development level, feasibility studies are almost universally used to examine the strength of market demand. In highly competitive markets, and that is all of them today, such studies are an essential preliminary to the financing process for new projects. Investors who are considering an existing project might find the cost of a feasibility study ($5,000 and up) to be one of the best investments they can make.

These studies are often used as justifying documents; their main focus is to prove to equity and debt investors that capital ought to be committed to a particular project. In the purest sense, however, they are an objective look at the demand and supply factors in a market area. This is what they cover:

Demand Elements

Market size in area and numbers.   An aerial view of the three- to five-mile market area is useful in viewing the density and land use characteristics of the area.

Residential Market Characteristics (current and trend):

- Population size
- Number of households
- Size of single-family homes; number with basements, number without basements
- Number of apartment units
- Size of apartment units
- Occupancy level of all residential units

- Occupancy costs per square foot
- Income levels
- Mobility of population (In many areas 15–17 percent of the population moves each year; this stimulates demand during the 100 days of summer.)

Commercial Market Characteristics (current and trend):

- Amount and type of retail, office and industrial space in square feet
- Space per employee
- Rent level per square foot
- Occupancy level for office, retail and industrial space
- Demand survey questionnaire distributed and results tabulated. Should reveal the type of space needed, rent level, propensity to rent. This is a critical procedure. The value of primary (self-gathered) market data is hard to overestimate, particularly in light of the gap between facts and folklore discussed in the Existing Projects section later in the chapter.

Supply Elements

The competitive survey includes:

- Number of self-storage facilities in the market area by square feet and number of units
- Types of units available by size (unit mix) and by type (climate-controlled, multistory, business centers, etc.)
- Rent per square foot by unit sizes
- Occupancy level and seasonal occupancy pattern
- Absorption time (It can take two to four years to achieve 85–90 percent occupancy; some projects have never exceeded 80 percent.)
- Age and condition of competitive projects
- Quality of on-site and off-site management
- Services offered

Financial Feasibility

- Total scheduled income
- Expenses

- Unit mix rent schedule

The numbers are never the whole story. It is the supply/demand drive behind the numbers that will make or break your investment, assuming that location, design, management and other "givens" are on track.

Other Considerations

Land values:

- Comparable sales data
- Available competitive sites
- Potential competitive sites (conversion possibilities, teardowns, etc.)

Government rules, regulations, taxation:

- Roads and highways. Check anything that might affect the nature or quality of the traffic past the site.
- Zoning: attitudes, timing, approval process
- Current taxation and the likelihood of unusual fee increases

Existing Projects

The self-storage investment is the mother lode of success for those who believe in personal research prior to investing. No other real estate product type has had quite so much misinformation circulated about its supply and demand characteristics.

Because of the oversupply that now exists and the propensity of many fee-driven developers to build into an overbuilt market, thereby quickly increasing the competition, an examination of the entire original feasibility study, if it is still available (check with the consultant who did it), is the very least that a prudent investor should do. Comparing that study with current conditions is the wisest course today.

When analyzing demand, it is common to look at the trends that underlie it. The trends listed below are those that many in the industry say drive demand and will account for its growth. Six of them do not favor self-storage today and the other two are weak to neutral demand drivers.

Yet these are the trends that are constantly cited as the power behind the demand for storage space:

- The declining size of dwelling units
- High commercial rents
- The increase in new business formations
- An increasing propensity to rent self-storage space
- Population mobility
- A rising divorce rate
- The acquisitiveness of the American public
- An increase in the amount of leisure time

Three of the most often-encountered of these trends are the persistent decline in dwelling unit size, which, if true, fosters a need for more storage space; rising commercial rents; and new business formations. They deserve a closer look.

In an extensive industry literature review, not one writer who mentioned dwelling unit size (through 1991) failed to point out that the average size of U.S. dwelling units was declining. This decline augurs well for self-storage demand, they argued. The facts on dwelling unit size, however, have been sharply different.

Single-family dwelling units increased in size every year between 1978 and 1991, with the lone exception of 1980–1982, when a decline in size occurred. Multifamily units declined in size from 1982–1984. Table 8.2 details this history. There is no strong trend (on a national basis) toward smaller dwelling size that is pumping up the demand for self-storage units. It is natural, however, for dwelling unit size to decrease during a prolonged recession, because homebuilders cut down on unit sizes so as to offer lower prices during such times. But so far this has been a short-lived phenomenon.

During the late eighties and early nineties, it was also popular to drag out a list of the high current rents for office space and suggest that office users would naturally want to use self-storage space in lieu of expensive office space for the storage of records, supplies and surplus items. The facts, even at that time, did not support those assumptions. Office rents peaked nationally in about 1982 at approximately $27 per square foot (in some areas they hit $40), but rents have declined since then by 50 percent or more in many areas. Similarly, research and development rents hit their own peak in 1983 and have declined steadily through 1991. It is true that

Table 8.2   Newly Constructed U.S. Dwelling Units: 1978 to 1991
(in median square feet)

Year	Single-Family Units	Multifamily Units
1978	1,655	863
1979	1,645	893
1980	1,595	915
1981	1,550	930
1982	1,520	925
1983	1,565	893
1984	1,605	871
1985	1,605	882
1986	1,660	876
1987	1,755	920
1988	1,810	940
1989	1,850	940
1990	1,905	955
1991	N/A	N/A

Source: U.S. Department of Commerce, Economics and Statistics Administration, Bureau of the Census, *Characteristics of New Housing*, Current Construction Reports, C25-9013 (June 1991).

some classes of real estate maintained their ability to support modest rent increases for some time while office rents were declining, but the recession of the early nineties eventually caught up with all types of real estate and removed high and rising rents as a demand driver. The point is that this "fact" was not true for most of the time it was used, and anyone doing the bare minimum of independent investigation could have easily discovered the truth.

The story for new business formations is much the same. They do not seem to be a source of increased demand for the self-storage industry. Unfortunately, there is no reliable public source for data on new business formations either nationally or regionally. The best source was the Dun & Bradstreet Corporation, which published such data from 1985 to 1987 but then had to suspend the series because of database difficulties; the organization hopes to renew it in the near future. In the meantime, investors can get some minimal information from their own state's Department of Finance. Intuitive evidence indicates that new business formations have not been increasing rapidly. Whatever the truth, it isn't available to affect investment in self-storage facilities.

New business formations undoubtedly account for some of the demand for storage space, but this and other common demand sources will only be news when some significant change takes place in the normal amount of such activities. During the early 1990s new business formations actually declined slightly, yet we continued to encounter, in loan applications and in speeches, the happy idea that small businesses were blossoming on every corner and that this would fuel increased demand for storage space. It simply was not true based on available data.

Americans are neither much more mobile nor are they getting divorces in numbers that depart from long-established norms. Nevertheless, these are two "trends" often cited to support the notion that the demand for storage space is skyrocketing. There is no doubt that people move around and get divorced, and this has some effect on the demand for self-storage space. The real question is whether that demand is changing. In the case of mobility, there has been no substantial change in the percentage of the population that moved in a given year for at least ten years. Divorces continue to occur, but they are not on the increase per 1,000 of population. In 1979 the rate was 5.3 divorces per 1,000; it is about 4.7 per 1,000 today, according to a Roper poll done in 1991.

There is ample evidence that Americans are an acquisitive people, but there is no proof that this trait has taken a quantum leap and will, therefore, fuel increased demand for the storage of surplus goods.

Any investor encountering rose-colored demand indicators, like those just discussed, should be immediately suspicious of the viability of the project being pitched. But these statistics will continue to appear, and one wonders why. The only answer that comes close to making sense is in two parts. Part one says that some of these statistics, like declining dwelling unit size, were once accurate (if only for a brief time) and the transient trend was picked up by some writer on the industry. Part two of the explanation is that most people are too busy or disinclined to do their own research, preferring instead to copy "facts" they see in other articles. In this way, misinformation is perpetuated and even institutionalized to a point where most uncritical people believe it to be true. It is this pathway to misinformation that gobbles up the capital of so many uninformed investors. Unfortunately, this path is not unique to the self-storage investment.

Demand Propensity

One important basis for estimating demand is the propensity of the population to rent self-storage space. Certain rules of thumb have been developed about this propensity, and these rules are given a kind of legitimacy by periodic, official-sounding revisions; the per capita propensity revisions are usually upward.

The industry generally accepts the idea that the propensity to rent self-storage space has been rising since 1975, when it was said to be one square foot per capita, to somewhere around two to two and one-half square feet today. It is a somewhat over-studied statistic; one analyst breaks propensity into six residential segments and sets a low to high range for each segment. You can hardly get more legitimate than that. Unfortunately, these propensity figures are of limited use, because they are drawn from less-than-valid sources. Investors are right to look askance at such data; they should question its value very carefully—especially if it is based on the use of false assumptions, as has been shown to be the case in so much of the justifying information on demand tendencies.

Market Area

The self-storage business is a neighborhood business. Close to 85 percent of your tenants will come from your primary trading area. The key question is, How big is the neighborhood?

There is no general agreement on the size of the primary market, but fortunately the range is narrow—a three-mile to five-mile radius. The difference in population between a three-mile and a five-mile circle can, of course, be huge.

Market size seems to change depending upon who is describing it. Optimistic developers tend to look at a larger area in order to "pump up" the financial pro forma. Lenders and appraisers often see a smaller primary market.

Because of the serious financial risk from overestimating the market area, investors will want to determine the smallest area that will support the income performance they require. If a facility is projected to do well serving a three-mile area, you are better off than if you had to depend upon a five-mile market. The bigger the market area, the more certain it is that competition will move into it.

It is possible that public awareness of this type of real estate product is still low. If that is true (and it would take very convincing proof to make the case), then a rise in demand might occur without a concurrent increase in population. While this argument is occasionally advanced, it is a highly subjective consideration and should not be the basis for tipping an investment decision one way or another.

The advertising campaigns in recent years, which are as much a sign of oversupply as they are of anything else, might be seen as an attempt to build market size by increasing public awareness. The results achieved indicate that demand can be expanded somewhat by advertising. The signs are encouraging enough to ensure that there will be more space-available ads in the future.

Population alone is not enough to justify a project. A rapidly growing local population is sometimes cited as justification for a new facility, and it may well be reason to develop one. Expanding population must be viewed critically to determine if it is based upon the need for workers from a broadly diversified economy or for one large employer who could be here today and gone tomorrow. Betting your capital in a narrowly diversified market will more often result in big losses than in big gains. The same is true for investment bets made where disposable income is stagnant or falling.

Income level is directly related to storage space demand. The strongest demand will come from middle-income families. If they are prospering, so will you, given a balanced supply.

Financial Analysis

No amount of talk about market niches or special areas of untapped demand will change the fact that this product type, like virtually every other real estate product type, is in oversupply. Careful analysis of the numbers is an essential step in your decision-making process; it is by no means the most critical step. The assumptions you make about supply and demand factors and the definition of market size are far more important than massaging the numbers.

Table 8.3   Income and Expense Ratios—Average-Size Project (30,000 to 50,000 square feet)

Item	Percent
Gross scheduled income (GSI)	100% (97% rent; 3% miscellaneous)
Vacancy allowance	10% to 20%
Expenses	(As a percent of GSA)
Real estate taxes	6% to 10.5%
Insurance	1% to 1.5%
Advertising	2% to 3%
Maintenance	2% to 3%
On-site management	4% to 6%
Off-site management	5% to 6%
Miscellaneous (telephone, accounting, legal, licenses, etc.)	2% to 2.5%
Total	23.5% to 34.5%

Table 8.3 sets forth the broad areas of income and expense. These pro forma guidelines have some usefulness, but no pro forma ever predicts failure. Given that 100 percent of the numbers you see will project success, the trick is to test individual items against some reasonable yardstick and then adjust the numbers to realistic expectations. Table 8.3 will help you do that.

Investment Characteristics

There are six important investment characteristics: development cost, cash flow, management, tenant turnover, resale and liquidity.

Development cost.   Cost of development is quite low relative to the rent that can be charged and comparison to the production costs of other forms of improved real estate. A self-storage unit will generate rents ranging from $.50 to about $1.35 per square foot per month. It costs from $25 to $45 a foot to build the project, including land. An apartment building often costs two to three times as much to build, but will achieve rents that are the same or less than those achieved by the self-storage project.

Cash flow.   One of the overpowering attractions of self-storage is its potential for huge cash flow. If vacancy plus expenses ranges from 35 percent to 55 percent of gross income, then an unleveraged project will show 45 percent to 65 percent in pretax cash flow. If maximum debt financing is used, the leveraged cash flow is 9.5 percent to 21.5 percent. Cash does not flow evenly throughout the year, however. In most areas there is a decided seasonality, with the summer months, from June through September, being the period of highest occupancy.

In today's competitive market, it may take two to five years to reach the 80–90 percent occupancy levels needed to produce these generous cash flows. These kind of returns, however, are not being enjoyed by those who own a limited partnership interest in unleveraged private storage facilities; pretax returns of 8 percent to 9 percent are most common for such investments. Perhaps this return differential, as well as the 1986 tax law, has something to do with the virtual disappearance of syndications from the real estate investment landscape.

Management.   This type of real estate is frequently rated as somewhat less than management-intensive. But that opinion is open to serious question when one considers that most projects require the use of a full-time on-site (not necessarily resident) manager plus off-site management. As competition has strengthened, the role of the on-site manager has become more critical, necessitating, in many cases, a more marketing-oriented person. This could eventually raise employee costs. In any event, whether you agree that the management job is intensive or not, most operating statements of professionally managed projects contain an 8 percent to 12 percent management charge, which equates to about one-third of the operating expenses. That's about as intensive as it can get.

Tenant turnover.   Turnover is quite high, rivaling or exceeding that experienced with unfurnished garden apartments. The average length of occupancy is about seven months. It is not unusual to have 10 percent of your total units turn over monthly.

Resale.   Resale prospects are uncertain. The resale market is not as vigorous as that for apartments. In many areas there have been too few sales to form a comparable sales base of information. It appears, however, that projects are often offered at a 9 percent capitalization rate, while most sales are made at between 11 percent and 13 percent. Sale prices seem to reach about 120 percent of development costs. If this is generally accurate, then the data in Table 8.1 ought to be reexamined with this fact in mind. At 120 percent (or even 130 percent) of development cost, the current capitalized value of the industry is closer to the value achieved using the 13 percent estimate than it is to any higher number.

Liquidity.   Liquidity is a major concern. One has to consider the marketplace's unfamiliarity with this investment type and the syndication structure used for many of these projects. Those who own projects without partners and those who are in small (fewer than 20 investors) syndications may have an easier time selling their interests. Those who are in the big syndications are at the mercy of the syndicator.

Even in a slow market modest bank loans are usually available, but financing is never easy. The usual financial structure is 100 percent equity; this, of course, severely limits the number of buyers (and the price received) as well as lengthening the time it takes to sell.

Since the Tax Reform Act of 1986, syndication investments have lost their allure. One result of this is that the sponsors who are left have almost nothing to do, especially the smaller ones. This increases their tendency to hang on to the projects they have (if they are performing) and thus stretch the investors' holding period to the legal limit. For many investors who put IRA or Keogh money into self-storage investments and are now approaching retirement, it must seem that this type of investment has about as much chance at liquidity as the million-year-old ice under the polar caps.

Design and Construction

Competition is intense. Marketing is king today. But before much marketing can be done, a marketable product must be designed and built. The day is long gone when you could get by with using shipping containers in an open field as a storage facility. Terminal ugliness is out, good-looking business facilities are in.

Self-storage projects get about 85 percent of their tenants from their fairly small primary trading area. Of these tenants, 50–60 percent are generated by the project itself (drive-bys); the balance come from the *Yellow Pages* and other advertising, not the least of which is a decent color brochure.

Over 90 percent of what a potential customer considers when choosing one project over another is the visual impact of the buildings and the site. The project must attract the favorable attention of potential tenants as they drive past it on the way to and from work or as they go about their local business. The value of a superior location and project design are hard to inflate, given the overwhelming importance of drive-by traffic. Yet, as has been observed by others, this product type originated in Texas 35 years ago, and the projects built today are not much different from that first one.

Considering the very basic product being provided, it is a challenge to cost-effectively differentiate it from its competition. But before considering how to do something new and different, you should have a firm understanding of what it is the customer wants.

The Site

It is a mistake to build or buy a good project on a bad site; it will never do really well. To give yourself the maximum opportunity to succeed, you must select a site that has high visibility on a major surface street and enough frontage to allow easy access. The instant impression customers get as they drive by should be that it is easy to get in and out of.

Customers feel most comfortable entering a site that offers an entry driveway that will accommodate several vehicles (some with trailers) at once. Potential customers are often inexperienced in towing a trailer or driving a big, boxy rental truck, and they want a site that is laid out with wide lanes between the storage buildings and lots of turnaround space at the end of those lanes. Interior driveway widths will run from 12 to 35 feet; the best width is 25 feet.

The best shape for a site is the rectangle or square. Exceptionally deep sites can be used if the street frontage is wide enough. Odd-shaped sites should be avoided, because it is hard to get good building coverage on them and they are difficult to lay out.

It is a mistake to think that you are "land banking" when you buy a storage facility. If the site is good as a storage facility, it will likely remain so during many changes in the area. As the area builds up, it will only become more valuable for what it is. If there is a windfall profit from a land sale some 30 or 40 years from today, it will be an unexpected and fortuitous event. Buy self-storage for what it is and run it to maximize your long-term profits, and you will make more money than you ever could fantasizing about how some office or retail developer is going to come along and make you rich by overpaying for your land.

The average site is two acres and will support a building coverage of about 40 percent. At this lot size and coverage, you get a project of about 35,000 square feet quite comfortably. The maximum building coverage ratio is 50 percent. The closer to 40 percent you are, the more convenient the layout will be for the customers.

The Site Plan

Sites are generally laid out with a series of long, narrow buildings separated by access and loading/unloading driveways. There is usually a minimum of interior landscaping.

Customers favor the "fortress" layout, with buildings placed around the site's perimeter. When this type of layout is used, little security fencing is needed, because the walls of the buildings make the area look highly secure. One way to destroy that secure appearance is to let graffiti accumulate on the exterior walls.

The resident manager's house (if there is one) is located near the front entrance so that customers have easy access to the manager without having to enter the storage premises. This also gives the manager a good view of the entry and exit, which are usually electronically controlled, card-access gates.

Many projects offer a full range of business services (copying, secretarial, faxing, conference room, etc.) as well as moving equipment and truck rental. These extra services and products can produce a significant amount of revenue. In many cases, resident managers have been eliminated and replaced by a strong daily staff, and their residences have been converted to retail space and a business center.

The Buildings

Customers like the look and strength of masonry or concrete structures. They also prefer standing-seam steel roofs and steel demising partitions. All of these features contribute to a sense of security, and they also lower maintenance costs.

Buildings can be almost any length but should be a multiple of 10, 11, 12.5 or 15 feet deep. Interior buildings can be twice the size of any of these standard depths to create double-loaded buildings of 20, 22, 25 or 30 feet that can be divided into rentable units of half that depth. Door widths are 3 to 4 feet for the 5-foot-wide units and generally 8 to 8.5 feet (not standard) for the 10-foot and 12-foot spaces. All doors must have two secure locking devices. Ceiling heights are 8.5 to 10 feet, although some projects have 12-foot ceilings.

Security

A self-storage facility must project a feeling of security. All property lines (in nonfortress projects) should have at least a six-foot fence. Good exterior lighting is a must. Many tenants will not see the project at night, so the impression of adequate lighting that they get during the day is critical. Modern projects provide interior lighting for the units and easy access to electrical outlets for use when the tenant is storing or removing goods from his or her unit. Older projects seldom have electrical outlets inside the unit, although installing in-unit, timer-controlled electricity is a popular retrofit. Fire extinguishers should be plentiful and in easy-to-see locations. Most operators have little choice in this matter, as they must meet local fire regulations. A few extra extinguishers is an inexpensive way to cater to tenants' need to feel safe.

Differentiating the Project

With the overbuilt condition that exists in almost every market, you have to capture more than your share of the business to succeed. Successful operators know that the project itself is their best marketing tool, and they pay special attention to design techniques that will give potential customers a feeling of wanting to do business with their facility.

The areas most susceptible to innovative design are the manager's quarters, the entry drive, the frontage and the site plan. The cost of added architectural elements that will make these areas more effective is quite low. But even if they were to add 15 percent to the cost of your project, which they won't, the increased "curb appeal" would be worth it.

Lush, fresh-looking landscaping featuring seasonal color all along the frontage will add visual impact and set you apart from your competitors, while increasing the recognition factor for your project. Consider some interior landscaping to relieve the starkness usually encountered once the customer passes through the entry gate.

Good color graphics on the buildings and the use of modern colors is another way the project can be made to sell itself better.

Good maintenance sells. This includes keeping all the storage unit doors freshly painted and in excellent repair, as well as making certain the site is kept free from trash and junk. Cleanliness sends a message that you care; it makes people feel that, somehow, this project is better than the one down the street.

Other Considerations

Thought should be given to the project sign and to all marketing literature. Homemade computer-generated price lists and typed lists of the project's features simply won't work. When a customer walks through the front door of the project office, he or she should walk into a bright, clean, well-organized space that is equipped with quality signage and the very best in marketing materials. You have to give your potential customers written materials that say, "We care about this business and about providing you with the very best in the most convenient way."

Trends and Conclusions

The industry is mature, overbuilt and highly competitive. The days of developing a self-storage project and selling it at an inflated price to uninformed investors looking for tax benefits are gone.

Supply

- Total supply will grow more slowly. Industry size will be fortunate to increase much more than 2–3 percent per year—a far cry from the heady 15 percent growth common in the early years.
- Mom-and-pop influence on the industry will decline as competition continues to increase.
- More intense competition will come from new projects built closer to the customer base.
- Use of modular units will increase, as will the conversion of existing properties to self-storage facilities.
- Supply will be restricted by a lack of financing until more balance is achieved between supply and demand.

- More larger projects of 60,000 to 100,000 square feet will be built in urban areas.

Demand

- The current oversupply condition will persist through the 1990s.
- Demand will grow at 3 percent annually until the late nineties.
- More advertising will be used in an attempt to stimulate demand; this will increase the pressure on smaller operators.
- Feasibility studies will become more important.

New Products and Services

- Business services will be added to those facilities where a market for them can be detected.
- Customers want longer hours that give them early-morning access and entry up to 8 or 9 P.M. in many markets.
- The conversion of multistory older buildings to self-storage will continue, but at a much slower pace.
- Climate-controlled facilities will increase because they "pro forma" well and because there is some flicker of demand for them in a few markets.
- More on-site storage services, such as individual door alarms, electricity in the unit, etc., will be offered to lure customers to projects. There is a growing demand for heated units in many markets. The demand for extra services includes an increase in the availability of truck rentals.
- Tenants also want to be able to charge their rental on a credit card; at least one major operator does not provide this service. Tenants also want a fully computerized billing service.
- There is greater sensitivity to project appearance, especially cleanliness. Some operators will have to hire extra people to improve, or just maintain, the appearance of their facilities. Overall quality of facilities will increase as operators respond to competitive pressures.

Investment Opportunities

- Availability of projects to second-generation investors will be greater as competitive pressures work to convince original investors to sell.

- Cash flows from both operations and resale are likely to shrink. Cap rates will rise.
- Consolidation of ownership into fewer hands will occur as the industry matures and the pioneers sell out.
- Local taxes are likely to rise as governments look farther afield for revenue. This will affect business license fees and special assessments.

The current imbalance between supply and demand is creating opportunities for astute investors with an abundance of marketing sense to buy existing developments at prices that make it possible to earn a profit.

C H A P T E R
9

Housing for the Elderly

In this chapter we examine housing for the elderly. We cover its history in the United States since 1900, the supply and demand situation today, design considerations, financing, the developer's role and trends in the industry.

The elderly are the second biggest demographic discovery of this century. There are more of them; they are living longer and healthier lives; they have more money to spend than at any time in our history; and their lifestyles are changing dramatically. All of this adds up to an important housing market segment.

Providing suitable housing for our older population has emerged as a small but growing part of the housing market, and it's one that many developers and most investors are unfamiliar with. It is a market with good potential for long-term growth and for serious short-term oversupply. Developer and lender enthusiasm for the strong potential of senior housing plus a scarcity of profitable development alternatives during the recent real estate slump have prompted speculators to overbuild demand in many areas.

Because of low birth rates during the Great Depression and throughout World War II, the number of elderly is not growing as rapidly today as it will in the years 2000 to 2035. Perhaps for this reason many developers have expanded this market segment by including people as young as 50.

There are actually two senior markets. The first is a maturing market, or preretirement group, which consists of those aged 50 to 65—elderly in training, so to speak. A large number are still actively employed, but their housing needs have changed; "empty nesters" is a popular descriptive term for this group.

The second segment consists of those who are 65 and older. The 65+ group is often further divided into three basic groups. The complete breakdown looks like this:

1. Group 1—The preretirement market; 50 to 64 years old; empty nesters.
2. Group 2—The 65+ market, which divides into:
   - the "young-old," 65 to 75, often called first-generation retirees;
   - the elderly, 76 to 84 years old; and
   - The "old-old," 85+.

Each of these groups has different housing needs, which you will find discussed in the Supply and Demand section.

Senior Housing Choices

Retirement communities.   To meet the needs of older Americans, four basic housing alternatives have emerged. The first, and best known, is the retirement community. These are minicities such as Leisure World and Sun City (in California and Arizona), developed for the upper-middle-income and affluent preretiree and retiree. This housing, to the casual observer, looks like housing built for the 25 to 44 age group.

Congregate housing.   In the second category is congregate housing, which are group-living facilities designed to serve a homogeneous population. These projects are much smaller than retirement communities and are often available on a for-rent or for-purchase basis. Congregate housing provides a living unit plus basic services such as meals, group transportation, and recreational and social activities.

Lifecare living.   The third alternative is lifecare living. Lifecare, as it was originally conceived, provides elderly residents with a living unit plus on-site medical care. Both services were guaranteed for life. Such facilities commonly collected an upfront entry fee of $20,000 to $200,000 or more and a monthly maintenance fee of $150 to about $450. Most entry fees were nonrefundable; they provided the "endowment" for the project. This concept has experienced the greatest difficulty. It has been marked with some well-publicized bankruptcies, which have brought about fundamental changes in both the concept of lifecare and the nature of the sponsorship for such projects.

Most lifecare projects were originally sponsored and operated by nonprofit entities. Many of them were religious organizations that had little or no business experience. This lack of expertise, combined with longer life expectancies and rapidly rising operating costs, led to frequent financial disaster.

The lifecare industry, however, is not dead. It is estimated to consist of anywhere from 325 to 700 projects scattered throughout the country. The average project serves about 200 residents.

No-limit, long-term medical care is no longer a feature of the most successful lifecare projects; it's pay-as-you-receive today. The nonrefundable entry fee has given way to higher, but refundable, fees. The failures of the past have laid the groundwork for a strong, financially successful expansion of this senior housing alternative. It is starting to attract participation from many large, well-financed corporations in the lodging, food service and healthcare industries.

Aging in place, skilled nursing facilities, adaptive-use housing and granny flats.   The fourth housing option is really a catchall category, but it is the biggest segment of all. It consists of at least three approaches:

1. Those who stay in their own homes and try to adapt them to their changing lifestyle. At least 90 percent of all elderly solve their housing problem this way; they age in place.
2. Skilled nursing facilities for the very old or for those who are unable to live independently. Only 5 percent of the elderly live in such facilities, and only 20 percent will ever be in one. It is the housing alternative most feared by the aging.
3. Adaptive use of all types, such as shared housing, group living, conversion of nonresidential properties into one of the three primary housing solutions, granny flats (sometimes called elder cottages)

and accessory housing of every imaginable type. Shared housing and group living are the boardinghouse concept adapted to senior housing. Granny flats are, technically, temporary construction designed to accommodate the needs of aging relatives by converting a portion of a single-family home to an apartment or by moving a separate living unit, perhaps a manufactured home or mobile home, onto the site of an existing single-family home. When the need for the elderly housing comes to an end, the temporary housing is supposed to be removed. Unfortunately, it does not always work that way, even though most communities have imposed strict time limits on such living arrangements to avoid permanently changing the character of their neighborhoods.

Granny housing proliferates quickly in high-amenity communities (such as resort cities) and is used, by many owners, as a way of increasing residential density. The tenants are, in such cases, seldom "grannies"; they are merely tenants helping to add to the cash flow of the homeowner. The proliferation of illegal granny flats has been so severe in some communities that the government has had to declare them legal retroactively or face long, often losing, court battles. Such activity tends to confirm the idea that the senior housing market would expand dramatically if producers were able to provide low-cost, well-located housing.

The granny flat phenomenon bodes well for small developers who do rehabilitation and conversion work. It also favors the producers of mobile homes and manufactured housing.

A Short History

The history of senior housing seems to indicate that the past is the future. In 1900, care of the elderly was the responsibility of the immediate family. The year 2000 might resemble 1900, because the costs of caring for and housing our elderly, using current social programs, may become a burden society can't carry. Table 9.1 shows one of the reasons for this. The ratio of working people to retired people from 1960 to 2080 is shrinking.

Costs for elder care continue to rise and the number of working people available to pay those costs continues to decline. Inevitably there will be efforts, at all levels of government, to force a greater reliance on private

Table 9.1 Ratios of Total Population and Labor Force to Over-65 Age Group

Year	Total Pop: Over 65	Labor Force: Over 65
1960	10:1	4:1
1965	10:1	4:1
1970	10:1	4:1
1975	9:1	4:1
1980	8:1	4:1
1985	7:1	3:1
1990	7:1	3:1
1995	7:1	3:1
2000	7:1	3:1
2010	7:1	3:1
2030	4:1	2:1
2050	4:1	2:1
2080	4:1	2:1

Source: U.S. Department of Commerce, Bureau of the Census, *Current Population Reports,* Series
P-25, No. 965.

resources in meeting elderly needs. Public policy at the federal level, such
as plans to encourage greater personal savings, extending the retirement
age, elimination of mandatory retirement, and tax incentives that force a
reliance on personal resources, will continue to be the focus of much
legislative activity.

State and local governments will come under pressure to make changes
in their land planning laws that will make it easier for profit-making
entities to produce the needed housing.

Figure 9.1 shows the evolution of elderly housing since the late 1800s.

Demand Factors

In this section you will find demographic factors, market characteristics,
influences on demand, the role of market research and investment characteristics of senior housing.

Figure 9.1   Senior Housing in the United States: A Short History

1880s	Chancellor Otto Von Bismarck of Prussia decreed (as a political ploy) that all persons reaching the age of 65 would get a life pension. Life expectancy at the time was 47 years. Nevertheless, this political act has set the retirement age in most countries up to the present time.
Late 1800s	First retirement housing project in the United States sponsored by a religious organization to provide for retired clergy.
1900	Life expectancy at birth (United States) was 47 years.
1900 to 1930	Heavy immigration of young adults contributed to the size of the elderly population from 1965 to the present.
1935	Social Security Act adopted.
1937	Housing Act of 1937; first federal involvement in housing for the elderly.
1940s	G.I. bill increases education level of young adults. Low-cost housing loans encourage children to establish separate homes, which most often were in the suburbs. Marks the start of the loss of family togetherness. Laid the foundation for today's senior housing market.
1950	Retirement housing market develops as World War I generation begins to reach retirement age. Choices of suitable retirement facilities in customer's home town were limited. Out-of-area retirement communities did well.
1954	First planned active-adult retirement community built in Arizona by Elmer Johnson and Ben Schleifer.
1956	FHA 207 program begins. Federal Housing Administration authorized to insure mortgages on senior housing.
1958	First public housing project designed specifically for the elderly.
1959	HUD 202 program. National Housing Act of 1959 enacted. Authorized direct loans to nonprofit sponsors of senior housing.
1960	First sizable retirement community (the 1954 project was the inspiration) built by Del Webb in Sun City, Arizona.

Figure 9.1   Senior Housing in the United States: A Short History (continued)

1970	First federal congregate-housing law passed. No funds provided for purchase and preparation of meals. Did little to stimulate production of congregate housing.
1974	National Housing Act of 1959 revised to allow 40-year loans to nonprofit sponsors to build or renovate senior housing.
1975	Permanent financing source for HUD 2023 program provided.
1978	Housing Services Act of 1978 gave impetus to congregate housing by providing money for meals and some services. Thirty-eight congregate developments were built in the following 36 months.
1979	About 100 lifecare projects in operation.
Late 1970s	More retirement housing built. Senior housing options increased. Some landmark financial failures occurred.
1980	Subsidized housing projects begin to decline as a percentage of total housing built. Uniform Barrier-Free Design Act drafted and made available to all states. American National Standards Institute revised Elderly Housing Design Standards (ANSI 1). HUD issues revised design criteria.
1984 to 1989	Lower construction costs stimulate production of senior housing.
1985	One person in ten is 65 years of age or older. The 65+ age group grows at the rate of 5,000 per day.
1986	From 325 to 700 lifecare projects in operation. Approximately 865 congregate housing projects in the United States. Over 20,000 nursing homes in operation.
	Life expectancy at birth is 74 years.
1990 to 1992	Construction declines dramatically in the face of overbuilding and a recession. Vacancies and unsold units increase substantially.

The Demographic Story

Few senior-citizen projects appeal to a nationwide customer base; therefore, national statistics are of little value except to indicate the absolute size of the market and how it will develop over time. National data leaves little room for doubt about the vigor of long-term demand. Investors can accept, as a well-established fact, that the elderly population is both growing in size and getting older.

Population statistics show that the older-American segment is increasing at a rate twice that of the total U.S. population. The 25 to 44 age group is still the best housing segment, but this will change gradually. As our population matures, the 55+ group will exert more influence on the character of the housing market. The full impact of this change may not be felt for 10 to 15 years, but its influence will be exerted long before then. At the moment, however, the elderly population is more of a market influence than a strong market segment.

Investors need to go slowly in the short run. The current market may not be as deep as some developers think. Table 9.2 shows three possible demand curves for the period 1985 to 2030. The assumption behind this table is that demand will expand as population grows. It also assumes that effective demand will increase over time.

The expected growth of the elderly population makes it likely that errors will be made in estimating the demand that comes from those who have the money to pay for elderly housing. Dynamic growth in a market segment seems to create its own kind of optimism. The fact remains, however, that not everyone is a potential customer for senior housing.

Effective demand ranges from 1 to 3 percent of the elderly population. The exact percentage depends upon the price and quality relationship of the accommodations offered. Based upon current senior housing offerings, demand is from 1 to 2 percent of the population group. Those who want such housing and have the money to pay for it apparently still do not have a strong opinion of the value being offered.

Interpretation of Table 9.2 should probably include the assumption that, at the low estimates, market supply will continue to be basically unresponsive to the true needs of the potential customer base and, further, that supply will be almost totally responsive to customer needs at the high level. It is also assumed that the percentage of wealth controlled by the

Table 9.2 Estimate of Effective Demand: 1985 to 2030

Source: Grubb & Ellis Company. Used by permission.

over-55 age group will remain fairly steady and that the tendency toward early retirement will continue until at least the year 2000.

Other Market Considerations

Market characteristics also include income considerations, the extent of government subsidy activity, location choices, the product types most likely to be in demand and the average age at entry of retirement residents.

Older Americans as a class are not poor, even though there are many elderly who are poor. The over-55 age group controls about 80 percent of all deposits in banks and savings and loan associations. Over 75 percent own their own home; more than 60 percent of that group own it free of any debt. On top of this, the average cash income of those 65 and above is about $20,000. When considered together with their equity position and their reduced need for material things, this group has enough to pay for reasonably priced elderly housing.

The preretired or early-retiree segment is the most affluent, and they are the target most developers try to hit. They have the equity and/or the income, and their lifestyle closely resembles that of the 25 to 44 age group.

Lower-income elderly must get government assistance in the form of housing cost supplements and other welfare grants. Providing housing to the low-income segment is by no means a nonprofit or even a low-profit activity. Even those programs that limit current cash return (to 8 percent or thereabouts) offer prospects for eventual capital gains. Interviews with many providers of subsidized housing revealed a high level of satisfaction with profitability. Government subsidies of all types are declining, however, as a percentage of the total housing market. It is unlikely that the production of subsidized housing will cease, but it does not appear to be a long-term growth industry.

Location Choices

Some markets offer far less promise than others. One of the poorest situations to be in is a market characterized by low apartment rents, since more than 70 percent of senior housing is in the form of rentals.

The Sun Belt has attracted a lot of attention but it has no monopoly on senior housing, even though some of the most visible retirement communities have been built in such areas. The sunshine states got a lot of play in the late 1960s and throughout the seventies and eighties as the nation's primary retirement centers. That market activity, however, was concentrated on a few highly visible retirement developments that catered to affluent preretirees and the young-old. Numerous market surveys that asked people where they would like to retire also seemed to point to the Sun Belt as having potentially the best long-term market for senior housing. But what people say and what they actually do are often different; it certainly is with the location choices made by retirees.

Over 92 percent of all retirees will never relocate more than 200 miles from their lifetime homes. The vast majority (over 90 percent) will age in place; they will not move at all. At least one conclusion seems obvious: There is no dominant retirement area in this country. The market is everywhere.

There is a definite current trend among the elderly toward living in or near metropolitan areas. But virtually every city, town, village and hamlet has, or will soon have, a retirement project of some kind. The apparent preference for metropolitan areas adds to the risk for those investors who choose rural and small-town locations.

Product Types

No one product type has universal appeal to the elderly market. The diversity among older Americans creates demand for numerous housing products. If, for example, you are appealing to the well-to-do empty-nest market segment, you will have the best chance of success if you can provide low-cost to moderate-cost single-family homes or duplex units under $100,000 and close to 2,000 square feet in size. This product holds appeal for the affluent elderly who are leaving a 3,000–4,000-foot home. They will also respond to well-designed cluster housing.

The middle-income buyer will look at congregate care facilities that provide a high degree of security, the prospects of good resale value (if they are for-sale units) and an array of basic services, such as housekeeping, two or three meals daily, limited group transportation, and the opportunity for recreational and social activities. The more the facilities look like a single-family home, the faster they will sell or rent. That is not to suggest that medium- to high-density midrise or high-rise projects won't work, but the demand is more intense for low-density, single-story developments.

Lifecare facilities have regained some favor. They present a market opportunity that should be fairly steady at about 100 projects nationally per year for the next ten years. This assumes an average project size of 200 units. If production costs continue to decline and operating costs stabilize, this part of the industry could do well. There is, however, a huge potential for overbuilding.

The biggest demand for the next 15 years, perhaps longer, will come from the 70+ market segment. This favors lifecare and nursing home projects. Even though only 5 percent of the elderly population will ever reside in a nursing home permanently, the twin trends of the 65+ population increasing at about 5,000 per day and longer life expectancy indicate a solid future for the nursing home.

The average age at entry to retirement facilities is:

Retirement villages	58
Congregate housing	62
Lifecare projects	77
Nursing homes	83

Table 9.3 The Senior Housing Market: Current and Future Status

Age Group	Product Type	Current Status	Future Status
50 to 65	Retirement communities	Adequate supply	Good demand after 2000
	High-quality single-family homes for empty nesters	Overbuilt in most markets	See above
	Quality cluster housing	Overbuilt in most markets	See above
66 to 75	Congregate facilities; sale or rent	Fair demand in big markets	No significant demand increase until 2000
	Lifecare facilities	Appears to be demand for 100+ projects annually	Demand improvement in 1995
75 plus	Lifecare	See above	See above
	Nursing Homes	About 20,000 in operation	Reasonably good demand from 1990 on

The senior housing market is a mystery to most investors because of the number of product types and market segments. Table 9.3 summarizes the current situation and forecasts the future for senior housing.

Influences on Demand

The demand for nonmedical elderly housing is influenced by these factors:

- The number of income-qualified persons who live in the market area and who are willing to move (from 1 to 3 percent of the total over-55 population)
- The quality of the project's location as determined by proximity to shopping, financial and medical services; the level of crime in the area; the general desirability of the neighborhood; driving time to

children and friends; and access to recreational, cultural and social services
- The tendency of most elderly to stay where they are—to age in place
- The physical decline of the neighborhoods now occupied by elderly persons
- The extent to which the housing used or owned by the elderly becomes unsuitable because of high upkeep and other operating costs
- The availability of affordable housing that meets the needs of the target market (if superior housing solutions at moderate cost are offered the demand expands)
- The level of competition—i.e., the absolute number, and cost, of senior housing units in the area without regard to suitability
- The quality of the marketing effort

The history of some projects that have failed (many of them lifecare projects) indicates that their decline most often stemmed from a poor understanding of demand rather than from poor operating techniques. A lack of market research appears to be the number-one cause of failure.

Market Research

Few developers or other sponsors do effective market research, claiming that it costs too much. Many give it lip service and prepare a "once over lightly"–type report, because their lender won't provide financing without some kind of feasibility study. The failure rate for real estate projects during the past five years suggests that the costs they are trying to avoid are not nearly so high as the costs they actually incur when a project fails.

Few real estate products are as dependent upon research for success as senior housing. The market is broad but not very deep; it is also highly segmented and diverse. The amenities and services demanded vary considerably among the three or four major market segments. And, while all senior housing projects are extremely management-intensive, the best management can't make a poorly located, badly designed or unneeded project succeed.

Without high-quality, independent market research, the best management teams cannot be attracted. Those who attempt to handle an ill-conceived project start out with three strikes against them. In the section on design, you will find more detail on what the elderly customer wants.

Investment Characteristics

An investor can participate in senior housing investments as the sole owner of a project or with a developer through a joint venture or syndication. Whatever vehicle you choose, it is important to know the hallmark of a good project and the kind of return you should receive.

An annual cash flow of 10 percent is not an unreasonable goal; total return, including resale profit, of 14 to 22 percent is achievable. Annual appreciation assumptions should not exceed 2 or 3 percent in today's investment climate. Some investors won't accept any appreciation assumption. The holding period is normally seven to ten years for nonmedical projects and four to five years for nursing homes. Typical loan-to-value ratios are 50 to 70 percent.

Supply Factors

There is no shortage of housing for the elderly, nor is one expected to develop in the foreseeable future. Some markets are not yet saturated, but given the shallowness of demand, it doesn't take long to overbuild a market. If any shortage exists, it is in low-income senior housing; this shortage will persist.

A varied group of sponsors is involved in providing for this market. It includes an array of nonprofit religious and charitable organizations, universities, colleges, nursing homes with excess land, private hospital corporations, low-income housing developers, experienced retirement community developers, homebuilders of all types, syndicators, doctors and individual investors.

The supply function has become a for-profit activity as the supply of subsidized funds has dried up and the cost of revenue bond financing, with its unending contact with the bureaucracy, has become less desirable.

The creation of new senior housing is, in some respects, countercyclical. Whenever the mainstream housing market slows down, home developers look for market niches in which they can continue to produce a housing product. Housing for the elderly is such a niche. The slowness in the housing market over the past two years has reactivated developer interest in senior housing.

Design Considerations

This section is not intended to turn you into an architectural expert, but rather to help you know enough to make an intelligent choice when faced with competing investments. You must have a working knowledge of what constitutes good interior and exterior design to ensure a good chance of long-term investment success. Much senior housing is poorly designed, and often substantial operating problems result.

Next to location, design is the single most important element to be considered during the development process. (This presupposes that adequate market research has been done and that an operating plan has been created before the design process begins.)

A potential investor would do well to ask, "Who did you use as an independent consultant?" Such a question might uncover how seriously the sponsor has approached the design challenge. Highly qualified consultants are available to help architects understand the needs of the market the project seeks to serve. Elderly buyers or renters are far more experienced at selecting housing than are the first-time or second-time buyers most housing providers usually deal with.

It is difficult to design a project that will appeal to every segment of the market. The wants and needs of the "young-old" differ from those of the second- or third-generation elderly. A project that focuses on one market segment has more chance of success than one that tries to cater to the entire market. It is a sound investment rule to invest only in those projects that have a clearly defined target market and avoid those that generalize.

Because the diversity among the elderly is so great, it is difficult to specify design features that are "surefire." Some features are more applicable to second- and third-generation elderly than they are to the preretired or just retired. Following are design areas that investors ought to be familiar with.

Interiors

The affluent elderly are a small percentage of the market. If the project is designed to attract them, it should be luxurious and loaded with recreational amenities. The wealthy tend to buy or rent downsized versions of their former homes. Units of 2,000 to 2,500 square feet are popular, and two bedrooms are a must.

The majority of the market is middle-income. This is what they want:

- Privacy within the living unit, whether it is for sale or for rent. The ability to have an area to oneself is important to older couples. The privacy issue extends to the congregate living format, where the number-one issue is a private toilet area. Shared baths, however, are acceptable.
- Common areas, both indoors and out, that provide for some measure of privacy while encouraging residents to mix. The privacy issue may explain why efficiency units are far less popular than one-bedroom plans and why nursing homes are so disliked by the majority of people.
- Security both inside and outside the living unit. An emergency call system and smoke alarms are essential.
- A liberal use of natural light in the individual living units and in all common areas. Corridors and lobbies ought to have views of the outside.
- Careful attention to artificial light levels. As people age, they need access to more light.
- Low-cost occupancy features that can make a big difference in comfort levels, such as:
  - Cross-ventilation in all rooms rather than air-conditioning, except in those climates where air-conditioning is a must.
  - Individually controlled heating. The elderly vary greatly in how they perceive heat and cold.
  - Well-insulated structures to keep fuel costs down and assist in noise control. Energy-efficiency rules make this mandatory today.
  - Liberal use of stained woodwork rather than high-maintenance painted surfaces.
- Lots of unbroken wall space to make furniture placement easy. An open-space plan (with due consideration to the privacy issue) that maximizes ease of movement with a wheelchair is usually successful. Small, walled areas should be avoided.
- Careful attention to avoiding barriers such as numerous steps, multiple living levels, uneven walking surfaces, thick carpet (which is hard to walk on as people get older), hard-to-open doors (lever handles are good) and difficult-to-operate plumbing fixtures.
- Unobtrusive safety features (if they are too obvious, they work against a sale at some age levels) such as large bathrooms, seats in

all showers, nonslip floors, wide doors and halls. Grab-rails and railings do not sell well and, in fact, are a hindrance to a sale or rental to the preretired or just-retired. Installing the bracing for them is a good idea, but it won't sell or rent many units. Electrical outlets and switches that are accessible without bending over are popular.

- Storage space. It is almost impossible to provide too much closet or display space. The elderly have a lot of prized possessions. Built-in bookcases are popular.
- Flexibility. The ability to adjust shelving, closet rods, and even bath and kitchen counter heights is a salable feature.
- Kitchens. A kitchen is a powerful amenity in all product types except nursing homes. Compact kitchens with at least 30 inches of counter space (usable while seated) and which are visible to the dining and living room areas are the most popular. You can avoid installing most kitchen gadgets, including, in many cases, dishwashers. Many of the elderly don't generate a lot of dirty dishes and don't want the expense of operating one. Top-mounted freezers should be avoided. All appliances should have front-mounted, easy-to-read dials and gauges. In projects without kitchens, residents respond well to a snack bar (not just a coin-operated machine) or some area where they can buy snacks whenever they feel like it.
- Laundry facilities. These should be located on the main living level, not in a basement.
- Mail delivery. Provide easy access to mail delivery areas. Large graphics on the housing units and mailboxes make it easy for residents to identify their units and mail slots.
- Elevators in any multistory project; you can get by without them in a two-story building. Elevators must be large enough for wheelchairs and must have slow-operating doors.
- Bathrooms. Most people want only one bathroom; the affluent elderly will want at least two. Separating the toilet area from the tub or shower is popular. Mirrors should start at the 40-inch level, and there should be a dressing table and basin that allow a seated person to use them. Showers are more popular than bathtubs.
- Entry doors that are recessed to give protection against the weather and to impart a sense of ownership (even in a high-rise project). Peepholes at two levels, one usable by a seated person, are appreciated. All entries must be well lit.

- Sufficient space. The median unit size is 600 to 650 square feet; the trend is toward a larger size. Typical unit sizes are as follows:
  –Efficiency units—Median is 415 square feet; the range is 325 to 450 square feet.
  –One-bedroom units—Median is 600 square feet; the range is 520 to 740 square feet.
  –Two-bedroom units—Median is 900 square feet; the range is 750 to 1,100 square feet.

The single-family residence is the most popular senior housing option. Duplexes sell and rent well and cluster housing, with buildings up to four units, is quite salable or rentable. The least-desired housing is multistory, especially high-rise.

Those projects that feature a healthcare facility generally have one of about 21,000 square feet; the size range is 13,000 to 30,000 square feet. It is typically a 60-bed center divided into a short-term stay area and a long-term care area.

Activity centers in congregate and lifecare facilities average 30,000 square feet; the range is 15,000 to 50,000 square feet. A space allocation of 125 feet per resident is a good rule of thumb.

Exteriors

Site sizes range from one to two acres for a small, in-town congregate project to hundreds or even thousands of acres for a retirement village or city. The median lot size for an in-city lifecare project is six acres; those located in rural areas have a median size of 29 acres.

Density varies widely. It ranges from 6.5 units per acre for rural projects to up to 50 units per acre for metropolitan developments. High-density projects are generally the most profitable. It is possible to design pleasant environments at 35 to 50 units per acre, but it can't be done without using a midrise or high-rise format.

Project size varies from 50 to 200 units; a 150-unit project is, perhaps, the most easily managed. Absorption time for successful projects ranges from 18 to 24 months. The rental or sale of four to six units per month is common.

The need for a lot of parking area decreases as the entry age of the residents rises. In congregate projects appealing to the 65+ plus segment, a parking ratio of one space for every three units is satisfactory. Most projects that have tried to reduce parking to one space for every four units have eventually run short of parking. Vehicle access to unit entries is quite important; covered access is desirable but not essential. All walkways leading to the parking area should be smooth surfaces without any steps.

Because many elderly are either on limited budgets or prefer to do other things with their time, it is wise to provide low-maintenance exteriors. Brick construction or stucco finishes are good; stained, rather than painted, exterior wood trim is excellent.

A small yard or access to a garden plot will help sell or rent the units. The cluster format lends itself well to small backyards.

Open areas that are accessible but still offer some measure of privacy are popular. Golf courses are overrated and overdone. Few elderly play golf, and those that do seldom play championship golf. Courses are valuable as open spaces and will be used for walking if paths are provided. In many cases, projects could succeed if the money scheduled to be spent on a golf course were put into the living units and improvement of the common areas. In a number of surveys on what the elderly really want, golf courses failed to rank among the ten most desired features. Indoor swimming pools usually rank ahead of golf courses and even they are well down on the list. A lot more people play cards, listen to music, dance and socialize than play golf.

When judging the overall desirability of a project, don't be taken in by the scope of the outdoor common areas. The best-designed common areas won't make up for a lack of adequate space or privacy in the living units.

The old are not a lot different from the young in their housing needs. Enough differences exist to justify developing projects especially for the elderly, but few plans will succeed if they are designed merely to serve the old.

Financing

It is much easier to design a good project than to finance one. Few lenders understand housing for the elderly. There is a lot of lender skepticism, and the underwriting standards are often conservative. It is not unusual to receive loan commitments that contain debt coverage ratios of from 1.25:1 to 1.5:1. A loan-to-value ratio of 50 to 70 percent is common. During real estate boom times, you might see LTVs of 80 percent. Due dates on conventional loans will be 10 to 15 years, with amortization based on 25 to 30 years.

Lenders want to be satisfied in three main areas: experience, liability and equity. Inexperienced sponsors can get loans, but it's a difficult task. Experience in building and operating senior housing projects counts very heavily. The developer's résumé will be carefully read and checked out. Sponsors without experience will have to show that they have used a qualified consultant, that they have a strong operating manager and that they can all work as a team.

Sources of Financing

Until recently, government funding was the main source of loans, but government activity in this area has declined. Both direct loan and indirect loan programs, such as tax-exempt bonds, are likely to continue to be scarce. The supply of conventional funds is adequate, but loan funds are not easy to get.

Entry fees as a financing source must be carefully handled to avoid their being declared current income by federal and state taxing agencies. Nonrefundable entry fees are particularly susceptible to IRS scrutiny. Today, most entry fees are either fully or partially refundable. When entry fees are fully refundable, they tend to be larger than the nonrefundable fee would have been. The issue of entry fees and how they should be handled is a matter for your tax counsel to advise you on. No tax advice is intended from the brief discussion in this chapter.

The issue of financing—at least individual unit financing—is often moot, because at least 50 percent of buyers will pay cash for their units.

Investor Checklist

Listed below are some critical issues you should investigate before investing in a senior housing project.

- *Marketing costs.* Are the reserves for marketing activity high enough? Initial marketing costs can be very high, and absorption frequently takes longer than estimated. The customers are difficult to reach and slow to make up their minds.

- *Operating reserves.* Are they sufficient to carry the project for at least 24 months?
- *The operating plan.* Is it adequate? Can the promises made to residents (especially in lifecare projects) be kept if turnover is lower than forecast? Is management experienced enough to react quickly to rising costs by increasing monthly fees so as to keep reserves adequate? Lengthening life spans have a way of putting tremendous strain on operating budgets.
- *Healthcare.* Is the facility promising too much? Continued huge increases in healthcare costs put the feasibility of providing such services in doubt.

Trends and Conclusions

Housing for the elderly, like all real estate product types, is continually evolving. The trends and forecast statements listed below summarize the major points from this chapter.

Competition

- The competition for residents will increase as an oversupply of senior housing is created in most major markets.
- Elderly consumers will become more selective and demanding as their numbers grow. Greater concern over the financial strength and operating experience of project sponsors will be one result.
- More adaptive-use senior housing will be created.
- Hospitals and nursing homes with excess land will be sought after as project sponsors.
- Universities and colleges will develop on-campus senior housing.

Government Involvement

- The amount of direct aid for senior housing will remain at a low level, but demands for more benefits will not diminish. This should lead to a relaxation of zoning laws and, possibly, tax incentives of all kinds designed to shift elderly care costs to the private sector. This trend will be evident long before 2030, when the senior population is expected to hit a high point.

- Senior housing will most likely be stimulated by friendly regulation, not by subsidy.
- Minimum size standards will be enacted for long-term care facilities. A 50-bed minimum is likely.
- Regulation of long-term care facilities will increase.
- New public policies will encourage later retirement.
- All levels of government will discover that the lifecare concept is more cost-effective than welfare, food stamps and huge housing subsidies.

Congregate and Lifecare

- A pay-as-you-receive system will completely replace remaining one-price systems.
- More projects will be built that do not provide any healthcare services.
- The lifecare concept will change to eliminate its insurance aspect. Specified amounts of eligibility will replace unlimited healthcare eligibility.
- The elderly will rely on long-term healthcare insurance.

Design and Location

- The manufactured-housing industry will benefit from an increase in the popularity of elder cottages.
- Superprojects (more than 15,000 residents) will decline in number.
- The best sites will continue to be in and around major metropolitan areas.
- Developers who ignore the principles of good design and solid market research will not survive the next five years.
- The apparent fascination with Sun Belt markets will be replaced by hometown development.

Deal Structures and Financing

- Joint ventures between medical providers, nonprofit entities and for-profit developers will occur more frequently.
- Conventional financing will be the chief source of development capital.

- The amount of equity required per project will remain high.
- More attention will be given to interior design elements and services. Expensive exterior amenities, like golf courses, will decline in popularity.

Market Size

- The market will expand gradually as the elderly population increases and as the facilities offered become more affordable and better suited to their needs.
- Lower construction costs, interest costs and operating expenses will eventually combine to create a miniboom in senior housing.

Management

- The demand for skilled on-site management will increase.
- The need for off-site asset managers will grow.

PART
III

Investment Value and Transaction Structure

CHAPTER
10
Determining Value

If you are convinced that a long and complicated analysis is the way to a profit, you can skip this chapter, because it is not about esoteric, highly sophisticated financial analysis programs. This chapter is about how to make a common-sense financial evaluation of an income-producing property that will result in the acquisition of a profitable long-term investment. Here you will discover how successful investors figure out what works.

This is not to suggest that sophisticated analysis techniques have no value; they are immensely valuable in the hands of someone who understands them and real estate as well. That, however, is not a commonly found combination. Fortunately, you don't have to have that combination of skills to succeed. In fact, it is possible that far more money has been made in real estate by people who scratch a few numbers on the back of an envelope to come up with a purchase price than has ever been made by the so-called "number crunchers."

When you buy an investment property, you are not buying a yield so much as you are buying the assumptions that are behind that yield. The numbers are important, but the facts behind those numbers are what make the investment work over time. If you have paid sufficient attention to examining the essential supply and demand factors of a proposed investment, you won't need to massage the numbers much.

For the cash buyer, there are two important return figures: current return and total return. Current return, which is also called cash flow, is net operating income (NOI), which is simply the difference between gross income and all expenses. Total return is the amount you earn after you add resale profit (or an assumed appreciation rate if you haven't yet sold the investment). One hopes the rate of appreciation is greater than the rate of inflation. The concept of total return leads to two analysis techniques that seek to measure it: the internal rate of return (IRR) and net present value (NPV). You need a basic understanding of both these techniques.

The result of an IRR calculation is an interest rate that equates the cost of the investment with the present value of future benefits. You are solving for an interest rate. For example, the IRR of the following would be 10 percent:

Initial investment:	$100
Annual return from all factors:	$ 10
Value at end of period:	$110

Few investors are relying upon IRR calculations today; current return is the target now. That emphasis is not misplaced. The higher the current return, the higher the IRR will be if income and expense are at least stable. In an IRR calculation, "early" money increases yield and "late" money decreases it.

NPV is the dollar difference between initial cost and the present value of future benefits at a selected interest rate.

In an NPV calculation, you stipulate the interest rate and solve for the difference in a dollar amount. If the NPV is a positive number, you have achieved a rate that is higher than your target return rate.

The leveraged buyer is concerned with one other return measure. If a property is financed, the current cash return is reduced by the amount of the loan payment. The percentage return on investment may be more or less than the current free and clear return depending upon the interest rate and amortization schedule in effect. Here is a comparative example:

Free and Clear	Item	Leveraged
$100,000	Property value	$100,000
$ 12,000	Net operating income	$ 12,000
None	Loan payment	$ 7,200
$ 12,000	Cash return	$ 4,800

If the investment was purchased with 10 percent down and loan payments at 8 percent interest-only terms, the investor is earning an annual cash-on-cash return of $4,800 on a $10,000 initial investment. If, however, the loan terms require a payment of $10,000 per year, the cash-on-cash return declines substantially.

The positive leverage illustrated here can be quickly reversed if income falls or expenses rise rapidly. For simplicity, the example ignores the effects of taxes and inflation, deflation or appreciation. In addition, taxes are ignored here because taxes do not create value, even though the after-tax return is occasionally enhanced by a temporary advantage created by some tax law. Positive tax effects are a bonus; often a fleeting one.

None of these return measures are of any value if your assumptions as to current or future income and expenses are wrong. Successful investors have a rigid approach to financial analysis. They verify all items of income and expense and compare each item to a guideline based upon their experience with the property being analyzed. Before they ever get to the financial analysis step, they have made an extensive investigation into the long-term prospects for the property based upon the economic and demographic trends they see.

Income is tested against comparable rents in the area and against the trends that could cause it to rise or fall over the expected holding period. Expenses are compared to operating averages for similar property based either on the investor's experience or on data published by such sources as the Building Owners and Managers Association (BOMA), the local apartment house association or the International Council of Shopping Centers, or by consulting with active property managers in the area. Expenses are also viewed against a background of research information on economic and demographic trends. Some guidelines for income and expense will be listed later in the chapter.

Capitalizing Net Income

Once both income and expense have been tested and adjusted, you will have some confidence that the NOI is likely to be valid for current and future conditions. Value is determined by capitalizing this NOI at a satisfactory rate of return. If the NOI is $100,000 (and there is no reason to believe it will decline) and the desired initial rate of return is 12 percent, the purchase price goal will be $833,333. A target purchase price range is then set; in this example, the range might be $800,000 to $850,000. The range is necessary to avoid too rigid an approach to the acquisition price, which might prevent you from successfully negotiating the acquisition.

It may seem simplistic, even anticlimactic, after all your supply/demand investigation, but that is all there is to it. About all a more sophisticated analysis can do is verify the worth of your decision (given the current return is high enough).

Income and Expense

The critical analysis element is a valid income and expense role, and it is not too difficult to establish this. Income is derived from space rent, either base or percentage, and revenue associated with that rent, such as income from parking, laundry rooms, storage or anything else related to occupancy.

Income is sometimes segregated, as in the case of retail property that generates both a base rent and a percentage or overage rent, and capitalized at different rates. This has some validity, because there is a "certainty" difference between receiving the contract, or base, rent and the percentage rent. Some investors feel that percentage income has less value, because it is speculative rent that is usually wiped out by increased competition in the area. If the contract rent is capitalized at 10 percent, they may cap the percentage rent at 25 percent—or they may give it no value at all, as is sometimes the case in neighborhood or strip retail.

It is important to know that the rents being represented are those actually being paid by the tenants as well as to verify that they compare to current rents being paid at other comparable properties. Again, you also need to make assumptions about the likelihood that these rents will rise or fall over your holding period. The usual holding period assumption is ten years, but you can set it at seven or less. It does no good to analyze too far into the future, because the assumptions won't hold up as the time gets extended. Your feasibility study uncovers rental data through three main sources:

1. A tenant offset statement
2. A comparable rent survey
3. An analysis of economic and demographic trends

Your financial analysis flows from and completes your feasibility study.

The two mistakes that have been made in the past relative to income analysis are:

1. failing to see a potential for rent increases; and
2. failing to see that rents are declining or are likely to decline, or that the rents being represented are inflated—i.e., not really market rents.

The first error may cause you to be less aggressive than you need to be to acquire the investment; the second will cause you to overpay.

The comparable rent survey, if done properly, will help you avoid mistake number one. There is no easy way to do this survey. It is face-to-face, door-to-door, hard, grinding work that takes a certain amount of skill to do well. If rent surveys ever become easy work (you discover some published data that is "just right"), you are on your way to making an error. The best surveys are the ones you do yourself.

There is room for the use of published data. Its proper role is to establish some rough guidelines. You should never bet your capital on it.

To make a good judgment on the adequacy and potential of the rent roll, you need to have both the rent being paid and the square footage of the space being rented. You also have to know if the lease is month-to-month or for a fixed term, and if there are any renewal options. A rent of $500 per month for an apartment may seem quite fair until you learn that it is a 1,000-square-foot unit and the average monthly rent per square foot in the area is 85 cents.

In all commercial property, the lease is the investment. This document contains provisions that govern virtually every element of income and expense. Therefore, it is necessary to read every lease—even if they are all on the same form. Your safest assumption is that no two leases are identical. Make a checklist that details all sources of income and expense as well as termination and renewal rights, plus the length of each lease. Your checklist must also include the size of the space rented. The lease will include the amount of any security deposit that, under certain circumstances, will have to be returned to the tenant when he or she successfully completes the lease.

Fundamental to any inquiry into current income is positive verification that the rents represented are actually being paid by the tenant and that they have not been increased by free rent or excessive landlord-provided tenant improvements or other concessions. There is often a substantial difference between effective rent and contract rent. Most prospective purchasers send inquiries to all the tenants asking them to verify the rent they pay and also asking them to set forth any unsatisfied claims they assert against the current owner. This inquiry, called an estoppel certificate, can contain questions regarding the amount of free rent received and the extent of tenant improvements provided. The tenant is required, under the terms of most leases, to answer such questions promptly.

Excessive free rent and above-standard tenant improvements have the effect of raising rent. Where such concessions have been used, the contract rent is not the same as the effective rent—and the tenant may not be willing to renew at the contract rent unless rents have risen during his or her lease term. If, for example, the contract rent is $100 per month for a one-year lease and the tenant was given one month of free rent, the effective rent is $1,100.00 ÷ 12 = $91.67 monthly. The effective rent is 8.33 percent less than the contract rent, and unless rents have risen 9.09 percent in a year, the tenant is not likely to renew at $100 a month. Ignoring the effective rent is how some buyers overpay. One of the easiest ways to uncover discrepancies between contract and effective rent is to have accurate data on current comparable rents. Some ideas on how to do a comparable rent survey are discussed in the section on apartment buildings in this chapter.

You can also overpay for a property if you base your purchase price on current effective rents and fail to consider what rents are likely to be when the leases renew. If lease rates have declined and are still heading downward, you will have to estimate the decline to avoid overpaying for the property. Failure to anticipate rent declines is what hurt many investors who bought bargain-priced office buildings two or three years ago. When you buy an investment property, you are betting your money on the quality of your assumptions. More will be said about income as we examine how expenses are evaluated. It is difficult, and often misleading, to separate income and expense and discuss one to the exclusion of the other.

Expense Guidelines

Each property type has its own expense array. An extensive choice of guidelines is available to help you determine what items of expense are common for the property type you are considering and how much each item should cost both as a percent of total expenses and by the square foot of rented space. Regardless of the guidelines available, however, the cost of operating each property (and the amount of income each will generate) will vary with age, condition, location and the management style of the owner.

Many investors have a "seat-of-the-pants" idea of what it costs to operate a property, and they use this perception to make a rough estimate of value during the early stage of a purchase investigation. Midrise office building investors, for example, may figure that operating expenses will be between $8 and $9 per square foot of leased space, so when they look at a property capable of producing $14 to $15 a square foot gross rent, they quickly see an NOI of between $6 and $7 a square foot. If their return target is 10 percent, they will try for a purchase price of $60 to $70 a square foot. This is a simplistic way of determining value, but it is quite useful as a screening device.

Apartment buyers do much the same thing. A B-grade unfurnished apartment investor may use 35 percent to 40 percent as the percent of adjusted gross income it takes to run a building. If a property has an adjusted gross of $50,000, they will see an NOI of $30,000 to $32,500 and a value of $300,000 to $389,000 if their return on investment target is 9 to 10 percent. Apartment buyers will also use other rough value estimators, such as price per unit, price per square foot and the gross rent multiplier.

Regardless of how you arrive at a preliminary idea of value, it is always important to examine every item of expense notwithstanding the nature of the lease. Even in a triple-net investment, the owner is ultimately responsible for all operating expenses and will pay them all if he has no tenants for a while. This may seem an obvious point, but many investors have gone into triple-net investments without an adequate investigation of the expenses, only to be jolted out of their reverie when the tenant defaults.

An investor should "pay himself first" when considering a property. If you need a 10 percent return, then only 90 percent of the income stream is left to pay the lenders and the vendors. It looks like this:

Gross income	100%
Vacancy and collection losses	15%
Adjusted gross	85%
All expenses	40%
Net operating income (NOI)	45%
Available for debt service	40%

Your return doesn't come first in the real world. You get what's left over. Your only protection against being forced to live on inadequate financial scraps is the kind of job you do analyzing the supply/demand elements and the work you do to make sure that the investment is not doomed by too little NOI and/or too much debt service. While fanciness may not be necessary, thoroughness and accuracy at this stage of your investment investigation are the key to long-term investment health.

Apartment Buildings

The major items of income and expense were reviewed in Chapter 1. At the time a purchase is being considered, the income stream must be closely examined to determine three things:

1. Is the rent roll accurate?
2. Is it in line with current market conditions?
3. Will the rent roll increase or decrease over the expected holding period (usually seven to ten years)?

Direct verification will usually answer the first question and, if done correctly, uncover any concessions. A comparable rent survey will reveal the answer to question two if the properties surveyed are truly comparable and if the survey is accurate and current. The usefulness of a comparable rent review begins with an accurate representation of the rents being

Table 10.1 Subject Property Rent Roll

Type of Unit	Number of Units	Monthly Rent	Size of Unit in Square Feet	Rent per Square Foot	Vacancy
Bachelor/ Studio	4	$450	500	$.90	0
One-bedroom	12	$550	625	$.88	1
Two-bedroom	8	$675	910	$.74	1
Totals	24				2

earned at the subject property. Such a presentation might look like Table 10.1.

To simplify the example, information such as tenant name, type of lease and furnished or unfurnished (assume an unfurnished building) has been omitted so we can focus on the rent dollars being paid.

Once you have established the correct rents for the property under consideration, you need to compare it to at least four similar properties in the market area. Table 10.2 shows how such a survey might look. It doesn't matter how big or how small the project is, this method of displaying comparables will work. All you need to do, when the survey has been completed, is to compare the current "comps" to the subject property and interpret the results.

Can these rents be sustained over time, or will they improve or decline? Presumably, the answer to the last question is satisfactory or you wouldn't have come this far in the acquisition process. If a decline in rents is expected, the price you pay should reflect the increased risk created by this uncertainty. But timing problems can occur. When, for example, you are trying to buy near the bottom of a cycle, the question becomes one of making an informed judgment. If you decide to wait until the market "bottoms out," you may find that the property you want will have been bought by someone else.

Table 10.2   Comparable Properties Rent Roll

Item	Property 1: 28 Units	Property 2: 22 Units	Property 3: 24 Units	Property 4: 20 Units	Average
Bachelors/Studios	6	2	4	None	3
Rent	$ 425	$350	$450		$408
Square feet	520	480	510		503
Rent per foot	$.81	$.73	$.88		$.80
Vacancies	1	0	2		1
One-bedroom	12	10	10	12	11
Rent	$530	$520	$530	$485	$516
Square feet	625	650	630	610	629
Rent per foot	$.85	$.80	$.84	$.80	$.82
Vacancies	2	0	1	1	1
Two-bedroom	10	10	10	8	9.5
Rent	$650	$650	$630	$610	$635
Square feet	875	890	870	915	888
Rent per foot	$ .76	$.71	$.76	$.74	$.74
Vacancies	0	1	1	1	.75

Office Buildings

An outline of office building income and expense items was presented in
Chapter 2. Office income differs from apartment income in that office
leases may be either gross or net. A gross lease means that the tenant pays
the agreed rent each month and nothing more—i.e., all expenses are paid
by the landlord and are included in the contract rent. If the lease is net,
the tenant pays his or her base rent and pro rata share of all expenses,
which are usually estimated, divided into a monthly sum and paid in
advance with the rent. The operating expenses are referred to as common-
area maintenance charges, or CAM. A pure net lease means the tenant
pays all expenses (except marketing costs); this arrangement is often
called a triple-net (NNN). Net leases can, of course, embrace any division

of expense between landlord and tenant. In some cases, the tenant pays certain expenses and the landlord pays others. Determining who has the responsibility for paying operating expenses is an excellent reason to read all leases carefully.

Gross lease may be modified to stipulate that the tenant is responsible for paying the taxes and insurance while the landlord pays all other expenses.

When the tenant pays expenses in addition to his or her base rent, some analysts include these obligations in gross income and then "net them out" by listing each individual expense in the operating expense list.

Before you close the books on your verification of income, it is essential that you audit the square footage leased or vacant. This is a necessary step for all types of property. At the very least, all rented and vacant space should add up to the leasable area of the property. Countless errors are made in measuring space, and unfortunately, many of these errors expand the size of the building. There is no way you can have a high degree of confidence in your income assumption until you know exactly how much space each tenant has and how much each is paying for. The BOMA standard is normally used to measure office space.

There are at least four good sources of expense guideline information that will help you to compare the expenses being represented to the experiences of other operators.

1. The Society of Industrial and Office REALTORS® (SIOR)
2. The Building Owners and Managers Association (BOMA)
3. The Institute of Real Estate Management (IREM)
4. The National Association of Office and Industrial Parks

You will need to temper this data with your own experience in the local market and also test it against the experience of other local owners by discussing expense levels with them or by checking with some reliable property management companies.

Both BOMA's and IREM's list of income and expense items vary somewhat from the generic list provided in Chapter 2. BOMA's income and expense array for downtown buildings looks like this:

Income
  Office area
  Retail area

    Other areas
        Total Rent
    Miscellaneous income
        Total Income
Expense
    Cleaning
    Repairs and maintenance
    All utilities
    Roads/Grounds/Security
    Administrative
        Total Operating Expenses
    Fixed expenses
        Total Fixed Operating Expenses
    Leasing expense
    Total payroll
    Total contract expense (cleaning, repair/maintenance, etc.)

You will find BOMA's data in the publication *BOMA Experience Exchange Report,* which is published yearly.
   IREM's chart of income and expense looks like this:

Income
    Gross spendable income
    Less: Vacancies and delinquent rent
        Total Rent
Expenses
    All utilities
    Janitorial payroll/contract
    Maintenance and repair
    Management fee
    Administrative payroll
    Insurance
        Net Operating Costs
    Real estate taxes
        Total Operating Costs

This data is published annually by the National Association of REALTORS® Institute of Real Estate Management in a report called "Income/Expense Analysis: Office Buildings, Downtown & Suburban."

Both these sources and the SIOR divide their data by area, city, building type and size, which makes the data quite useful to investors. If the property contains some retail space, you will be able to get good guideline data from the International Council of Shopping Centers, which publishes an annual "Operating Cost Analysis Report."

Industrial Buildings

The Society of Industrial and Office REALTORS® and the Urban Land Institute (ULI) are sources of income and expense guideline data. Local REALTORS® and property management firms, plus your own experience and investigation, are the best sources of local data.

Industrial, like offices and retail, may be rented on a gross or net basis. Just as in the case of office buildings, some owners treat CAM charges as "other income," and then detail the expenses to net them out of the operating budget. Regardless of how they are handled, from an analytical standpoint, meticulous records must be maintained that will survive any tenant challenges; such challenges become more numerous when economic activity slows down. It is normally easy to determine the revenue being received from CAM charges and to verify the associated expenses, because this data is often kept in computer files to make it easier to calculate and to bill.

Just as is the case for office property, you must carefully verify the amount of gross and net leasable square footage in the project or building. It is essential that a comparison be made between your measurements and the total leased space per the lease agreements (plus any vacancies). Often the net rentable area of an industrial building is calculated differently from how BOMA suggests it be done for office space. Quite often industrial space is measured from outside wall to outside wall, and all enclosed space (such as covered entryways) is commonly included in leasable area. It is important that the leases follow established practices in your area and that they be consistent in this regard.

A comparable rent survey must be done to validate the current rent roll and a comparable sales survey should be assembled to help establish current price per square foot and the current cap rate. The comparable sales survey is only included to save time and avoid repetition, but it is needed for all property types. Table 10.3 is an example of a comparable sales survey. The data will be most reliable if you gather it yourself from

Table 10.3   Comparable Sales Survey

Item	

Item	No. 1	No. 2	No. 3	No. 4	Averages	Subject
	\multicolumn{6}{Properties and Addresses}
Price (in 000s)	$1,980	$2,100	$1,910	$2,000	$1,998	$1,975
Lot size*	110,000	100,000	108,000	100,000	104,500	107,000
Building size	50,000	50,000	50,000	50,000	50,000	50,000
Price*	$39.60	$42.00	$38.20	$40.00	$39.95	$39.50
Date of sale	8/93	2/93	2/93	6/93		10/93

*In square feet

the public records and from interviews with the buyers and sellers who were involved in each transaction. Professional organizations in some marketing areas gather this data and sell it to interested parties. If you use such data, it should be confirmed.

The problem of true comparability haunts all such sales surveys regardless of the property type. In spite of the difficulty of assembling a sufficient number of current and truly comparable sales, such surveys are almost universally used and have a great usefulness to investors. To be useful, the comparable properties must be in similar locations, of the same construction and age, have equal amenities and be on similar lot sizes. Properties that are not exactly similar may be used as comps, but it is then necessary to introduce adjustments to equalize the differences; these adjustments tend to weaken the value of the comparison.

A comparable sales survey may fully justify the proposed purchase price (as in Table 10.3) and still not justify the purchase. Even though all the other recent purchases were similar or virtually identical, all that may be happening is that investors, like lemmings, may be following one another to disaster. Just a few years ago, when the signs of overbuilding and weakening demand were all around us, carefully crafted financial analyses consistently supported a decision to buy. What has been said earlier bears further emphasis: *It is not the numbers but the assumptions behind the numbers that are important.*

A simplified income and expense array appears below.

Gross Scheduled Income
   Less: Vacancy and Collection Loss
      Adjusted Gross Income

Expenses
   All Operating Expense
   Other Expense
      Total Expense
      Net Operating Income

Operating expense consists of the usual items of management, repairs and maintenance, and any utilities or other expenses that the owner is responsible for. Other expense consists of taxes and insurance if the owner is responsible for them.

Value is determined by capitalizing the net income at the rate of return you are seeking to earn. This estimate of value is compared to the prices revealed in your comparable sales analysis. Investors need avoid adjusting their "hurdle" or minimum acceptable return rate to match market conditions lest they fall victim to the "greater fool" method of establishing price. It is presumed that the return you seek to earn is realistic given current and expected future conditions. Sometimes your opinion of value simply will not match the market, and you will have to refrain from investing because prices are just too high. During a down market, you may find that you are perfectly willing to buy at a price that will provide you a fair long-term return and you appear to be alone in the market. This is especially true near the bottom of a declining market, and it takes a good deal of faith in your research and judgment to take advantage of such times.

You may also find during a down market that many investments are available at less than the cost of reproducing them at current land and construction costs. Such information is interesting but of little value unless you expect a period of sharply increased demand.

Retail

Retail has the most varied revenue sources. In addition, operating expenses can vary from other types of property, because they will often include marketing costs to increase customer traffic. One of the best sources of income and expense guideline data is the International Council of Shopping Centers (ICSC), which publishes data by region and by the type and size of the center. The Urban Land Institute (ULI) also publishes valuable information in a publication called *Dollars and Cents of Shop-*

ping Centers. Revenue and expense items are shown in dollars per square foot and as a percentage of total revenue for each type of retail.

The most complete income menu is that for a regional center; in simplified form it looks like this:

Income
    Rental income from base rent
    Rental income from percentage rents
       Total Rental Income
    Common-area maintenance income
    Insurance reimbursement
    CPI and other escalation income
    Property tax charges
    Charges for roof and structure repairs
    Income from utility sales
    Tenant association charges
    Miscellaneous income
       Total Income

Not all income and expense statements will contain every item listed above, but the list is complete enough to cover most of them, including those few centers with quadruple-net leases (requiring tenants to pay a pro rata share of roof and structural maintenance expenses).

The list of expenses looks like this:

Expenses
    Building maintenance
    Maintenance of common areas and parking lot
    Utility costs (includes central utilities)
    Advertising and promotion
    Real estate taxes
    Insurance
    Management fee
    Leasing fees
       Total Operating Expense
       Net Operating Income

These items of income and expense cover all regional centers and many community and power centers. Neighborhood centers, strip commercial and some freestanding properties may have a simpler list quite similar to the generic list used for apartment buildings.

An accurate accounting of expenses is always necessary to maximize cash flow. Accuracy is especially important in retail wherever CAM and other chargebacks are in effect. Errors have been so common in CAM charges that a new business has emerged just to make sure that these charges are accurate and based upon the lease provisions that authorize them.

Conclusion

Many intricate methods exist for analyzing an income property, and many of them are useful to the sophisticated investor. In spite of all the hardware, software and brainpower applied, poor investments are made every day. You won't be among those who acquire an unsatisfactory property if you spend more time investigating the basic supply and demand drivers and concentrate on current return. Establishing a reliable net operating income and capitalizing it at a rate that compensates you for the expected risk should ensure a reasonable chance of success. The keys to investment success will always be to look at the right things and to keep it simple.

C H A P T E R
11

Real Estate Finance
in the 1990s

The river of capital that runs through real estate does not flow without numerous twists and turns. Change is the norm; it must be expected and planned for. Unfortunately, most investors give in to the all-too-human tendency to believe that whatever conditions prevail today will last almost forever—or at least until they have made a killing and moved on.

The euphoria generated by the relatively easy-money periods of the 1970s and 1980s had to diminish. Change was inevitable, if for no other reason (and there were many other reasons) than such huge amounts of capital will always cause a surplus to be created. Builders define demand by the availability of debt and equity money, not by effective demand; hence the market has a structural bias toward surplus. Nonspeculative investors, either equity or debt, need to concern themselves with this bias and pay much more attention to the fundamentals of supply and demand. You can't make a long-term profit if you let yourself be swept along in the supercharged atmosphere of easy money.

It is not impossible to forecast when supply will overwhelm demand. When such conditions threaten, long-term investors must restrict investing and start their sales program before the situation gets critical.

Figure 11.1   Real Estate Finance: A Recent History

The 1970s

- Savings and loans (S&Ls) specialized in home mortgage lending.
- Commercial banks made construction loans and some permanent loans.
- Bank loans, and most other short-term real estate loans, were contingent upon the borrower getting a permanent loan from some other source, such as an insurance company.
- Concerns over the supply of funds and the level of interest rates were the most important factors in the loan market.
- Foreign investors were present in the market but not in overwhelming numbers.
- Inflation was high and capital was generally plentiful.

The 1980s

- S&Ls were deregulated and became active in commercial real estate lending and development.
- Banks became more aggressive lenders.
- Insurance companies expanded their activity in both the debt and equity markets.
- Foreign investors were four times more active in the equity and debt markets than in the 1970s.
- Many lenders made short-term construction loans without being covered by a long-term take-out commitment.
- Radical tax law changes were enacted in 1986.
- Pension funds, both domestic and foreign, increased equity and debt participation.
- Bullet loans were used frequently.

The 1990s

- Full extent of the S&L scandal became apparent.
- Regulatory vigilance increased.
- A net outflow of capital occurred. The amount of real estate mortgage debt decreased.
- New, tougher underwriting standards were adopted.
- Construction activity declined by 50 percent, often more, in most markets.
- Real estate prices began to soften.

Similarly, it is relatively easy to see when supply is lagging and demand is building so that investments can be made near the beginning of the cycle. In spite of our ability to predict supply and demand trends, no investor can completely avoid experiencing some of the negative effects of an overbuilt market; but those who build portfolios on the basis of supply and demand, rather than on the availability of capital, will always do better than those who "go with the flow."

It is tempting to forget the past, ignore the present and look ahead to the bright new world of the 21st century, but that would be a mistake—and those who make it will not only likely be wrong about what they see for the future, they will also be paralyzed into inaction and thus miss the opportunities presented by the evolving market.

This chapter is about real estate finance in the nineties; where it has been, where it is and where it is going. Market conditions will change; they have already changed from when this was written. Nevertheless, an examination of the current condition and recent history of the real estate finance market has immense dollar value. It helps to form insights that will lead to a successful investment philosophy. Figure 11.1 is a condensed recent history of the real estate finance market.

In part one of the chapter, you will find a description of the situation that existed in mid-1992 in the investment real estate market. Part two covers the major factors that have combined to create current conditions. Part three focuses on where the market is heading; we examine the "credit crunch" of the early nineties and list the alternative loan sources that were available. This section also contains a list of who the "new" lending players are likely to be for the rest of this decade. Part four lists the trends and a synopsis of conclusions.

The Current Situation

There has been a shortage of loan dollars in the midst of plenty. Commercial banks and many savings and loans, according to their managers, are sitting on a mountain of money, but they are not anxious to commit much of it to commercial real estate loans. Some observers, including the National Association of REALTORS® (NAR), have noted a serious real estate credit crunch and claim that it is widespread. Others, however, say that the restricted availability of real estate credit is by no means nation-wide; some regions, like the Northeast, have been more seriously affected than others. The truth seems to be that the crisis in real estate finance is not due to a shortage of loan funds but is one of confidence, on the part of both lenders and buyers, in the integrity of investment real estate in a severely overbuilt market.

Construction lending is at a virtual standstill, having dropped, in most regions, more than 50 percent in the past two years. It is just about impossible to find a construction loan for any type of speculative real estate project today. Rollover financing, which is needed to refinance the aptly named "bullet" loans taken out three, five or seven years previously, is extremely difficult to secure. The NAR has reported that 80 percent of those looking for such refinancing are having great trouble finding it. Insurance companies hold billions of dollars worth of these loans. The Travellers, which had $400 million of them come due in 1990, had to deal with $1.4 billion in 1991. The rollover financing difficulty is caused, in part, by the fact that when the lender has the property appraised, it quite often will not support a loan as large as the one made three to seven years before. In many cases it is turning into a showdown at the lender's corral, with the lender being told "Refinance it or take it back"—a Hobson's choice that is both slowing down the process and increasing the bor-rower's costs in almost all bullet loan refinancing. Reappraisal is but one problem for borrowers; the others are higher equity requirements, no credit lines, tighter loan draw requirements and no rolling maturities. All underwriting standards have been tightened, and far more attention is being paid to the borrower's credit history today.

In addition, a realignment of the "players" has occurred; this has complicated the process of searching for a loan in most areas, and in some areas (where the S&Ls dominated the loan market) it has created a situation that can only be described as desperate. The S&Ls are finished as commercial lenders, and the banks are hesitant to fill the gap left by their departure. Banks hold about $365 billion in commercial real estate loans, many of which are troubled, according to newly-vigilant regulators, and they do not seem overly anxious to go for $400 billion at this time. Although the banks are positioned to take a larger and larger share of the commercial real estate loan market, it will be a growing share of a smaller market.

Table 11.1 Commercial Property Loan Sources: 1989–1992 (all properties)

Lender	Fall 1989	Fall 1990	Summer 1991	Spring 1992
Pension funds	1%	1%	3%	2%
Insurance companies	8	14	11	7
Savings & loans	20	18	10	13
Industrial revenue bonds	1	1	<1	2
Commercial banks	31	36	29	37
Syndication	1	<1	1	1
Private investor	3	3	6	<1
Seller	29	22	34	28
Assumption	6	5	6	4

Source: National Association of REALTORS®, *Financing Investment Real Estate* (Washington, D.C., 1989–1992).

How have the sources for commercial real estate loans changed during this period of tight money? The NAR follows the loan market rather closely and publishes its findings two to three times yearly in a study titled *Financing Investment Real Estate*. All data come from closed transactions that occurred during the period of the study. An examination of the data from their 1989 through 1992 reports (see Table 11.1) shows how the lending sources have changed and how they varied from year to year during a lending crisis.

The current financing shortage had not fully developed in 1989, so it can serve as a base year for evaluating the changes that have occurred.

Since early 1989, borrowers have reported that all aspects of commercial real estate borrowing are tougher to deal with. The NAR has provided data that show the trends in debt-coverage ratios, loan-to-value ratios, interest rates and loan length. Table 11.2 shows what has happened in the past two years.

If the NAR data is correct, and we have no reason to doubt it, the changes between 1989 and 1992 are not as dramatic as the press coverage about the credit shortage might lead us to expect. In fact, it would not be unfair to say that the data are somewhat suggestive of a surplus credit condition. It appears that the credit crunch has a huge nonprice element to it.

Table 11.2   Debt-Coverage Ratios, Loan-to-Value Ratios, Loan Terms: Spring 1991 and Spring 1992 (all figures are mean)

Item ↓	Property Type									
	All Properties		Retail		Office		Industrial		Apartment	
Year →	'91	'92	'91	'92	'91	'92	'91	'92	'91	'92
DCR	1.29	1.30	1.24	1.37	1.35	1.28	1.20	1.35	1.19	1.24
LTV %	73.5	73.6	73.4	71.9	70.8	76.3	74.2	71.2	76.3	75.6
Loan Term (Years)	20	19	23	19	21	20	21	19	23	23

Source: National Association of REALTORS®, *Financing Investment Real Estate Survey,* (Washington, D.C., Spring 1991 and 1992).

The area of greatest change is in the loan-to-value ratios (LTV). All are down. Office buildings have declined by 300 basis points, while industrial has fallen by 500 points. It takes a lot more equity to close a deal today.

Debt-coverage ratios (DCR) are up for offices but have dropped in three out of the four regions NAR surveyed. Industrial property, which has been widely reported as faring the best during this recession, has actually done the worst in the loan markets, according to the NAR surveys.

Those who are interested in the direction the loan market is taking will find Table 11.3 of some interest. In this table you can see the changes that have been occurring by type of loan. The wraparound loan referred to is also called an all-inclusive loan in some parts of the country; "participating" means a loan that has any type of income participation by the lender. A comparison of 1989 and 1992 shows few radical changes in the type of loan made.

The Real Estate Finance Crisis

"Credit crunch" is a catchy phrase with wide popular appeal, and it was quickly adopted to describe the early 1990s situation in real estate finance. The term, however, is a generalized, broad-brush description of a fairly complex situation and, as such, is really of limited usefulness in understanding the financing problems of commercial real estate. The credit

Table 11.3   Types of Loans Made, All Lenders: 1989–1992

Loan Type	1989	1990	1991	1992
Fixed-rate	66%	69%	75%	65%
Adjustable-rate	34%	31%	25%	28%
Wraparound	5%	5%	10%	3%
Balloon payment	43%	31%	69%	34%
Equity participation	3%	2%	10%	3%

Source: National Association of REALTORS®, *Financing Investment Real Estate,* Spring, Summer and Fall ed., 1989–1992 (Washington, D.C.).

crunch has been characterized by a deep fear of lending, even to credit-worthy borrowers, by all classes of lenders. It has not been limited to real estate lending. Stories have been heard about businessmen who have never missed a principal or interest payment on any loan being refused normal operating credit. Other stories, which interest us more, are told of the great difficulty many people are having trying to find real estate loans.

It makes little sense to sit on the sidelines and decry the poor conditions that exist; all that does is freeze you out of the market. It is a time of change, and all times of change are times to make money—if you know how. One of the most useful lessons that can be learned from the ups and downs of the real estate finance market is that there is opportunity for profit in the midst of adversity. Tight money is a signal for buying and selling activity for many investors. These are the buyers and sellers who know that real estate has a cycle of from seven to ten years between its peaks and valleys. They buy near the beginning of the upward curve of the cycle and sell before the down trend is apparent to most investors.

Opportunity is plentiful for the contrarian investor during a financial crisis, because traditional loan sources dry up, transaction volume falls and prices decline. The market is not dead; there are always sellers who have to sell during such times because of death, divorce, bankruptcy and countless other reasons. Such sellers have to consider carrying the financing in order to facilitate any transaction (unless they can find the fabled all-cash buyer). Buyers are then the recipients of both favorable terms and lowered prices. Table 11.1 shows how seller-carried financing has increased since 1989.

Even though there is activity during a financing crisis, transaction volume declines, because some sellers simply do not offer their property for sale during a depressed market. They, too, know that real estate follows a cycle, and they try to "wait the market out." Such sellers are refusing to recognize a loss (or a lower profit than they want) by refusing to sell. This ostrich-like technique leads buyers to circulate the idea that no good buys are available. That, of course, is seldom true.

The gap between what buyers will pay and what sellers want widens. This gap is now between 10 and 15 percent. The closer it gets to ten percent, the more numerous possible deals become. Astute buyers are constantly testing the market looking for a narrowing of the price expectancy gap created by a tight money market.

The closer one examines a real estate credit shortage, the more one realizes that the facts are often quite different from the impression created by the daily papers or real estate periodicals. In the current situation, one might ask, "Would there have been a shortage of real estate credit even if no general credit crunch had developed?" The answer is yes.

Indeed, anyone who knows the true state of the imbalance between supply and demand for most types of investment real estate (and that must surely include all of us by now) would have to wonder why it should be otherwise. When the supply of a product increases beyond the level that buyers are willing to absorb, the price falls. That is not a new phenomenon; it is a fundamental economic law.

There is always lots of time to profit from a supply/demand imbalance. A surplus condition does not occur overnight; it often takes years to develop—just as a return to a more balanced relationship between supply and demand can take years. In many communities there is a nine- or ten-year supply of office space (in one small city there is a 69-year supply), and there are serious oversupplies of many other types of real estate in every region of the country. When this was recognized by the market, prices began to decline. Add to this a lender group that has been badly mauled by the underwriting errors made during the 1980s and it is not surprising that loans are hard to come by for some product types.

The production of speculative real estate is a "gut-level" business that has generally been guided by only one fundamental law: if financing is available, it gets built. Lenders, according to many observers, are the driving force behind supply. Put another way, the supply of speculative real estate is credit-driven and is not a result of some exhaustive study of supply and demand factors. As one financier put it, "I have never seen a negative feasibility report." Even in June of 1992, after it was clear to all that there was an oversupply in virtually every geographic area and product type, developers were still out beating the bushes looking for loans to develop more real estate. A University of California survey at that time showed that 84 percent of the national developers were looking for lenders to finance new projects.

When the availability of real estate credit is severely limited, the moans and groans heard in the market are led by those who want dollars to create more product or want money to sustain the surplus projects already built. These wails of distress are calls to investment action for the contrarian investor.

This does not mean that there are not real problems in the real estate finance marketplace today. But one man's problem is another man's opportunity—and the scarcity of rollover financing is such an opportunity. The difficulty in finding construction loans for speculative projects is another. Similarly, the shortage of loans for existing real estate in the $10 million-and-up category paralyzes that market while creating opportunities for those who have cash and who understand the future of commercial real estate.

The shortage of real estate credit will not last forever, but conditions have a way of reappearing, so it is useful to look at how the current environment evolved. The reasons for the real estate credit restraint that developed in the early nineties were as follows:

- The deregulation of the S&Ls in the early 1980s, which led, in part, to the oversupply of the nineties and massive failures of these institutions.
- The Tax Reform Act of 1986, which removed many artificial stimulants to the value of investment real estate.
- The reregulation of the S&Ls in 1989, which removed them as important players in the commercial real estate market.
- Overly aggressive regulations and auditing procedures in the wake of the S&L failures and the uncovering of many bank problems.
- Lender fear based on massive losses.
- Lack of lender profits.

The Future of Real Estate Finance

The future looks bright. Real estate lending is the most profitable activity in which a bank or any other lender can engage, and they will not stay out of it one day longer than they absolutely have to. The near future will see an adequate supply of credit for all real estate financing needs that are based on real, effective demand and that show a normal relationship between net operating income (NOI) and price. The suppliers of that credit may realign, but there will be plenty of them and they will have all the money needed for projects that make economic sense. The prospect of easier money in the near future means that transactions will be easier to make and profits will be realized from acquisitions made during the depressed period.

The relationship between NOI and price got out of balance in the 1980s. In the sixties and seventies the common capitalization rate was between 9 percent and 10 percent, and it changed very little over time. During the 1980s, capitalization rates for some types of quality property fell below 7 percent. This decline influenced the cap rate for second-tier properties, and real estate became generally overpriced even as the oversupply grew larger. As we suggested earlier, there is a huge backlog of buying power. Many buyers are sitting on the sidelines waiting for the sellers' perception of value to change. Once the sellers have come to a new understanding of the current value of their properties, a good deal of buying activity will occur, and there will be plenty of loan dollars to finance it.

Even in all the confusion that exists today, the future of real estate finance seems clear. A realignment of the credit suppliers is underway. As of today, the lending lineup looks like this:

- Commercial banks
- Sellers and private investors
- Loan assumptions
- Insurance companies and pension funds
- Savings and loans
- Syndication and industrial revenue bonds

By mid-decade, the lineup could look like this (listed in descending order by percent of total volume):

- Commercial banks

- Insurance companies
- Savings and loans
- Sellers
- Loan assumptions
- Private investors
- Pension funds
- Syndicators (includes securitization)

Savings and loans will continue to be a significant factor in small multi-family loans, while commercial banks will increase their share of virtually every type of real estate loan. Sellers will absorb 15–18 percent of total loan demand and will expand their role when credit shortages develop.

The current loan shortage and lender realignment will be resolved gradually as market surpluses begin to decline. It will not be necessary to achieve a perfect balance between supply and demand before the supply of loan funds for real estate increases. When a normal loan market reappears, it will not look that much different from the one that existed before the current crisis. The biggest difference will be the disappearance of the S&L as a significant force in the commercial real estate market. It is not beyond the realm of possibility, however, that when the S&Ls regain their financial health, and after some years of conservative and profitable residential real estate lending, we see them ask for (and probably get) the ability to make nonresidential loans again.

Trends and Conclusions

The major trends and conclusions covered in this chapter are shown below. They are divided into three main categories.

The Credit Crunch

- The oversupply condition in most property types has led to an undersupply of real estate credit.
- Rollover financing, construction lending and real estate loans in excess of $10 million have been the most seriously affected by the current credit shortage.
- Interest rates for commercial properties will decline but remain high relative to other assets so long as risk and loan demand remain high.

- The need to make a profit will prime the lending pump.
- The surplus property supply condition will not have to be fully dissipated before lending starts.

The Future of Real Estate Finance

- Commercial banks will be the largest investment real estate lenders in the 1990s.
- Seller-carried financing and loan assumptions will constitute a larger share of the real estate loan market for the next 18 to 24 months.
- Interest in securitization will increase, but it is not likely to be a big factor in commercial real estate finance due to a lack of standardized documentation.
- Syndication is likely to play a minor financing role in the next decade.
- Pension funds will make more of their loans directly, using their advisers, and will reduce the amount of capital they put in the life companies' guaranteed investment contracts.
- Internationalization of real estate finance will be complete during the first half of the 1990s. Foreign lenders will continue to play a role in the U.S. market.
- Corporate sale-leaseback activity will increase.
- Joint venture activity will also increase.
- Participation loans will grow in popularity.
- Savings and loans will not be commercial real estate lenders during the 1990s.
- Merchant building and build-to-suit activity will increase.
- A shortage of first-tier properties ensures that lender competition for their financing will continue. This does not mean that such properties are immune from price declines.
- More personal liability on real estate loans is a virtual certainty.
- Large, multiuse projects will be in lender favor during the 1990s.
- Small to midsize developers will continue to have difficulty attracting financing.
- "Creative lending" is dead; high-security lending lives.

Influences on Investment Values

- It is unlikely that significant federal tax relief will be enacted.

- Supply will grow more slowly as new construction continues to be depressed in the near term. Persistent surplus of office space, hotels and, in some markets, retail will accelerate the razing of many older properties. Additions to supply should also be restricted by a decline in the number of real estate developers.
- Capitalization rates will return to their historical norms of 9–10 percent for most investment property types.
- The budget deficit is more likely to rise than to fall. Interest rates will tend to be higher, rather than lower, in the long term.
- Tight money for the development of new projects is likely to continue well into the nineties.
- High equity requirements will also persist well into the 1990s.
- The renter's market will continue for all property types except multifamily housing.
- Yields on office buildings are likely to remain low well into this decade.
- Investment demand from real estate investment trusts and from wealthy individuals will increase.

C H A P T E R
12

The Environment and Investment Values

Nothing in our recent national experience, except perhaps the 1991 Gulf War, has captured the attention of the American public as much as the environmental movement. As we will see, it has been an expensive obsession.

Until the late 1970s, real estate had been traded for thousands of years with little concern for environmental conditions. Not anymore. Factors that were once obscure considerations have become of overriding importance.

Environmental issues have changed the way real estate is bought, sold, exchanged, leased or loaned upon. They have added what some think are staggering costs to the development, ownership and operation of all property. It is a strongly American phenomenon. No country in the world has accepted the economic burden of environmental protection assumed by the United States, even though activists in this country often state otherwise. Annual environmental protection costs are now at least $150 billion, and there is no doubt this number will increase.

Despite the massive costs involved, it is almost impossible to generalize about the effect they have on value. You can't get too specific, either, because concrete examples are usually dismissed by labeling them anecdotal. Further, environmental costs have so completely pervaded our economy that it is now difficult to separate them for study as an isolated factor.

As daunting a task as estimating the costs and their impact on investment values may be, that is exactly what we have attempted here. Our efforts have resulted in some measure of the financial impact of this social issue.

This chapter has six main sections. You are reading section one. In section two there is a brief review of the important legislation and legal decisions that have given the environmental movement its impetus. In part three you will find the cost of compliance and the effect this burden has on property value. This is followed by an examination of the audit or assessment process and the factors to consider in choosing an environmental consultant. The chapter ends with a look at how the principals in a real estate transaction are affected by environmental considerations and, finally, a trends and conclusions summary.

The Legal Foundation

The environmental movement is solidly grounded in American life. The movement has at least three deep piers under its foundation:

1. It has strong political support. Some reports have held that as many as 85 percent of voters strongly support environmentalism.
2. There is a large body of federal and state law behind the movement.
3. There are some court cases that give considerable additional support.

Legislatively, the movement can trace its ancestry at least to 1969, when the Environmental Policy Act was passed. This law required the administration to submit an annual report on the state of the environment. With that cornerstone, an entire bureaucracy was built.

In 1970 the Environmental Protection Agency (EPA) was born and the Clean Air Act was passed. The Comprehensive Environmental Response, Compensation and Liability Act (the Superfund Law, also known as CERCLA) was enacted in 1980, leading to the emergence of the environmental movement as we know it today. This was followed in 1986 by the

Superfund Amendments and Reauthorization Act (SARA). Other landmark laws were quick to appear.

Even before SARA, Congress passed the Resource Conservation and Recovery Act (RCRA) in 1984, which set up the procedure for tracking hazardous waste from its cradle to its grave. It also dealt with landfills and underground storage tanks. The EPA's recent regulations for the 6,000+ landfills nationwide stem from the authority granted in RCRA. The annual cost of these landfill regulations carried an initial estimate of approximately $400 million.

In 1987 the Water Quality Act was made law, and in 1990 the original Clean Air Act was amended by the Clean Air Act Amendments of 1990. Some critics have called this law an "environmental overkill" that will significantly add to the cost of doing business, thereby reducing the value of the properties used to do that business.

Another recent law, the Endangered Species Act, has drawn fire from property owners throughout the country because of its provision that actions must be taken without any consideration given to economic impact. This law, it is said, has given the no-growth and slow-growth segment of the environmental movement an overpowering, paralyzing tool that will inevitably add substantially to the costs of homes, schools, roads and all other property. Many observers have predicted legislative changes that will soften the economic impact of this law. Changes, if they come, may be slow getting here.

Administration of the areas designated as wetlands has also come under attack by affected property owners. At this writing there was legislation before Congress—the Comprehensive Wetlands Conservation and Management Act of 1991—that, if passed, would limit the negative impact of past federal administration of the wetlands. The law would redefine wetlands and provide for compensation to landowners who lose the economic benefits of their property through wetlands designation. Laws are often interpreted by the courts, and in the process some important changes in emphasis can occur. Environmental law has not been exempt from this process.

The cases one hears about most frequently focus on lender liability under CERCLA and SARA. So far, the lender has not been doing well. These are some of the notable cases:

1. *U.S. v. Fleet Sales* (1990)
2. *U.S. v. Maryland Bank and Trust* (1986)

3. *The Mirabiles Case* (1976)

All of these cases are briefly reviewed in the section called "The Parties: Special Considerations."

Other cases also threaten lender solvency and thus the marketability of real estate. On September 13, 1991, a Federal Appeals Court decision made insurers liable for hazardous waste cleanup costs under the provisions of their general liability insurance policies.

The Cost of Compliance/Effects on Value

Environmental costs are part of the economic fabric of our society; because they are woven into it so tightly, it is difficult to separate them and study their effect on any one area of the economy. Every human endeavor is touched by our concern about the environment. The food we eat, the transportation we use, our factories, our offices, our homes, the very air we breathe and the water we drink, the way we dispose of trash, our education, medical care, travel—all cost more due to environmental regulations. If all these things were well and wisely regulated in a cost-effective way, perhaps there would be little or no economic problem. But they aren't.

Many regulations are unnecessarily costly because the standards used (as in Dioxin) are arguably too stringent; in some cases the administration of the law is arbitrary and uneven. Some regulations create expensive problems the public seems all too willing to lay on the doorstep of private-property owners even though the problems were created by publicly supported laws that mandated the use of the materials now felt to be hazardous. One of the oldest examples of this is asbestos. The wetlands and acid rain issues are the most recent examples of asking private owners to bear costs for public programs. Attempts are being made to correct some of these problems.

Whatever the result of the fledgling attempts to straighten out some of the costly errors and inequities created by environmental regulation, we will still have costs that are deeply buried in our economy and are difficult to segregate; they are simply a part of "the cost of doing business." All costs rise on the floodtide of environmental regulation. It is a case (to borrow a phrase and turn it into an analogy) of "all ships rise on an incoming tide." If by some miracle we see rational thinking intrude on the political process, then we will see environmental costs decline as the tide ebbs. When this happens, real property owners may benefit from a small windfall profit, much as they did in California when Proposition 13 was passed in 1978. Already-sunken ships will not be helped by any tide, however.

At least partly for the reasons just given, there is no precise method for discovering the total cost of environmental laws and regulations. That, of course, is precisely what makes it so hard to deal with; in many ways the environmental movement is, to property, death by a thousand nicks. There is a way, however, to get a glimpse at these costs. Table 12.1 provides an incomplete, conservative (some might say fainthearted) estimate of the direct annual costs to property of our environmental efforts. At any reasonable capitalization rate, these costs represent a reduction in property value of from $741 billion to $821 billion. There are some offsets in direct benefits received, but many of these are overstated or the product of control or abatement work of doubtful value. It is not unusual, as is the case in air-quality regulation in Southern California, for example, for benefit estimates to vary by billions of dollars per year depending upon whether the source is the regulating agency or those being regulated.

Much is missing from the list in Table 12.1, because there is either no reasonable way to estimate the cost or because little mention of such costs is to be found in the literature. Among the missing are the effects of such laws as the Endangered Species Act, which could be the most expensive piece of environmental legislation ever passed. Nor is there any estimate of the full impact of the wetlands rules, or such things as the sick-building syndrome, open-space preservation, or the economic effect of regulating agencies turning over, at no cost, land and other property to various environmental efforts. Jonathan Adler (environmental analyst at the Competitive Enterprise Institute, Washington, D.C.), writing in the *Los Angeles Times* (August 19, 1991), estimates that the United States has spent $1 trillion on the environment since the 1970s.

It would be easy to double the dollar number in Table 12.1 simply by adding the following:

1. Annual solid waste management costs: $32 billion
2. Annual hazardous waste management costs: $15 billion
3. Annual water treatment costs: $27 billion
4. Amortized cost of decontaminating military sites: $17 to $57 billion (based on a 30-year cost of $500 billion to $1.7 trillion, University of Tennessee study, December 1991)

Table 12.1   The Cost of Compliance: Estimated Annual Cost (Nationally) of Selected Environmental Laws and Regulations

Item	Cost*	Based on
Environmental audits, engineering, testing	$18	5 million transactions × $500 plus EBJ** estimate
Acid rain	$4–$7	"60 Minutes," CBS News, Aug. 4, 1991
Asbestos abatement	$4	Removal cost only
Dioxin	$7–$8	Reference 74***
PCBs	$1	Cleanup only
Wetlands	$4	Unresolved taking claims, est. loss in property value
Assorted growth restrictions on housing	$15	Approximate value of new housing times 10%(1)
Regulatory costs	$.1	Federal only (2)
Radon	$1	Federal water regulations (3)
Lead in paint/plumbing	$20–$24	Removal cost (4)
TOTALS	$74.1–$82.1	References shown

Table Notes and Sources:
Cost* = Annual cost in billions of dollars.
**Environmental Business Journal*, Vol. 4, No. 4, April 1991.
***Ray, Dixie Lee, *Trashing the Planet* (Washington, D.C.: Regnery Gateway, 1991).
(1) *Not in My Backyard,* Department of Housing and Urban Development (Washington, D.C.: July 1991).
(2) Adler, Jonathan, from telephone conversation on Aug. 19, 1991.
(3) *Orange County Register,* Aug. 15, 1991, B 11.
(4) Mariano, Ann, "Paint Removal May Cost Billions," *Los Angeles Times,* Orange County Ed., Aug. 22, 1991, D 7 and D 8.

The total might be dismissed with the view that we are a rich country and can well afford $74 to $82 billion (or $150 billion) per year for the environment. Before such a "small" number is dismissed too casually, one might want to think about just how much a billion dollars represents. The *World Almanac* (1991) points out that if a company had $1 billion in A.D. 1 and spent $1,000 per day, it would not run out of money until the year 2800; and those figures do not give any earning power to the unexpended money after each day's spending spree.

Our earlier estimate of a $741 billion to $821 billion loss in value is supported, to some degree, by the Hazardous Materials Institute in Columbus, Ohio, which estimates the value loss to all property at 10 percent. Based on a total value estimate for all commercial property of $8.77 trillion in equity, the number for all property would be $974 billion (8.77 ÷ by .90 × 10%). It should be noted that the estimate of $8.77 trillion is of equity, not full market value, according to the National Association of REALTORS®.

If one wants to take the position that any estimated loss in value would not occur all at one time, one might take the $974 billion figure and spread it over ten years to give its full effect over a typical holding period. This adds $97.4 billion to the cost of environmental regulation, bringing the annual number to approximately $170 to $180 billion. This is not a precise figure, and it may or may not be a net figure; but it is as close as we are going to get until someone funds a study of this question.

If you believe that all value is created by and flows to the land, then you have to view these costs on a value-received basis. Unfortunately, the evidence suggests that full value is not being received. Much of our environmental legislation is socially inspired, politically correct activity that is not always based on good science. Good science is, in fact, often deliberately ignored by the environmental pressure groups and the politicians they pressure. While this chapter is not about the shortcomings of some environmental activities, such shortcomings are pertinent, because they are widespread and impose huge costs that find their way into the real estate income stream and lower market value. The likelihood of any change in public sentiment about these costs is important to investors.

Some additional examples may be needed to make the problem more tangible. Take the case of Dioxin, which was mentioned earlier. The American standard of control is 1,600 times as strict as that of the rest of the world, according to the World Health Organization. This imposes unusually high, and frequently unnecessary, cleanup costs on American property.

Times Beach, Missouri, is a notorious Dioxin contamination site. It now appears this community will absorb more than $200 million in direct costs plus the wrenching changes in over 2,000 lives that have already taken place. Judged by world standards, this cleanup was not necessary, according to many scientists, including those at the Centers for Disease Control. Nevertheless, Times Beach still lives on in its ability to send waves of potential disaster through the financial community. It was a

Times Beach case that led to the Friday the 13th Federal Appeals Court decision mentioned in the "Legal Foundation" section. This decision, if it survives appeal, has important implications both for insurance costs and for the ability to secure real estate loans.

Or consider the matter of acid rain. Responsible—even renowned— scientists have said for years that if it is a problem, it is a very small one. The U.S. Congress spent $570 million on a ten-year study of acid rain that involved approximately 3,000 scientists. Their report minimized the deleterious effect of the phenomenon, yet Congress passed the Clean Air Act Amendments of 1990 after considering their $570 million report for only about one hour. The cost to American property is estimated at $4 billion to $7 billion per year to control sulphur emissions.

If those examples are not enough to illustrate the point, think again about asbestos. Here investors can see the stark reality of a clash between emotions and scientific truth. Emotions won, and hundreds of billions have been spent, or will be spent, to remove asbestos from existing structures. The effect on building value is awesome. In one Southwest city, an office building containing asbestos was offered for sale at $28 million; it sold for approximately $10 million. Even giving full weight to the real estate recession going on at the time, this was a huge price reduction for a relatively young building.

After 10 or 15 years of timorous leadership, some government agencies are now saying that asbestos is often (*most* often, it turns out) best left in place and "managed." It is on this swing in public perception that those who buy asbestos-containing buildings at bargain prices are counting for a profit.

The question that investors must try to find an answer to is this: "In spite of the weak evidence supporting many major environmental initia- tives, will these issues go away or be reduced in economic intensity?" Will the environmental pendulum move away from its present position of overregulation at too high a cost? Will an environmental balance be found? Some think the move toward balance has already begun and will gain momentum if its cost-saving potential can be shown as a road to solving the real problems of the unemployed, the homeless, the elderly and those in need of education. If the emphasis on the environment changes and takes a more reasonable and less costly approach, there will be some slight windfall to those who own property. If nothing changes, some property values will die in the embrace of the environmentalists.

Environmental Audits/Assessments

When it comes to environmental considerations, nothing is more important than realizing the truth of the old saying, "If something appears to be too good to be true, it probably is." Many investors, in hot pursuit of a bargain, have learned that failing to investigate the environmental condition of a property can cause losses that occasionally exceed the cost of the property. It is also true that an assessment that reveals no environmental problems can add value or support it by removing uncertainty about actual or potential liability.

This potential for loss may have always been present to some degree, but even those with short memories can recall the "good old days" of only four or five years ago, when an average property was purchased with not much more investigation than a title search, a rent roll, a loan application, sometimes an appraisal and a termite report. Institutional investments went through a more extensive due-diligence process, but that antiquity pales when compared to what many feel is necessary today.

You can find almost as many explanations of what an environmental investigation consists of as there are names to describe the process. Audits, assessments and surveys are but a few of the popular names used to describe what is essentially the same investigative procedure. According to professionals, however, there is a distinction between *audit* and *assessment*. An audit, according to Richard Young, executive director of the National Registry of Environmental Professionals, is part of a continuing process used by manufacturing companies to monitor their environmental condition; it is usually performed by in-house staff. An assessment is a one-time investigation usually conducted by outside consultants to evaluate the environmental condition of real property. In this book, the three terms *audit, assessment* and *survey* are used synonymously.

An environmental investigation is not a completely new procedure; it has been fairly common, in one form or another, in many larger transactions for quite a few years. The audit's current level of importance has been an evolutionary process that was given great impetus by the passage of the Comprehensive Environmental Response, Compensation and Liability Act (CERCLA) in 1980 and by its "sister SARA," the Superfund Amendments and Reauthorization Act, which was passed in 1986; both were discussed earlier in the section "The Legal Foundation."

The potentially responsible parties defined in these laws and the possible liability ascribed to them makes it the best course for buyers, sellers, lenders and, occasionally, tenants to minimize their potential liability by getting an environmental assessment prior to being party to any significant event in the history of the property.

A full environmental assessment is an investigation by a competent person into the past and present environmental condition of the property in question and of any relevant nearby properties. Appropriate written reports will include all findings plus recommendations on steps needed to correct any adverse conditions, together with the estimated cost.

These assessments are generally subdivided into three parts, or phases, as the facts warrant. Most assessments are complete after part one. Some investors even dispense with part one and get a "windshield" or "express" survey; if no problems are found, they accept the survey as conclusive. Given the long history of varying uses that most properties experience, this fast-track method may not be prudent as a stand-alone assessment. In fact, most investors using the express method do so only to get a quick look at the property from an environmental viewpoint, and then proceed with phase one of the process.

Phase I Assessments

This stage has been called the "screening" phase, the "identification" phase, the "fact-finding" step, the "preliminary" phase and various other names. Here are some of the things addressed in phase I:

Record review. A review of all relevant government and private records that could provide evidence of possible environmental problems. Typical items examined are topographical and aerial maps, land-use maps, photos, reports on environmental problems and conditions on-site and off-site, relevant drawings, geological and hydrological records, business permits, occupancy permits, soil and water characteristics in the area, and anything else an inspection of the property suggests. It is not unusual for a record examination to span 40 to 60 years.

Property inspection. Inspection is meant to help uncover any signs of actual or potential pollution on or near the site. Most of the evidence is developed by simply looking around for such signs as discolored soil; stained buildings or drains; closed drains; evidence of above-ground or below-ground storage; and dead, dying or the absence of plant material.

All improvements will be inspected for indications of the use of asbestos, urea-formaldehyde, PCBs, the possible presence of radon and the like.

Title chain review. An inquiry into the ownership and land uses of the property for the last 40 to 60 years is common. The investigator looks for owner or user activity that could have generated toxic waste, such as gasoline storage, battery manufacturing, paint companies, cleaning plants, scrap metal dealers, chemical users, etc.

Identification of water sources, wetlands, etc. The consultant will sometimes plot the location of all drinking water reservoirs, water wells, wetlands or other environmentally sensitive areas that are close to the property. If endangered species are in the area, that will also be mentioned.

Identification of all hazardous waste sites. Phase I will sometimes also include a map locating all Superfund or other hazardous waste sites in the immediate area.

A written report on the findings from phase I is customary. Most properties do not require anything more than the phase I procedure, which can take from a few days to two or three weeks and cost from $3,000 to $15,000.

Phase II

Sampling, confirmation and testing are three of the names commonly used to describe this phase. The object is to gather exact information that will confirm or deny the findings of phase I. It can cost from $10,000 to $100,000 or more and take from 6 to 12 weeks, depending upon the size of the property and the capability of the consultant. These are some of the activities done in phase II:

Sampling and testing. This phase zeros in on the suspicions developed in phase one; the emphasis is on specialized testing and physical sampling. Tests will be conducted as needed for indoor and outdoor air quality; water quality at all appropriate locations; and soil condition, especially near any storage tanks or where any evidence of dumping or spillage has been seen. Building materials such as asbestos, urea-formaldehyde or PCBs will be noted, quantified, and sampled as required; noise levels both on-site and off-site may be monitored; geological conditions may be investigated; and sources of radioactive emissions may be noted and quantified.

All needed testing and sampling will be performed by experts in the field being investigated. It is not unusual for some outside labs and experts to be employed during this phase.

If phase I did not include a regulatory compliance review and an investigation into the uses of the property over the last 40 to 60 years, it will often be done now. Phase II will result in a written report that may run 50 pages or more.

Phase III

This is the defining, solution or plan-making phase. The objective is to bring together all information from phases I and II and create a report that includes recommendations as to what should be done to clean up the environmental problems and avoid them in the future. An estimate of the cost of the work and the time it will take should also be in the phase III report.

This phase does not involve doing the actual cleanup work; it is simply a summing up, a blueprint, and a time-and-money estimate. It can take from six months to a year and cost upwards of $100,000. Investors should get a "not-to-exceed" estimate for the cost of generating the phase III report. Whether the final report is a phase I, II or III, keep in mind that just because it recommends corrective action, your deal is not necessarily dead.

The Environmental Consultant

Investors, lenders and other potentially responsible parties depend on the skill and efficiency of the environmental consultant chosen to do any phase of the audit. This is a fairly new professional field, and there are, as yet, no universal professional standards for consultant qualifications or even for the content or format of their reports. However, it is important to recognize a competent consultant when you meet one. It is now quite common for lenders to require an environmental audit for a new loan or a refinance. Borrowers are generally required to use someone from the lender's approved list of consultants, but this list is no guarantee of your satisfaction.

Competent legal help is essential when environmental issues are a factor. One of the many reasons you need to work closely with an attorney is that you must set up the environmental inspection situation correctly if you hope to have it end well. This is true for buyer or seller. The offer to purchase, for example, should often contain provisions as to who is expected to pay for any assessment and cleanup work. It is also necessary to clearly set forth who hires the consultant and who coordinates his or her activities.

If written representations or warranties are needed relative to the environmental condition of the property, it is essential that these be properly drawn. If you agree to seller participation in future cleanup costs that stem from undiscovered contamination at the time of sale, it is vital that the seller's promise to pay be backed by the financial ability to do so. These are only a few of the environmental matters that must be covered in a purchase or sale and are set forth solely to reinforce the advice that you work with an attorney. The ideas and suggestions in this section are indicative and not exhaustive.

All consultants are not created equal. Below are nine guidelines to help you deal with this investment step.

Choosing a Consultant

"Environmental consultant" is a fairly new specialty; there are not yet many strong professional organizations or specific licensing laws in place, although some states do issue certificates to consultants who investigate asbestos contamination. There is, in short, no government agency, no one professional society that you can use as a complete source of credential information. You must know what to look for.

1. Make sure you get a written statement as to the education and qualifications of the consultant and the key members of his or her staff. Verify the truth of these assertions.
2. Get a written list of client references and call enough of them to satisfy yourself as to the consultant's ability to do the work.
3. Look at the range of services offered by the consultant and determine which are done in-house and which have to be contracted out. Determine the consultant's willingness to use your staff for work that must be contracted out.
4. Make sure you have a good understanding of what the consulting firm staff cannot do, and get a list of the sub-contractors they will use. Check these out.

5. Read some of the consultant's previous reports and see if you find them thorough and easy to understand.
6. Discuss with the consultant the procedure followed to keep all parties informed of the progress being made in the assessment.
7. Discuss with the consultant and some regulators the ability of the consultant to negotiate with the regulators.
8. Do not choose a consultant until you have interviewed at least three. You can find consultants through your attorney, title companies, the *Yellow Pages,* friends in your business and many other sources.
9. Finally, consider the balance between the consultant's private and government work. Some people feel that too much government work (above 25 to 30 percent of the total) fosters an "open checkbook" mentality that does not contribute to minimizing costs.

This list is by no means the last word on how to choose a consultant, but if you use it, it will put you ahead of the majority of people who have to use this specialty.

The Parties: Additional Considerations

Buyers

The environmental needs of most buyers are simple and few. They want to invest in a property that is free from environmental problems and thus limit their risk from this potential source of loss. They also want to avoid exposing themselves, their families, friends, employees and customers to any hazard connected with the property. Finally, when they are ready to sell, they want to be able to do so with little likelihood of discovering some environmental hazard that predates their time of ownership. To do these simple things, investors must take the steps necessary to protect themselves from liability. Here are some of those steps.

1. Don't buy a property without getting legal advice.
2. Negotiate. The existence of environmental problems may enhance your negotiating position and help you achieve a more acceptable price for the property. This negotiating power may, however, be of limited use except as a tool to terminate the buying process. And it

could kill the transaction; a lot of sellers are behind the curve on this problem.

3. The lender may be helpful. If a loan is involved, you will have a powerful ally. In environmental situations, however, the lender's main interest may be in withdrawing from further discussions about a loan.

4. If you start right, you will end right. Under current law, one of the areas of potential liability is the Environmental Protection Agency's ability to hold previous owners liable for all cleanup costs. One of the defenses against this is to be an "innocent purchaser" when you buy and to keep the property clean after you own it.

5. Get some information. Become knowledgeable as to the obvious visible signs of possible hazardous contamination, but don't be tempted to consider yourself an expert. Use a qualified consultant when you buy a property and as you operate it.

6. Remember that the amount of your possible liability for contaminated property has nothing to do with your initial investment or the property's price. The potential is often there for you to lose many times your original investment.

7. The liability net covers a lot of people with many different roles in a property's life. In some circumstances, officers, directors and stockholders can be held liable for the cost of cleaning up a property. The Manville Corporation bankruptcy could be instructive for shareholders.

Sellers

Sellers can no longer operate in the relatively carefree ways of the past, oblivious to the environmental condition of their property.

Almost all sellers were once buyers, and if they were careful ones, their problems as sellers should be few. Many sellers, however, have owned their properties since before the days of heightened environmental concern. The situation today demands that a seller be very careful about how environmental conditions are discovered, reported and handled. Here are seven other ideas:

1. Get a lawyer to advise you on the legal aspects of any sale or lease.

2. You might want to have an environmental audit done before you offer the property for sale. In this way, you will control the process

and its cost and be able to take adequate steps to clean up the property before a prospective purchaser does his or her own environmental investigation. Sellers who do assessments before attempting to sell have found that their properties often sell faster and for an amount that is closer to their original asking price. This will not eliminate the buyer's investigation at the time of purchase, in most cases, but it may act to transfer the costs of that one to the parties who benefit the most.

Not all sellers will choose to do the environmental work before they attempt to sell the property. For those who elect not to, perhaps this piece of information is worth considering: An EPA spokesperson who addressed a New York investor conference in the Fall of 1990 stated that 25 percent of the contaminated properties offered for sale do not sell.

3. The buyer will ask for proof. Well-advised buyers (and some tenants) are going to ask for immediate (and continuing) proof that the property is clean. Many of them will want an enforceable (funded) agreement to clean up any preexisting contamination discovered after the sale closes.

4. You can't get "a clean bill of health." No one will issue a statement that claims the property is now free of all contamination. About the best you can get is a general, qualified statement concerning environmental conditions on the property and relevant surrounding properties.

5. You won't be able to "sell it to the lender" by letting them foreclose, because you won't get a loan. You are not likely to be able to "borrow out of" the property by getting new loans. Nor is the buyer likely to finance part of the purchase price without satisfying the lender that the property is free from hazardous waste and other environmental problems and threats.

6. You are responsible for the condition of the property you are selling. You are the one who must prove you have marketable title. If adverse environmental conditions are found on your property, you are likely to be the first one the EPA deals with. You may have cost-recovery rights against previous owners or users who did the actual polluting; to date, however, the EPA has not shown any great inclination to bring lawsuits that would apportion the costs among the possibly responsible parties.

7. You need to limit after-sale liability in some way. Some sellers have been able to set up time and dollar limits; others have cost-sharing arrangements with the new owner. Only the negotiations will reveal what is possible in a given case.

The Lender

The lender has two environmental objectives: to make loans on properties that are "clean," and to make sure the property stays clean at least during the life of the loan. Traditionally, the lender's main concerns have been with the borrower's ability to repay the loan and with the value of the collateral that secures the loan. Unfortunately, lenders' pursuit of these traditional goals in the past sometimes put them in a position of being liable for the costs of environmental cleanup associated with their collateral. Three recent cases touch on this problem; they deal with "overmanagement" and foreclosure.

1. *The Mirabiles Case* (1976). This case sought to establish the rule that if a lender was substantially involved in the day-to-day business affairs of its debtor, the lender (Mellon Bank) could be deemed a responsible party under CERCLA and SARA.
2. *U.S. v. Maryland Trust* (1986). The EPA sued for Superfund cleanup costs on a property the bank owned through foreclosure. The EPA won. The bank was held to be in "...a position to investigate and discover potential problems in its secured properties." Although not a part of this decision, there is a large body of opinion that believes lenders can protect themselves through their loan covenants.
3. *U.S. v. Fleet Factors Corporation* (1990). The decision stated that a secured lender could be held liable under CERCLA, even without foreclosing, if it participated in the financial management of the borrower's business.

Lenders are now environmentally wary to the point that many of them will not make loans on properties that have any environmental contamination; some won't consider a loan for properties that *ever* had a problem. In a recent interview, appraiser Peter Patchin of Minneapolis reported that one major insurance lender explained its environmental policy as "NO! The Federal Appeals Court decision of September 13, 1991, will not help to loosen these kinds of attitudes."

It does appear, however, that lenders are making progress in their effort to protect themselves from unending environmental cleanup claims. They are avoiding problem properties, tightening up their loan documents and working for legislation to blunt the harmful court cases. It is unlikely that lenders will end up with the role of the nation's environmental police force, as they once feared they might.

Trends and Conclusions

This section is organized by topic for your convenience. The trends and conclusions come from the text and the research, some of which may not have been used in the chapter but is, nevertheless, summarized here.

Buyers, Sellers and Lenders

- An increasing number of states will enact laws requiring a transferor of real property to get a state environmental clearance before the transaction can be completed. That will tend to dampen the deal-making euphoria that sometimes causes environmental issues to be overlooked. Small deals will not be exempt.
- With or without mandating law, the need for an environmental assessment at resale or refinance will become almost universal.
- The practice of cleaning up a property before it is offered for sale will become more common.
- To smooth the course of future sale it would be wise, as you operate your property, to give the environmentalists very little to chew on.
- The number of speculators willing to buy "environmentally troubled" properties will continue to increase.
- The biggest potential liability will continue to rest with sellers and operators.
- The need for legal advice will continue to increase.
- Lenders will demand a warranty or representation from all borrowers that they have obeyed (in the case of a refinance) or will obey (all loans) all environmental laws and regulations.
- Problems stemming from environmental matters may get worse for lenders before they get better, but lenders will successfully avoid becoming the nation's environmental police force.

- Lender reluctance to lend on any property with a history of environmental problems will be strong for at least the next three to five years.

Audits and Assessments

- All insuring agencies will require some form of environmental assessment at resale or refinance.
- The need for assessments will increase. The trend is toward having an assessment performed at any change in ownership or loan status, or upon a substantial remodel.
- Federal insuring agencies will develop a standard format for simple assessments.
- Phase I activities will expand to include many of the functions now performed during phase II.
- Careful management of a property's environmental condition will become much more important to asset managers.
- The real difference between an audit and an assessment will become clearer.
- Environmental consulting, as a distinct activity, will grow far faster than the general real estate market, and buyers will come to accept that there is no such thing as a bargain assessment.

Laws and Regulations

- As the total costs of many environmental measures become more widely understood, it is likely that more moderate approaches will be adopted.
- Wetlands laws and the Endangered Species Act are likely to be revised to include greater attention to their economic impact.
- Dioxin standards will be revised to more closely reflect world standards. This will lower the compliance cost considerably.
- Regardless of any easing of regulatory pressure, it is likely that the cost of complying with all environmental rules will increase at a compounded rate of 11 percent.
- Emphasis on air-quality control is likely to continue to be strong. Excessive regulation in some areas will cause many firms to fail and weaken local real estate markets.
- The public's virtual unquestioning support for a host of environmental causes may weaken somewhat as more evidence of the

massive overreaction through regulatory overkill becomes available. This could lead to some slight lowering of compliance costs.

- The linear response theory for predicting human reaction to chemicals will be found less reliable than many had previously believed. This could lead to more balanced regulations at less cost.
- The drive to retrofit older commercial buildings with fire sprinklers will accelerate. This could lead to some expensive asbestos abatement expense.
- The removal of lead-based paint and plumbing joints containing lead solder will be advanced as a big issue in the 1990s.

Supply and Demand

- The combined effect of all housing regulations amounts to an approximate 20–35 percent increase in the price of housing units, depending upon location. It is unlikely this will be reduced by much. Apartment prices will be supported by this.
- Slow-growth and no-growth sentiments will continue to be a big cost factor. This will continue to be an important support for multifamily prices.
- It is unlikely that residential or other property prices would decline significantly if antigrowth and unnecessary environmental laws and regulations were to disappear. Most likely result would be a lowering of the rate of price increases.
- The percent of population that owns a house is not likely to increase over the next ten years; this steadies the demand for multifamily housing.

Value

- There is no way to accurately measure the precise effect of all the environmental laws and regulations on property values.
- The number of contaminated properties forfeited to the state for nonpayment of taxes will increase.

C H A P T E R
13
Exchanging:
Maximizing Wealth

For more than 80 years, real estate investors have been able to depend on one basic truth: Exchanging is the best way to maximize your wealth. Since 1913 the tax laws have been tilted in favor of the real estate exchange, and they still are, in spite of numerous changes. If you are interested in maximizing your wealth, it is far better to exchange than to sell and repurchase.

The Economic Recovery Tax Act of 1981 and the almost annual tax reform since that date have eroded some of the former benefits of exchanging and have made the decision to hold, sell and repurchase, or exchange somewhat closer calls, but exchanging is still the best way to increase your wealth.

Because the exchange choice requires a good deal more information than that needed to select holding or selling and repurchasing, this chapter covers the underlying rationale for exchanging, the reasons for and against doing it, the mechanics of a trade, and the impact of the 1984 Tax Reform Act and later tax changes on exchanging.

A Proper Trade Means No Tax

There is no federal income tax currently payable on a proper trade; there never has been. No tax is paid because no tax is due at the time the exchange is made. That's the central truth about exchanging. Endless arguments can be conducted over whether an exchange is tax-free or tax-deferred, but they are somewhat pointless exercises. There is no tax paid until a property is sold. A properly executed exchange is not a sale. The exchange is just as tax-free as a property you own but have not yet sold. There is one essential difference: If you hold property to avoid paying a tax, you put yourself in the inflexible position of not being able to change the nature of your holdings. Exchanging provides some degree of flexibility without taxation. For most literal thinkers, it is as Gerald J. Robinson suggests in *Federal Income Taxation of Real Estate:* "A tax postponed is a tax not paid."

For the real estate investor who adopts an exchange strategy, it is almost as if the 1913 income tax enactment had never been passed. Under federal tax law current income, including capital gain, is taxable. There is no current capital gain in an exchange if it is done correctly.

The absence of a tax, however, is only an advantage if it results in an increase in yield. To test for this, you need to perform a hold, sell or trade analysis that calculates the total cash flow from ownership and the IRR over the expected holding period. Every such analysis I have ever done clearly favors the exchange over all other alternatives, because the exchange preserves your equity and keeps it working for you.

The tax consequences of exchanges of investment property are determined under Section 1031 of the Internal Revenue Code (IRC). This section states, in part, that "no gain or loss shall be recognized if property held for productive use in trade or business is exchanged solely for property of like kind to be held for productive use in trade or business or for investment." In plain English, this means that if you trade one property for another, you currently don't have to pay any tax if you do it right.

Public Policy

There is nothing tricky, sneaky or dishonest about exchanging. In fact, if a real estate transaction is made, even an apparent sale and separate repurchase, it is mandatory that it be reported as an exchange if it meets the mechanical provisions of Section 1031 of the IRC. You cannot elect to handle the reporting of an exchange as you would an installment sale. An exchange, once it occurs, is not an elective event for tax reporting.

The underlying rationale for a nontaxable trade is that when property is traded for property, and no cash or anything else of value is involved, there simply is no change in your status as an investor. The party making the trade has merely continued his or her investment in an asset of the same sort as the one given up. The law is designed to avoid the inequity of forcing the taxpayer to pay a "toll" tax on a paper gain. The consensus of those who write about the underlying purpose of the exchange tax law is that if the exchange is properly done, you have a *realizable* gain but not a recognizable one.

The law's purpose has not always seemed quite so clear to the Internal Revenue Service, nor to at least one court. In its notorious Starker II decision (which is no longer applicable to delayed exchanges), the Ninth Circuit Appeals Court said that the underlying purpose of Section 1031 is not clear. Be that as it may, the law has been on the books for more than 80 years and has survived the challenge of thousands of court cases and IRS audits, and every session of Congress since 1913. Looking at the record, it is reasonable to assume that Section 1031 represents the clear will of the people.

Investors should never avoid exchanging out of fear or ignorance. The tax law has always permitted exchanges, but it is important to retain competent exchange advisers to ensure that transactions are done right. Good tax counsel, even at $200 per hour, is more than worth the money you spend for it.

Nor should you avoid exchanging out of fear of acquiring replacement property for more than it's worth. Profitable, straightforward exchanges with all properties at fair market value are made every day. The economics of fair market value are alive and well in a competently handled transaction. The assistance of a real estate broker who is experienced in exchanging is important to the point of being virtually indispensable.

Don't avoid exchanging because you have a fuzzy idea of its advantages. Most people who exchange have little trouble keeping focused on the benefits of this technique; all they have to do, if their perspective starts to dim, is remind themselves that the alternatives are to sell and face a big taxable event or to hold and be frozen in place, underutilizing their equity to avoid current taxes.

Background Data

Before discussing why people do or don't exchange, you need to know some essential background data.

- An exchange may be fully taxable, partially taxable or nontaxable.
- An exchange may be tax-free at the federal level but taxable at the state or local level.
- A trade need not be a trade for all parties. Your tax consequence in an exchange is unrelated to any other person's tax status.
- There is no limit on the number of exchanges you can make in a year or in a lifetime.
- Corporations can make exchanges; so can partnerships.
- Exchanges are not difficult to make if you deal with people who know how to make them.
- The properties being traded do not have to be in the United States.
- It is legal to make an exchange solely to save taxes.

The Reasons for Exchanging

There are many reasons to exchange and some not to; all the important considerations are discussed here. The overwhelming reason to trade is to avoid current taxes. If it is done correctly, there is no tax at the time of the transaction, and tax not paid is equity gained. By retaining the money that would have gone for taxes, you accomplish two things: You acquire a larger property and you get the time-value use of your equity. Both tend to maximize wealth.

Because an exchange investor gets to use money that a selling investor would pay out in immediate tax, it has been said that an exchanger gets an interest-free loan from the government. That's true, but it is also a loan that might never need to be repaid. You can make one exchange after another for your entire investing life (as long as the law does not change) and never pay a federal capital gain tax. What's more, your heirs (if the property is willed correctly) will pay no income tax when the property passes into their hands, and if they exchange forever (assuming the law is not changed), they will live a tax-free life—at least as to capital gains. Those who intend to minimize taxes throughout their lifetime by using the exchanging technique will also, in all probability, take advantage of estate planning to maximize the size of their estate after taxes.

Here are some other reasons:

- *To avoid setting a value*—Some owners who won't set a price or who can't get their price sometimes trade without any values being stated. This "no stated value" idea is sometimes used to dispose of problem properties; it's the "two $25,000 cats for one $50,000 dog" transaction. It is used to trade one problem for another that might be more acceptable.
- *To change locations*—People who are relocating can trade property in their old area for similar property in their new area, and thus continue their investment without paying any tax. There are, of course, normal transaction costs to pay. You may need cash in the amount of 7–10 percent of the value of the property traded to handle such costs.
- *To change property types*—You may use exchanging to move from one property type to another as long as you make a like-kind transaction and maintain the nature and intent of your investment. You might want to move from a non-tax-sheltered land investment into depreciable real estate. Another investor might want to trade a management-intensive property for one that requires less management.
- *Depreciation considerations*—You can increase depreciable basis by acquiring a bigger debt. You can defer depreciation recapture by trading. The general rule is that if no gain is recognized, no recapture will apply. You can increase depreciation by trading for a property with a higher building-to-land ratio.
- *To increase cash flow*—Some investors trade from a capital appreciation investment into one that provides immediate cash flow. Others may look for nontaxable cash flow by trading into a larger property and then refinancing it. Other trades are made solely to acquire a more easily financed property. It is also possible to increase cash flow by acquiring a property that is appreciating in value faster than the one given up.

Some corporations trade to conserve cash and possibly increase net worth. A company that sells one property to raise cash to buy another is unnecessarily adding to the cost of the new property by the amount of the tax paid on the disposition of the old property.

- *To consolidate or diversify holdings*—You may exchange many properties for one property, or one property for many others.
- *To facilitate a transfer*—In a tight money market, an exchange may be the only feasible way to dispose of one property and acquire another.

Some Reasons Against Exchanging

One hears a lot of reasons not to exchange; some are more valid than others. Here are several of them:

- *Exchanging is too difficult and time-consuming.* This isn't a reason, it's a rationalization. Both the difficulty and the time involved have been exaggerated by those who, for their own reasons, don't want to do exchanges. There is slightly more difficulty in doing a trade, and consequently some additional time is involved in completing one. The taxes you defer pay you well for your trouble.
- *The basis in the new property will be low.* The tax basis in the new property is the basis of the old increased by "boot" (unlike property), additional debt or added equity. To say that basis cannot be increased in a trade is to speak the language of the poor. The key issue in an exchange is whether the preservation of your equity will offset the loss of the full depreciation benefits acquired in a sale and repurchase. The numbers will always answer this question.
- *You may exchange yourself into a time when taxes are higher than they are now.* This argument assumes an eventual sale. Most knowledgeable advisers recommend that the only time to sell is when you have decided to get out of real estate altogether. If you are thinking about selling out someday, this may be a persuasive argument.
- *You can't recognize a loss when you exchange.* That's true. When you have a loss that you can offset against other income, you should probably sell. See your tax adviser if you are ever in this situation.
- *The cost of an exchange is higher than that of a sale.* It may be somewhat higher than a sale in most areas, but it is the bottom line that counts. If the nominally increased costs are fully considered and if yield improves, you should exchange.
- *I will overpay for property in an exchange.* Not likely—especially if you have a good broker and other qualified advisers. In any event, you are the one who makes the final pricing decision. Exchanging

does not add value to any property; the basic rule is "If it won't sell, it won't trade." Most exchanges depend upon a third-party "cash-out" buyer to make them work. This fact alone just about guarantees that fair market value will enter into the transaction.

- *Everyone I talk to advises against an exchange.* You are talking to the wrong people. Don't do business with people who haven't done exchanges. Tax advisers who are overly cautious often haven't done many (or any) trades. Real estate brokers whose only interest is a quick commission are the wrong ones to work with.
- Deal with professionals who know exchanging. That is not to say that inexperienced but well-trained people could not help you execute a profitable trade. Such people can be very useful (at least you will get a lot of their time) if they are backed up by senior people or experienced, involved management.
- *I don't know anything about exchanging.* That's just an excuse. It's easy to learn about exchanging. Numerous books and articles are available. All you have to do is start reading.

The Elements of an Exchange

When is a transaction an exchange? There are some surprising answers. The problem is the almost unvarying tendency of the IRS to call it an exchange when there is a loss, but to tag it as a sale when there is a gain. If you don't follow the rules, you will be at their mercy.

It is essential that a tax-free exchange meet the mechanical and technical tests normally applied to such a transaction. If all the elements aren't there, you may wind up with an exchange, but it will be a long and costly process to prove it if your transaction is challenged.

The three most important tests of a trade are:

1. It must structured in *form* as an exchange. It can't be a series of independent sales and separate purchases that you decide to treat as an exchange "after the fact."
2. The properties traded must be like-kind.
3. The properties must be used in a trade or business or be held as an investment.

In the recent past, there was a strong conflict between the position of the IRS on some of these tests and the findings of various courts. The situation is clearer now, thanks to the Tax Reform Act of 1984 and the regulations that followed it.

Form versus Substance

The road to an exchange is not paved with good intentions; intent to exchange is not enough. What actually happened, in form and substance, is what will rule the day if you are challenged on an audit and eventually get to court. The Carlton case (*Carlton v. U.S.*, 385 Fed 238, 5th Circuit, 1967) is a classic case in which substance won. The Carlton transaction was written up as a trade, but the court determined that the facts did not support the words used to document the case. Words alone do not make a trade.

The Alderson case (*James Alderson, et al. v. Commissioner*, 317 F2d 790, 1963), on the other hand, started out as a sale transaction and was amended into an exchange prior to closing. The court held it to be an exchange.

The history of exchanging shows the courts to have been fairly lenient in characterizing a transaction as an exchange. You should, however, do everything you can to structure your transaction to qualify (or not qualify—remember, Section 1031 is mandatory) as a trade. The basic idea is to avoid interminable IRS procedures and court appearances, which are both expensive and time-consuming. Even victory is costly.

Major Considerations

While exchanges are not nearly so difficult as some people make them out to be, there are technical areas that must be handled correctly.

Some of the major considerations in an exchange are the like-kind issue, boot, primarily-for-sale determination, interdependent transactions, and the form versus substance issue that we just discussed.

The like-kind issue. Before a transaction can qualify as an exchange, the properties involved must be "like kind." Section 1.1031 of the IRS Regulations sets out the criteria for like kind and the taxpayer makes the judgment, subject to IRS review.

Like kind refers to the nature or character of the property, not to its grade or quality. It is one of the key provisions of Section 1031, and it has been the target of recent IRS attempts to limit its scope.

The fact that real estate is improved or unimproved is not material to the like-kind question. Simply stated, the like-kind rule says you may trade one piece of investment real estate for another. At least one court has said that Section 1031 was not intended to draw any distinctions between parcels of real property, however dissimilar they may be in location, attributes and capacity for profitable use (*Commissioner v. Chrichton,* 122 F2d 181, 1941). It is a matter of usage and intent as well as whether the property is held for investment or inventory. Check with your tax adviser. The best general advice is to avoid the gray areas.

It is customary to explain like kind by giving examples of what it is and is not. Figure 13.1 contains such examples.

In general, the IRS has followed state law in the matter of what constitutes real property. If the state says it's real property, then it is. About the only exception to this is in the life estate area.

Boot; unlike property.   Boot is any kind of unlike property received or given in an exchange. Cash, net mortgage relief and personal property are examples of boot. Boot received is bad; it requires taxes to be paid currently. If there is anything good about boot, it's that it increases your land and building basis.

The receipt of unlike property in an exchange has the effect of partially disqualifying a transaction from the full tax-deferral benefits of Section 1031. The receipt of boot, however, does not invalidate a trade.

Your gain in an exchange is taxable to the extent of any boot received, but your losses, if any, can't be recognized even if the transaction is only partially qualified as an exchange.

If there is any depreciation recapture in a trade, you have boot, and you face a potentially higher rate of tax. The gain (boot) is taxed as ordinary income rather than capital gain to the amount of the depreciation recapture.

Primarily-for-sale property.   Dealers in real estate can't benefit from Section 1031, as to their resale inventory, nor can they be held to nonrecognition of losses.

Real estate is "stock-in-trade" or inventory if it is held primarily for sale to others. The houses sold by a residential developer are an example of primarily-for-sale property. So are the building lots of a land developer.

Figure 13.1 Like Kind: What It Is, What It Isn't

1. These are like kind:
   - Real estate is like kind to real estate. Personal property is like kind to personal property.
   - A leasehold of 30 years or more is like kind to a fee interest.
   - A mineral interest in land
   - Real property held as an investment is like kind to all other real property to be held as an investment. For example, an apartment building may be traded for vacant land or an office building may be exchanged for retail.
   - Water rights
   - Tenant-in-common interests
   - The trade of real estate by a trustee on behalf of a one-beneficiary land trust
2. These are not like kind:
   - Corporate stocks, bonds, certificates of trust or beneficial interest
   - Business inventory such as real estate held for resale
   - A joint venture
   - A life estate where the life expectancy is less than 30 years
   - An exchange of personal property for real property
   - An assignment of oil royalties
   - Real estate partnership interests
3. These are gray areas:
   - An option to buy real estate
   - Water rights, air rights and other property-related rights in states that have not declared them to be real property

---

It is possible to be both a dealer and an investor. You could, for example, hold considerable property primarily for resale and still hold other property for investment or for productive use in your trade or business.

Once again, motive, or intent, is not necessarily the best guideline. The determination of whether a taxpayer holds a property for Section 1031 purpose or primarily for sale depends on the exact circumstances surrounding a particular transaction, as well as the supporting documentation and the form of the transaction.

It may sound as if the primarily-for-sale determination involves a lot of judgment, but most cases are surrounded by a considerable amount of factual evidence.

Interdependent transactions.   This is the concept often used by the IRS to tie two seemingly independent transactions, such as a sale and a separate purchase, into one transaction and declare them a Section 1031 exchange. It is particularly important to avoid interdependent transactions if you have a taxable loss.

To qualify as an exchange, the disposition of one property and the acquisition of its replacement must be a mutually interdependent transaction. The interdependent transaction trap is just one more reason to retain good tax counsel.

Constructive receipt of cash.   The unilateral right to receive cash is as good as the receipt of cash for tax purposes. This issue is central to any delayed exchange and is often crucial in a multiparty trade.

The receipt of cash is boot. In order to avoid the constructive receipt of cash, there must be a substantial restriction on the exchanging party's right to receive cash other than the mere passage of time.

Types of Exchanges

Exchanging is much more orderly since the passage of the Tax Reform Act of 1984. There are basically three types of exchanges:

1. The simultaneous or concurrent exchange
2. The delayed exchange
3. The reverse exchange

The delayed or "Starker-type" exchange is by far the most common.

The simultaneous exchange.   In this type of exchange, *A* trades with *B* and both transactions close simultaneously. For many years, this was the only kind of exchange that really fit the criteria used by the IRS. The hardships, difficulties and legal maneuvering caused by this narrow definition were massive. In practice, of course, it is quite rare to find two investors who have exactly what the other wants and who want to get together and make a trade.

The delayed exchange.   This is the classic exchange format. It is the A-B-C third-party cash-out type of trade. In this transaction sequence, A trades with B to acquire B's property, and B sells A's old property to C, the cash-out buyer. The result is:

- A gets a Section 1031 trade.
- B has a taxable sale.
- C has a purchase.

Done correctly, it will qualify as a tax-deferred exchange.

Unfortunately, B is not always readily available—or, if the new property is available, cash-out buyer C is not always around. Hence the delayed exchange, which is now authorized under the Tax Reform Act of 1984. In one form of the delayed exchange, A sells to C and inserts a clause into the sales agreement that the seller (A) has the right to execute an IRC Section 1031 exchange at no additional cost or liability to the buyer (C). This means that C may end up acquiring title from someone other than A.

The safest, most conservative way to do the delayed exchange is to structure it as an exchange from the very beginning, with the provision that if no exchange property is located, the transaction will close as a sale.

The tax law requires that A identify the replacement property within 45 days of the close of escrow (as used here, "escrow" and "closing procedure" are identical terms) for the property he or she is giving up, and that the acquisition of a replacement property be completed within 180 days from the close of escrow or before the due date (including all extensions) of the exchanging party's tax return for the year of sale. The 180 days includes the 45-day identification period.

The central problem of a delayed exchange is to avoid constructive receipt of the sales proceeds when A sells to C. This is accomplished through the use of an accommodator/qualified intermediary who acts as a middleman to hold the sales proceeds. The accommodator retains all cash generated by the sale to C and purchases the replacement property of B. A potential problem with using an accommodator is the possibility that the funds being held will be lost to fraud or business failure. One solution is to purchase a letter of credit protecting against such a loss.

Exchanging parties should avoid using individuals as accommodators, as such persons could become incapacitated or die. Partnerships also present some risk, because the liabilities of the partnership could jeopardize the exchange. An accommodator should be a corporation set up to handle Section 1031 exchanges. Investors should get legal advice on this area.

The IRS has issued numerous regulations to implement the 1984 tax law. In July of 1990, they issued regulations covering the following:

- The three-property rule
- The 200 percent rule
- The 95 percent rule
- The 45-day exemption rule
- Criteria for a qualified intermediary
- Related-party definition
- Receipt of interest on sales proceeds
- Replacement property production

Each of these rulings affects a critical aspect of the delayed exchange. Together, they represent eight more reasons to retain qualified counsel.

The reverse exchange.   Occasionally a taxpayer will find the replacement property before the exchange property buyer is located. This is particularly true in a market of highly motivated sellers. In such a case, an exchanging party can still fashion a trade if money is available to carry it out.

Here is one way it can be done:

1. The taxpayer provides funds to an accommodator to purchase the new property.
2. The intermediary holds title to the new property while the trader finds a buyer for the old property. It's an *A-I-B* sequence: *A* is the potential exchanger, *I* is the intermediary and *B* is the cash-out buyer.

I buys the property *A* wants with the money provided by *A*. *B* is found and *A* trades his or her old property to *I* for the new property. *I* sells the old property to *B*. This can be done as either a simultaneous or concurrent exchange and is subject to all the laws and regulations pertaining to exchanges, including the 45/180-day rule.

Success Techniques, Basic Ideas, Principles of Exchanging

The following list of success techniques is heavily influenced by the principles set forth in John T. Reed's book *Aggressive Tax Avoidance*, published by Reed Publishing, Danville, California. The ideas are used by permission.

- If your tax savings is insignificant, sell rather than trade.
- Don't trade if you are selling at a loss.
- Make your purchase contracts flexible. Word all your real estate contracts to allow for an exchange even if you have no intention of exchanging.
- Don't look for an exchange property without a detailed criteria sheet on what you want to acquire.
- Price your old property right. If it won't sell, it won't trade.
- Don't let ignorance and fear (yours or other people's) stand in the way of exchanging.
- Trouble and inconvenience are not valid reasons for not trading.
- Deal with tax advisers and real estate agents who have done some exchanging.
- You can exchange even if the other party to the transaction doesn't really want to make a trade.
- Remember that there is no perfect investment. You don't need to find one to complete your trade.
- Whenever possible, have all properties escrowed at the same place and all title policies issued through the same insurer. Don't make this a deal-killer, however.
- There is no limit to the number of exchanges you may make in a month, year or lifetime.
- Don't start the process until you've analyzed your options with a hold, sell or trade analysis.

Exchanging is the one sure way to maximize your total wealth. It may seem somewhat technical and complicated at first, but the process is really quite straightforward and simple, especially if you work with good advisers.

Index